A New Renaissance

Also by David Lorimer:

Radical Prince: The Practical Vision of the Prince of Wales
Spirit of Science: From Experiment to Experience
Thinking Beyond the Brain: A Wider Science of Consciousness

A New Renaissance

Transforming Science, Spirit and Society

Edited by David Lorimer
and Oliver Robinson

Floris Books

First published by Floris Books in 2010

British Library CIP data available

ISBN 978-086315-759-2

Printed in Great Britain
by CPI Antony Rowe

CONTENTS

Introduction: The Choice Before Us

DAVID LORIMER

David Lorimer is a writer, lecturer and editor who is programme director of the Scientific and Medical Network. Originally a merchant banker then a teacher of philosophy and modern languages at Winchester College, he is the author and editor of a dozen books, including The Spirit of Science, Thinking Beyond the Brain *and* Science, Consciousness and Ultimate Reality. *He has a longstanding interest in the perennial wisdom and has translated and edited books about the Bulgarian sage Peter Deunov. He is also a member of the International Futures Forum and Vice-President of Wrekin Trust. His book on the ideas and work of the Prince of Wales —* Radical Prince *— has been translated into Dutch, Spanish and French. He is the creator of the Learning for Life Values Poster Programme, which has reached over 50,000 young people in the last five years. See* www. learningforlife.org.uk/awards/ *and* www.davidlorimer.net

In November 1936, as Hitler was on the rise, Sir Winston Churchill presciently warned: 'Owing to past neglect, in the face of the plainest warnings, we have now entered upon a time of great danger ... The era of procrastination, of half-measures, of soothing and baffling expedients, of delays, is coming to a close. In its place we are entering a period of consequences ... We cannot avoid this period, we are in it now ...'

I recently visited the Churchill Museum in London, where these words are graphically brought to life. We now know that Churchill was right to sound these warnings. Now, some seventy-five years later, we face a wide-ranging cultural crisis with ecological, social, economic and political dimensions. The founders of the Scientific and Medical Network (SMN) — George Blaker, Peter Leggett, Sir Kelvin Spencer and Patrick Shackleton — were born around a century ago and also lived through this turbulent war period. They were all deep thinkers, probing beneath the surface to examine not merely the symptoms of our cultural crisis but also what they saw as the underlying causes in terms of the philosophical assumptions we hold about the nature of reality.

They founded the SMN in 1973 — it was one of the earliest informal networks — as a forum to question the materialistic assumptions of science and medicine and explore wider conceptions of reality that were open to the implications spiritual experience, healing, complementary medicine and parapsychological phenomena. This gave them what they called a wider horizon: a broader and indeed a deeper understanding. Many meetings and seminars have been held in the intervening years, including our flagship conferences Mystics and Scientists and Beyond the Brain. A regular newsletter launched, as the SMN grew from its original base of fifty members to become an international group with several hundred members. *Network Review* is now a 72-page full-colour journal published three times a year.

The contributors to this volume follow in this 35-year tradition of enquiry, building on earlier volumes published in 1998 and 2001 — *The Spirit of Science* (derived from the first twenty Mystics and Scientists conferences) and *Thinking beyond the Brain* (compiled from contributions to the Beyond the Brain conferences). In the one hundredth issue of *Network Review* (Summer 2009), we published an article/manifesto by Oliver Robinson, John Clarke and myself entitled 'Crisis as Opportunity: Seizing the Moment for a New Renaissance', which is republished here as an Appendix. This new volume has arisen in response to a call for papers at the end of the manifesto. The fundamental argument advanced across the book is that the present cultural crisis represents an unprecedented opportunity for us to bring forward and make a transition to a new worldview — new thinking and values appropriate for the twenty-first century. This worldview transition is centred on our core values and fundamental relationships:

how we connect with the inner realm and our innate wisdom, how we connect with each other, and how we connect with the Earth.*

Among the global community, there is now widespread agreement that we are facing mounting challenges at many levels; but the crisis we face is not just financial, social, ecological and economic; it goes much deeper. The recent financial and economic crisis reflects not simply a crisis of confidence, a crisis of trust, but more profoundly, I believe, a crisis of values, a crisis of meaning and purpose, which means a crisis in the predominant Western outlook or worldview, since it is our collective values and attitudes that have got us to this point of meltdown. This situation, I believe, calls for a fundamental re-examination of the values that we have lived by in the past fifty years.

Kenneth Clark, the presenter of the pioneering BBC series *Civilization*, first broadcast in 1969, remarked that:

> lack of confidence, more than anything else, kills a civilization. We can destroy ourselves by cynicism and disillusion, just as effectively as by bombs. [Our] trouble today is that there is still no centre. The moral and intellectual failure of Marxism has left us with no alternative to heroic materialism, and that isn't enough.

Or, as Cecil Collins (1994) put it:

> We have to contact the centre of our being because there we have contact with the centre of the universe. Because we are cut off from our centre and from the centre of the universe we feel, and are, exiles imprisoned in the world of multiplicity and mere existence, longing to awake and journey back to the centre which is our heart and our home.

Our modern worldview, developed in Europe in the seventeenth century, is dominated by the idea that human beings are separate

---

*The SMN website is establishing a special blog area where other essays will be posted, along with contributions to an ongoing open discussion of the issues.

from Nature, when we are in fact wholly embedded in it. This modern outlook proposes that the world, human beings and other organisms are best understood using the metaphor of the machine, for instance that brains are really computers. This mechanistic outlook detaches us from Nature and gives our economic system permission to exploit, manipulate and attempt to control Nature rather than work in harmony with its laws.

Even as early as 1795, William Strickland wrote about his journey up the Hudson River. Speaking about the settlers in this area, he comments that:

> in the first place he drives away or destroys the more humanized
> native, the rightful proprietor of the soil; in the next place he
> thoughtlessly and rapaciously exterminates all living animals
> that can afford profit, or maintenance to man, he then extirpates
> the woods that clothe and ornament the country, and that to any
> but himself would be of greatest value, and finally he exhausts
> and wears out the soil, and with the devastation he has thus
> committed usually meets with his own ruin ... it is then left to
> him only to sally forth and seek frontiers, a new country which
> he may again devour. (Strickland 1971)

This is a chillingly prophetic passage of what is now happening on a worldwide scale.

In his book *Collapse: How Societies Choose to Fail or Succeed,* Jared Diamond (2005) examines the conditions that have brought about the survival or collapse of previous cultures. Among the key factors he identifies in precipitating collapse are deforestation, soil exhaustion, over-population, social inequality, inappropriate values and climate change. Does this sound familiar?

Central to Diamond's argument, however, is that cultures always have an element of choice; there are no inevitable outcomes. Past cultures that have collapsed have failed to recognize new problems when they arise, since they do not fit past experience and so are all too easily ignored or denied. Then, significantly, they have failed to cope even when the solutions are obvious. In other words these cultures have exhibited failures of foresight and failures of political and moral will.

Diamond explains that two types of choices have been crucial

10

in tipping previous outcomes towards success or failure: the first is long-term planning, and the second a willingness to reconsider core values. We know that our present situation is unique. For the first time our problems are global. The human footprint is everywhere. What happens in one place very soon affects what happens somewhere else. Information travels almost instantaneously worldwide. We have long-term scenarios and forecasts, now we need co-ordinated long-term planning. And we are coming to a growing realization that our world-view and values are deficient and need to be reconsidered.

For the last two hundred years the West has promoted the ideal of progress and development: social progress, educational progress, economic progress, political progress, scientific progress, technical progress, medical progress. Rooted in the ideals of the Enlightenment and allied to Science, Reason, Liberty and Democracy, Progress has inspired generations of reformers and idealists. During that period, and especially in the last fifty years, we have made extraordinary advances, especially in the fields of science, medicine, technology and communications. However, at this point we need to take a closer look at our current models of progress and ask ourselves if they now need to be refined. Climate change, resource depletion, ecosystem degradation, poverty, population growth, rapid urbanization, financial crises and economic challenges cannot be separated from one another. Under these circumstances, and facing as we do such a broad range of interlinked challenges, it is clear that our dominant worldview, which reflects our modern quest for technology-led progress through endless economic growth, is in need of a radical overhaul. If Lord Clark is right that we have lost our centre and that heroic materialism is not enough, then what are the ways forward? The great theologian, missionary doctor and musician Dr Albert Schweitzer reflected that:

> Three kinds of progress are significant for culture: progress in knowledge and technology; progress in the socialization of man; progress in spirituality. The last is the most important ... technical progress, extension of knowledge, does indeed represent progress, but not in fundamentals. The essential thing is that we become more finely and deeply human. (Schweitzer 1965)

In this volume, we offer a number of wide-ranging commentaries and proposals on the need for a new worldview, or, to use a different metaphor, a New Renaissance. Philosophically, the Florentine Renaissance marked a rebirth of Platonism and Esotericism with the work of Marsilio Ficino and Pico della Mirandola and an interconnected understanding of Nature as alive. In our time we find a similar resurgence of spiritual and esoteric philosophies, this time from different cultures, and a renewed understanding of interconnectedness in physics, biology, systems theory and the Gaia hypothesis. Just like the Renaissance thinkers, we now see ourselves again as creative participants in Nature rather than as detached spectators.

For convenience and clarity we have grouped the chapters under the following headings:

- The context and manifestations of the crisis
- Consciousness and mind in science and medicine
- Spirituality and new understandings of the sacred
- Global and local transformation: governance, economics and education

In this context, Shelley's famous lines, 'life like a dome of many-coloured glass stains the white radiance of eternity', spring to mind. The reader will find that different authors depict various facets of our situation, but a similar light of insight and wisdom shines through. Some readers may find it useful at this stage to scan through the Manifesto before the main body of essays in order to gain a better understanding of our starting-point. It can also serve as a summary statement at the end of the book.

This volume argues overall that our new worldview or a New Renaissance needs to be based on balance and harmony rather than on endless expansion, on sustainability rather than on excessive consumption, on partnership and co-operation as well as on enterprise and competition. It will balance the inner and the outer, the spiritual and the material, heart and head, integrating contemplation with action, feeling and intuition with reason and analysis. As E.F. Schumacher pointed out, 'man is now far too clever to be able to survive without wisdom'.

The future does not just happen, it is the outcome of our choices, of human thinking and creativity. As the Indian philosopher and statesman Sarvepalli Radhakrishnan (1947) wrote:

There is nothing inevitable in human history. Neither progress nor decline is the law of life. The future lies open before us. We can let mankind destroy itself or weld it into a single family. We can give to our future glory or gloom. If we are to co-operate with the will of the universe, we must give up egocentric illusions of modern sovereign nations, give up parochial conceptions of society, and develop loyalty to the human community. After all, there is only one race and that is humanity.

Winston Churchill expressed the view that 'a pessimist sees the difficulty in every opportunity; an optimist sees the opportunity in every difficulty.' We currently face some very considerable difficulties and challenges, but also some unprecedented opportunities. It is our collective responsibility to seize them and forge a model of progress corresponding to all three senses advanced by Schweitzer: not only progress in knowledge and technology, but also progress in social and spiritual terms, a restoration of trust and a cultivation of wisdom and compassion.

References

Clark, Kenneth (1969) *Civilization*, BBC Books, London.
Collins, Cecil (1994) *The Vision of the Fool and Other Writings*, Golgonooza Press, Ipswich.
Diamond, Jared (2005) *Collapse: How Societies Choose to Fail or Succeed*, Allen Lane, London.
Lorimer, David (ed.) (1998) *The Spirit of Science: From Experiment to Experience*, Floris Books, Edinburgh.
Lorimer, David (ed.) (2001) *Thinking Beyond the Brain: A Wider Science of Consciousness*, Floris Books, Edinburgh.
Radhakrishnan, Sarvepalli (1947) *Religion and Society*, Allen and Unwin, London.
Schweitzer, Albert (1965) *The Teaching of Reverence for Life*, Peter Owen, London.
Strickland, William (1971) *Journal of a Tour in the United States of America, 1794-95*, New York Historical Press, NY.

PART 1

Worldviews in Transition

1. The World's Health Problem: An Integral Diagnosis

ERVIN LASZLO

Ervin Laszlo is Founder and President of The Club of Budapest, President of the WorldShift Network, Founder of the General Evolution Research Group, Co-Chair of the World Wisdom Council, Fellow of the World Academy of Arts and Sciences, Member of the International Academy of Philosophy of Science, Senator of the International Medici Academy, and Editor of the international periodical World Futures: The Journal of General Evolution. *He received the Peace Prize of Japan, the Goi Award, in 2002, the International Mandir of Peace Prize in Assisi in 2005, and was nominated for the Nobel Peace Prize in 2004. Formerly professor of philosophy, systems science and futures studies in various universities in the US, Europe, and the Far East, Laszlo is the author or co-author of fifty-four books and several hundred studies translated into twenty-three languages. He lives in Italy.*

In the last few years, and especially since the economic-financial crisis of the fall of 2008, it has become painfully clear that there is something seriously wrong with our world. The media is full of reports of crises, and various experts offer suggestions on what to do about them. But for the most part the diagnosis and the cure are highly sectoral and partial. There is talk about the financial crisis, and the overall economic crisis. Then of the environmental crisis and various resource-crises: energy, food, water, among others. There is also talk about consumerism, power-hunger, and greed. There is no integral, encompassing overview of what's wrong, and what's needed to correct it. This paper attempts a systemic analysis of the world's health problem. It reviews the factors that make the planet sick, and suggests the nature of the treatment that would heal it. An integral analysis shows that the contemporary world is (1) socially, economically, and ecologically unsustainable, (2) saddled with irrational behaviours, and (3) governed by obsolete beliefs, and aspirations. The elements of unsustainability are listed below.

Unsustainability in society

The contemporary world is polarized; there is a large and still growing gap between rich and poor, powerful and marginalized. The gap is expressed in economic terms, but it's a social reality. It depresses the quality of life, and even the chances of survival of vast populations. Wealth and income differences have reached staggering proportions. The combined wealth of the world's billionaires equals the income of nearly half the world's population: three billion poor people. Eighty percent of the global domestic product belongs to one billion people, and the remaining twenty percent is shared by nearly six billion.

Poverty has not diminished in absolute numbers. The World Bank estimates that of the total world population — currently nearly seven billion — 1.4 billion live on less than 1.25 dollars a day and an additional 1.6 billion on less than 2.50 dollars. In the poorest countries seventy-eight percent of the urban population subsists under life-threatening circumstances: one in three urban dwellers lives in slums, shantytowns, and urban ghettoes, and more than 900 million are classified as slum-dwellers.

The gap shows up in food and energy consumption, and in the load placed on natural resources. People in North America, Western Europe, and Japan consume 140 percent of their daily caloric requirement, and populations in countries such as Madagascar, Guyana, and Laos live on 70 percent. The average daily amount of commercial electrical energy consumed by Africans is half a kilowatt-hour (kWh) per person; the corresponding average for Asians and Latin Americans is 2 to 3 kWh, and for Americans, Europeans, Australians, and Japanese it's 8 kWh. The average American burns 5 tons of fossil fuel per year, in contrast with the 2.9 tons of the average German. The American places twice the environmental load of the Swede on the planet, three times that of the Italian, thirteen times the Brazilian, thirty-five times the Indian, and two hundred and eighty times the Haitian.

Social structures are breaking down in both the rich and the poor countries. In poor countries the struggle for economic survival destroys the traditional extended family. Women are obliged to leave the home in search of work. They are extensively exploited, given menial jobs for low pay. Fewer women than ever have remunerated jobs and more are forced to make ends meet in the 'informal sector.' According to the International Labour Organization fifty million children are employed for a pittance in factories, mines, and on the land, for the most part in Africa, Asia, and Latin America. Many more are forced to venture into the streets as beggars. In some countries destitute children are recruited as soldiers and forced into prostitution.

In the rich countries the gap between the rich and super-rich and the urban and rural poor is widening. Job security is disappearing, competition is intensifying, and family life is suffering. In the US the rate for first marriages ending in divorce is fifty percent, and about forty percent of children grow up in single-parent families for at least part of their childhood. More and more men and women find satisfaction and companionship outside rather than within the home.

Many of the functions of family life are taken over by outside interest groups. Child rearing is increasingly entrusted to kindergartens or community day-care centres. The provision of daily nourishment is shifting from the family kitchen to supermarkets, prepared food industries and fast food chains. Leisure-time activities are coloured by the marketing and public relations campaigns of commercial enterprises. Children's media exposure to TV, video games, and 'adult' themes is increasing, and it motivates violent and sexually exploitative behaviour.

Unsustainability in the economy

Resource use

The economy, in its original and basic sense, is the management of resources for the household (from the Greek *oikonomia*, where *oikos* is household, and *nemein* is manage). The global economy can be viewed as the system concerned with the management of the resources of humanity's household. In this context the global economy faces a structural crisis because, for the first time in history, the rising curve of humanity's demand exceeds the descending curve of global supply.

Until the present, human demand has been insignificant in relation to global resources. But in the six decades since World War II, more of the planet's resources have been consumed than in all of history before then. Human consumption is nearing, and in some cases has already surpassed, planetary maxima. The production of oil, fish, lumber, and other major resources has already peaked; 40% of the world's coral reefs are gone, and annually about 23 million acres of forest are lost. Ecologists also speak of 'peak water,' since henceforth the quantity of water suited for human use is bound to diminish.

According to the Fourth Global Environment Outlook of the UN Environment Programme average resource demand in the world is around 8.9 acres per person. This figure masks great disparities between rich and poor economies: resource availability drops to 1.23 acres in the poorest countries such as Bangladesh, and mounts to 25.5 acres in the United States and the oil-rich Arab states. However, the amount of land that could sustainably respond to human requirements — the 'Earth-share' of every man, woman and child on the planet — is 4.2 acres.

Reducing excessive resource use is made urgent by the rapid growth of the population. World population has increased from about 5 billion twenty-two years ago to nearly 7 billion today. Since the amount of available land remains constant — and is actually shrinking due to overpaving and erosion — the per capita availability of land for meeting human requirements has shrunk from 19.5 acres per person in 1900 to less than 5 acres today. This is the maximum share of the planet that's both physically available, and is sustainably exploitable.

The financial system

The precarious structure of the world's financial system is another factor in the unsustainability of the global economy. Instability in this system is not new, but it was not generally recognized until the credit crunch of 2008. The bubble that burst at that time had its roots in the low interest rates the Federal Reserve created to accomodate the after-effects of the burst of the previous Internet bubble, and this has led to an unprecedented and largely unanticipated boom in the US housing market. Ever more houses were sold, at ever higher prices, and with ever more profit for banks, brokers, and the whole financial sector. The lenders knew that many people would default on their payments, but they continued to entice prospective buyers in view of short-term profits. When this practice crashed, over 2 million jobs were lost almost immediately in the US alone. Worldwide the crash resulted in the greatest loss of wealth ever recorded apart from a major war: 2.8 trillion dollars.

The structural unsustainability of the world's financial system is of longer standing than the creation and burst of speculative bubbles: it's rooted in the imbalance of international trade. For the past several decades the United States has been running up a massive international debt to finance unrestrained domestic consumption. The excess of imports over exports has produced a staggering trade deficit with China and other newly industrialized Asian economies. The latter have exported more than they imported, and chalked up a large trade surplus. Presently Asian central banks are financing American overspending: they are captives of US fiscal policy.

This is not a sustainable condition. Already in 2005 the IMF's *Economic Outlook* noted that it's no longer a question of *whether* the world's economies will adjust, only *how* they will adjust. If measures are further delayed, the adjustment could be 'abrupt,' with hazardous consequences for global trade, economic development, and international security. Today abrupt adjustment has started, with consequences that prove hazardous for most of the world's economies.

Unsustainability in ecology

Social and economic unsustainability is exacerbated by the conditions human activity is creating in the environment. The planet's wealth is being progressively overexploited and exhausted.

(i) *Water.* The amount of water available for per capita consumption is diminishing. In 1950 there was a potential reserve of nearly 17,000 m3 of freshwater for every person then living. Since then the rate of water withdrawal has been more than double the rate of population growth, and in consequence in 1999 the per capita world water reserves decreased to 7,300 m^3. Today about one-third of the world's population doesn't have access to adequate supplies of clean water, and by 2025 two-thirds of the population will live under conditions of critical water scarcity. By then there may be only 4,800 m^3 of water reserves per person.

(ii) *Land.* There is a progressive loss of productive land. The Food and Agriculture Organization estimates that there are 7,490 million acres of high quality cropland available globally, seventy-one percent of it in the developing world. This quantity is decreasing due to soil erosion, destructuring, compaction, impoverishment, excessive desiccation, accumulation of toxic salts, leaching of nutritious elements, and inorganic and organic pollution owing to urban and industrial wastes. Worldwide, 12 to 17 million acres of cropland are lost per year. At this rate 741 million acres will be lost by mid-century, leaving 6.67 billion acres to support 8 to 9 billion people. This would be catastrophic, as the remaining 0.74 acres of productive land could not produce food beyond the level of bare subsistence.

(iii) *Air.* Changes in the chemical composition of the planet's atmosphere constitute another unsustainable trend. Since the middle of the nineteenth century oxygen has decreased mainly due to the burning of coal; it now dips to nineteen percent of total volume over impacted areas and twelve to seventeen percent over major cities. At six or seven percent of total volume, life can no longer be sustained. At the same time, the share of greenhouse gases is growing. Two hundred years of burning fossil fuels and cutting down large tracts of forest has increased the atmosphere's carbon dioxide content from about 280 parts per million to over 350 parts per million.

During the twentieth century human activity has injected one terraton of CO_2 into the atmosphere. Currently it's injecting another terraton in less than two decades. The rapid injection of carbon dioxide makes it impossible for the Earth's ecosystems to adjust. In the oceans, the explosive growth of CO_2 at the surface makes the water too acid for the survival of shell-forming organisms, the species that is the basis of the chain of life in the seas. On land, absorption is reduced by the destruction of the ecosystems that had previously sustained a stable climate. As much as 40 percent of the world's forest cover has disappeared, due to acid rain, urban sprawl, and the injection of a variety of toxins into the soil.

The influx of greenhouse gases from human activity is now matched by the influx from nature. In Siberia an area of permafrost spanning a million square kilometers started to melt for the first time since it formed at the end of the last ice age 11,000 years ago. A barren expanse of frozen peat is turning into a broken landscape of mud and lakes, over a thousand kilometres across. The area, the world's largest peat bog, is releasing as much methane into the atmosphere as all of human activity put together.

(iv) Global warming and climate change. Climate models show that even relatively minor changes in the composition of the atmosphere can produce major effects, including widespread harvest failures, water shortages, increased spread of diseases, the rise of the sea level, and the die-out of large tracts of forest. Currently the cumulative effect of the changes includes the greenhouse effect. A shield in the upper atmosphere prevents heat generated at the surface from escaping into surrounding space.

Global warming is an indisputable fact: in recent years the average global temperature has risen significantly, and the warming is accelerating. Currently debate centres on whether warming is due to human activity or to natural causes. There were other warming periods in the history of the Earth; geologists speak of alternating hot and cold stable states — 'hot-houses' and 'ice-houses.' The best known previous hot-house occurred 55 million years ago, when between one and two terratons of carbon dioxide were released into the air, most likely by the impact of a large meteorite. This caused temperatures to rise 8 degrees Celsius in the Arctic zones and 5 degrees in the tropics. It took about 200,000 years for temperatures to return to their previous level.

Conservative elements claim that today's warming is due to natural causes, at the most exacerbated by human activity. A new cycle in the fusion-processes that generate heat in the sun sends more solar radiation to Earth and heats up the atmosphere. However, whether the causes of global warming are natural or anthropogenic, warming creates a series of problems. It produces nefarious changes in the climate and has a negative impact on food production. There are storms and persistent rains in many parts of the world, and serious drought in others. The result is a significant drop in food production.

Low international food reserves exacerbate the problem. Quite apart from the economics of paying for the mounting cost of food imports, current stocks are not sufficient to cover the needs of the growing number of food-deficit countries.

Irrational behaviours

An integral diagnosis of what's wrong with the world must not fail to take account of the element of irrationality in the way we manage ourselves and the environment. We have created paradoxical, unjust, and basically intolerable conditions.

- Millions are suffering from overeating and obesity, and a thousand million go hungry.

- 6 million children die annually of starvation, and 155 million are overweight.

- There are millions of intelligent women ready to play a responsible role in society, but they don't get a fair chance in education, business, politics, and civic life.

- Vast herds of livestock, consisting in part of intelligent and sensitive animals, are brought into the world for the sole purpose of slaughtering them, a procedure that, apart from its questionable ethical and health implications, is wasting an enormous amount of resources (it takes 5,214 gallons of water and 16 pounds of grain and soy to produce one pound of beef, and not much less to produce a pound of pork).

- The wellbeing and possibly the very survival of humanity are in question, but most of us remain occupied or preoccupied with making money and holding on to our privileges.

- We fight cultural intolerance and religious fundamentalism in others, but have been, and many of us still are, willing to subscribe to virulent forms of nationalism under the banner of patriotism and national security.

- We tell children to abide by the golden rule 'treat others as you expect others to treat you,' but we seldom if ever treat other people, other states and other businesses as we expect other people, states and businesses to treat us.

- The problems we face call for the commitment and participation of every able-bodied human being, but we put millions out of work to save on the cost of labour.

- The problems we face also call for long-term solutions, but our criterion of success is the bottom line in annual or semi-annual corporate profit-and-loss statements.

- The planet is bathed in energy (if fully used, 40 minutes of the solar radiation reaching the Earth would cover all of humanity's energy needs for a whole year), and technologies are on-line to derive energy from sunlight, wind, tides, geothermics, and plants, but the global economy continues to run predominantly on polluting and finite fossil fuels.

- Hi-tech weapons that are more dangerous than the conflicts they could possibly resolve are being developed and stock-piled, at vast investment of money and resources.

- The ineffectiveness of military force to achieve economic and political objectives has been proven over and over again, yet the world's governments still spend over 1.2 trillion dollars a year on arms, wars and military establishments, and similar amounts on empire-building objectives thinly disguised as national defense and security projects.

Obsolete beliefs and aspirations

Some of the beliefs that guide action and aspiration in the contemporary world are now seriously obsolete and dangerously counterproductive. For example:

- *The planet is inexhaustible.* The long-standing belief that the Earth is an inexhaustible source of resources and an inexhaustible sink of wastes leads to the overmining of natural resources and the overloading of the biosphere's regenerative cycles.

- *Nature is a mechanism.* The belief that we can engineer nature like a building or a bridge is producing a plethora of unforeseen and vexing side-effects, such as the destruction of natural balances and the disappearance of untold living species.

- *Life is a struggle where only the fittest survive.* The (mal)adaptation of Darwin's theory of natural selection to society produces a growing gap between rich and poor, and concentrates wealth and power in the hands of a small group of smart but often unscrupulous managers and speculators.

- *The market distributes benefits.* Affluent people tend to hold on to the belief that the free market, governed by what Adam Smith called the 'invisible hand,' distributes the benefits of economic activity. When they do well for themselves, they maintain, they do well also for society. The poverty and marginalization of nearly half of the world's population is eloquent testimony to the fact that this tenet doesn't work in the context of today's power- and wealth-distorted global markets.

Opportunity — approaches towards healing our world

Crisis is not only danger: as the Chinese — whose word for crisis, *Wei-Ji* means both danger and opportunity — well know, crisis is also opportunity: the chance to renew, to change, and to innovate. A stable system, whether it's a society, a culture, or an ecosystem, has many defenses against change: its survival is associated with the status quo. For such a system crisis is danger. But for an unstable system crisis is opportunity. The conservative defences of the system are weaker; the system itself approaches the condition known in the systems sciences as chaos. In this condition even small fluctuations can catalyze major changes. In today's multi-unsustainable global system, crisis is the opportunity to produce timely transformation. It is the opportunity to engage in new thinking — to adopt new objectives in politics, in business, and in the personal sphere of our life.

The objectives of enlightened politics

Enlightened politics is democratic politics: it serves the genuine interests of the *demos*, the people. The genuine interests of the people include physical survival, meaningful relations in society, meaningful social and cultural identity, and remunerated and socially useful work. Safeguarding these interests calls for political objectives that ensure the physical availability and the economic accessibility of the required resources. Beyond the basic goals, enlightened politics is dedicated to objectives that are specific to a given place and time. In today's world this means commitment to economic, social, and ecological sustainability. An enlightened politics:

- Provides incentives for the use of alternative energy and resource-saving or recycling technologies, and technologies of low or zero toxin and waste emission;

- Gives priority to eco-labelled, organic, ethical, and fair-trade products;

- Works with the business community to promote practices that incorporate criteria of sustainability in the processes of design, production, marketing, and disposal of manufactured products and manufacturing by-products;

- Pays attention to the availability of natural common goods at acceptable cost, including energy, water, and land;

- Improves the quality and increases capacity of the public transportation system, creating realistic alternatives to the use (and overuse) of the private car;

- Channels funds to reconstruct and revitalize derelict or disadvantaged areas;

- Uses safe and efficient energy and resource technologies in public services, including electric power generation, transport, and communication;

- Monitors and regulates civil and industrial activities that destroy ecological balances and despoil or reduce wilderness areas;

- Applies strict criteria for urban design and construction, requiring renewable energy technologies and efficient insulation to be part of public housing and in licensing the construction of private dwellings, commercial buildings, and industrial plants; and

- Makes accessible fields, forests, rivers, streams, lakes and seas in the surroundings with adequate provisions for the integrity of ecological cycles and processes.

The social objectives of business

In the course of the last century business companies have progressively excluded themselves from concern with and responsibility for society, seeking only their own profit and growth. The classical objective was to make money for the owners of the company. This 'shareholder philosophy' has become a major source of malaise in the world. It polarizes society and leads to the unrestrained exploitation of resources.

A shift in the objectives of business, from corporate profit and growth, to public benefit, is still viewed with scepticism, yet it's entirely possible. The social spirit is not extinct among managers. A hundred years ago a Rockefeller, a Vanderbilt, a Ford, a Mellon, and a Carnegie didn't think of himself purely as a businessman, out to get the maximum money for himself and his family; he considered himself a builder of society, a force for the common good. As IBM founder Thomas J. Watson Sr. said, companies were not created 'just to make money' but to 'knit together the whole fabric of civilization.' Today a Bill Gates, a Warren Buffett and other business leaders create charitable Foundations to champion humanitarian causes, much like Rockefeller, Ford, Carnegie and others did before them. But this in itself is no longer sufficient. In the 1920s and 30s nobody suspected that a company pursuing its own interests would have negative consequences for society. Society obviously had need of motor cars, gasoline, steel, and the other products and services provided by the major companies. For business people being public spirited didn't involve changing the orientation of their company; at the most it meant ensuring fair treatment for workers and staff, and espousing selected social causes on the side.

Today it's not enough to 'do good' as peripheral philanthropy while being narrowly focussed on 'doing well' in the marketplace. The damage done by companies staying with short-term profit-maximizing strategies is not made good by funding charitable causes, however good these may be. The need is for those who have the wealth and the power to control major businesses to become a force for the public good not by philanthropy, but by re-orienting their companies.

The social objective is not an arbitrary step in the development of management philosophy: it's a logical development of the shift from a narrow shareholder to a broader shareholder philosophy. This shift would bring the business companies into the fold of societal actors dedicated to furthering human wellbeing as well as ecological sustainability.

The objectives of individual responsibility

Some aspects of the individual's life have become public business. What one person does affects others, and either helps to heal the world, or exacerbates its malady. Responsible individuals espouse sustainable objectives in their own life. They live in a way that satisfies their basic needs without detracting from the opportunity of other people to satisfy theirs. They respect the right to life and development of all people, wherever they live, and whatever their ethnic origin, sex, citizenship, and belief system. They safeguard the right to life and a healthy environment of all the things that live and grow on Earth. They pursue happiness, freedom, and personal fulfilment in consideration of the similar pursuits of their fellows in their community, country and culture, and they choose their work or profession and commit their time and talents to activities that are useful and beneficial to their community and do not harm other people, other communities, and the environment.

When it comes to interacting with the world of business, responsible individuals are highly selective. They only patronize and do business with companies that honestly and accurately represent the long-term benefits and costs of their products and services, reporting on their safety, social consequences, environmental toxicity, reusability and recyclability. They actively seek to reduce pollution and environmental damage and minimize waste; they consult their employees and collaborators when formulating their goals and objectives; they take an active interest in the lives of their employees; and they take an active interest also in their host communities, encouraging employees to devote part of their time to social work and the improvement of the local environment.

The deeper cause

Unsustainability in society, in the economy and in the ecology, the irrationality of many elements of human behaviour, and the obsolescence of dominant beliefs and aspirations are symptoms of the disease that afflicts our planet, but they are not the cause of the disease. The cause lies deeper — it lies in the way we think. Einstein said that we can't solve a problem with the same kind of thinking that generated the problem. We can apply this to the contemporary world: we can't heal our planet and ourselves with the same kind of thinking that created our malady. Here 'thinking' is intended in an inclusive way: it's the totality of our perceptions, values, beliefs, and aspirations. It refers to our *consciousness*.

Today's predominantly materialistic and ego-centred consciousness is obsolete and must change. Fortunately, the consciousness that dominated the world for the past one hundred years is not a permanent feature of the human species. For most of the twenty or fifty thousand years that humans had possessed a higher form of culture and consciousness, they didn't think of themselves as separate from the world around them. They lived in the conviction that the world is one, and that we are an intrinsic part of it. The radical separation of a thinking, feeling human being from an unthinking and unfeeling world came only with the modern age, and came mainly in the West. It prompted the uninhibited exploitation of unthinking and unfeeling nature by the thinking and feeling, and therefore superior, human race. Insightful people have never accepted this narrowly anthropocentric view, whether they were artists, poets, mystics, or scientists. Giordano Bruno, Leonardo da Vinci, Galileo Galilei, Isaac Newton, Nicolas Copernicus, and in more recent times Albert Einstein, gave eloquent testimony of their belief that the world around us, though in many respects still mysterious, is intrinsically whole and meaningful.

The dominant consciousness of humankind could shift again in the coming years; and there are indications that it has already begun to shift. The new cultures emerging at the creative margins of society have a mindset very different from the materialistic, narrowly self-interested consciousness of the mainstream. Social psychologists, experimental parapsychologists, sociologists, and even physicians and brain researchers are discovering a different kind of perception and awareness in people, especially in young people and children: 'integral consciousness,' 'extended mind,' 'nonlocal consciousness,' 'holotropic mind,' 'infinite mind,' or 'boundless mind.'

The consciousness now emerging bears out the predictions of a few remarkable thinkers and spiritual people. The Indian sage Sri Aurobindo viewed the emergence and spread of what he termed 'superconsciousness' (the kind of consciousness that surfaces in samadhi, satori, and similar states of meditation) as the mark of the next evolutionary stage of human consciousness. The Swiss philosopher Jean Gebser defined the next stage as the coming of four-dimensional integral consciousness, arising from the prior stages of archaic, magical, and mythical consciousness. The American mystic Richard Bucke portrayed this stage as cosmic consciousness, beyond the simple consciousness of animals and the self-consciousness of contemporary humans, and social scientists Chris Cowan and Don Beck elaborated the colourful scheme called spiral dynamics. According to them consciousness evolved from the strategic 'orange' stage, which is materialistic, consumerist, and success-, image-, status-, and growth-oriented, to the consensual 'green' stage of egalitarianism and orientation toward feelings, authenticity, sharing, caring, and community, and is now shifting to the ecological 'yellow' stage where it's focussed on natural systems, self-organization, multiple realities, and knowledge. In the future it would reach the holistic 'turquoise' stage of collective individualism, cosmic spirituality, and Earth changes.

Many spiritual traditions speak about the coming of a new consciousness as well. The Mayan elders predict that the coming era will be an era when the ether, the long-neglected fifth element of the universe, will become dominant. 'Whereas the four traditional elements [air, water, fire, and earth]... have dominated various epochs in the past,' said Mayan spokesperson and high-priest Carlos Barrios, 'there will be a fifth element to reckon with in the time of the Fifth Sun: ether.' Ether is a medium, he pointed out, it permeates all space and transmits waves of energy in a wide range of frequencies. An important task at this time is 'to learn to sense or see the energy of everyone and everything: people, plants, animals. This becomes increasingly important as we draw close to the World of the Fifth Sun, for it is associated with the element ether — the realm where energy lives and weaves.'

Coincidentally, but perhaps not accidentally, physicists are discovering that the ether was not correctly discarded one hundred years ago when experiments failed to detect the friction it was predicted to cause in the rotation of the Earth — the place of the ether is not replaced by empty space, the vacuum. What physicists now call the quantum vacuum is far from empty space: according to grand-unified theories it's the unified field, the womb of all the fields and forces of nature. It contains a staggering concentration of energy, and carries and transmits information.

In Sanskrit and Hindu philosophy the ether was considered the most fundamental of the five elements; the one out of which all the others arose. The ether was known as *Akasha*, the element that also *connects* all things — as the 'Akashic Field' — and conserves the *memory* of all things — as the 'Akashic Records.' Today, in the form of a cosmic energy- and information-field, the ether regains the pre-eminent status it had enjoyed three thousand years ago.

A consciousness that recognizes our connections through the ether — an 'Akashic' consciousness — is a consciousness of connectedness and of belonging, ultimately, of oneness with people and nature. It's the transpersonal consciousness foreseen by mystics and philosophers and supported by discoveries at the leading edge of science. The evolution of this consciousness in the human family is a precondition of healing our seriously damaged but not incurably sick planet.

References

Laszlo, Ervin (2008) *Quantum Shift in the Global Brain*, Inner Traditions, Rochester, VT; (2009); *WorldShift 2012*, Inner Traditions, Rochester, VT.

2. Celebrating Crisis: Towards a Culture of Cooperation

ELISABET SAHTOURIS

Elisabet Sahtouris PhD (www.sahtouris.com) *is an internationally known evolution biologist, futurist, author and speaker living in Spain. With a post-doctoral degree at the American Museum of Natural History, she taught at MIT and the University of Massachusetts, contributed to the NOVA-Horizon TV series, is a fellow of the World Business Academy, and a member of the World Wisdom Council. Her venues include the World Bank, UN, Boeing, Siemens, Hewlett-Packard, South African Rand Bank, Caux Round Table, Tokyo International Forum, the governments of Australia, New Zealand and the Netherlands, Sao Paulo business schools and State of the World Forums. Author of* EarthDance: Living Systems in Evolution; A Walk Through Time: From Stardust to Us; *and* Biology Revisioned *with Willis Harman.*

We could be celebrating at least three major crises — in energy, economy and climate — now confronting us simultaneously, globally, adding up to the greatest challenge in all human history. That *challenge* itself is what I believe we should celebrate. Why? Because nothing short of a fundamental review, revisioning and revising of our entire way of life on planet Earth is required to face these three interrelated challenges successfully. That makes this an amazing time of opportunity to create the world we all deeply want! Is this an idle dream, an airy-fairy 'create your own reality' pitch?

Guess what? We humans created the reality we have *now*. It was not imposed on us by fate or any other outside agency. While some may still claim we had nothing to do with global warming, few would deny we have ravaged our planet's ecosystems and loaded our air with pollutants. How many would claim we had no choice in how to produce our energy, or insist that Mother Nature inflicted our money system on us? We humans dreamed up and then realized our economic systems, including our technological path via the exploitation of nature and our focus on consumerism.

Some human systems were created such that they remained sustainable over thousands of years, while our currently dominant one has proven unsustainable in only a few hundred years. The recognition that our current way of life is unsustainable is a new and vital insight, without which we could not see any need to change the way we live on our astonishingly provident planet, now ravaged to a critical point. So I celebrate our recognition of our unsustainability together with the enormous creativity of our species, which has already proven itself resourceful again and again in its relatively brief evolutionary/ historic trajectory. In that regard, we follow in the footsteps of many a biological ancestor species, as we will see, and as I hope, will give us inspiration and guidance on the road ahead of us.

Economic basics

What is an economy? I will venture to define the essence of an economy as the relationships involved in the acquisition of raw materials, their transformation into useful products, their distribution and use or consumption, and the disposal and/or recycling of what is not consumed. This definition — and this is very important to understand — is as applicable to our human economy as to nature's ecosystemic economies, as well as to the astonishingly complex economies operating within our own bodies.

Earth has four billion years of experience in economics and may well have something to teach us. Just for starters, nature recycles *everything* not consumed, which is why it has managed to create endless diversity and resilience, with ever greater complexity, using the same set of finite raw materials for all that time. Furthermore, with us or without us, she is likely to continue doing so for as long as the benevolent sun shines upon her, despite — or perhaps because — she suffers periodic crises that drive her creativity. Let's look at how Earth faces these crises.

Before we do, let me point out that Earth's economy is a truly global economy, composed of many and diverse interconnected local ecosystemic economies woven together by global systems of air, water, climate/weather, tectonics, migrations and — not least important — a single biological gene pool. While most of the history of biology and biological evolution has been about 'rabbits in habitats,' we are finally coming to understand 'rhabitats' — the holistic economies of nature embedded within each other all the way up to its global economy.

Crisis as opportunity in nature

We are facing an onrushing Hot Age. Around fifty-five million years ago, Earth had its last Hot Age. In between, since the advent of humanity, our species faced and survived at least a dozen Ice Ages. Only since the last Ice Age has there been the long — from a human perspective — benign, stable climate in which known human civilizations evolved. It was possible because the last Hot Age plus an Earth-rocking meteor, extinguished the massive reptiles and kicked off a creative wave of mammalian evolution. Crisis for some was opportunity for others in nature's resourceful ways.

In the much older 520-million-year-old Cambrian era Burgess Shale, found between two peaks in the Canadian Rockies near Banff, Canada, lies fossil testimony to one of the greatest 'opportunity' responses to crisis in all Earth's history. Interesting that it, too, happened during a time of warm seas and no polar ice — such as we ourselves may be facing — occurring relatively shortly after a 'snowball Earth' climate. In this Cambrian period before land plants and animals appeared, marine invertebrate life reached a fully modern range of basic anatomical variety that more than 500 million years of subsequent evolution has not enlarged. The fossil record of this 'Cambrian Explosion' shows a radiation of animals to fill in vacant niches, left empty as an extinction had cleared out the pre-existing fauna. Once again, crisis for some; opportunity for others.

Let's continue deeper yet into the past. By the Cambrian era, Earthlife had already been through well over half its evolutionary trajectory in years. In fact, for the first half of Earth's biological evolution — for roughly two billion years — archebacteria had the whole world to themselves. They evolved amazing lifestyle diversity in their massive proliferation from the depths of the oceans to the highest mountain peaks and even the highest life ever reached in the air, dramatically changing whole landscapes and shallow seafloors as well as the chemical composition of the atmosphere. Their impact is yet to be truly understood outside the halls of science, although they pioneered economic situations and technologies such as harnessing solar energy, building electric motors and developing the first World Wide Web of information exchange we claim as human firsts, as I will describe. My point here is that archebacteria, at the beginning of Earthlife's evolution, were first to make extraordinary responses to global crises — *crises of their own making*, we should note, unlike the later great extinctions.

The first major such response was to a global food shortage that occurred because the first archebacteria, after spreading all over Earth, were eating up all the free food — the sugars and acids chemically produced via solar UV radiation. Their amazing response was to draw on their own gene pool to change their metabolic pathways such that they could harness solar energy to produce food in the process well known to us as photosynthesis. If we could copy it at a human scale, according to Daniel Nocera at M.I.T., it could fill all our energy needs as long as Earth and we ourselves live.

Before photosynthesis, bacteria had to dwell in seawater or underground, away from burning sunlight. To function in sunlight, the new photosynthesizers were driven to invent enzymes functioning as sunscreens to protect themselves as they lived off the sun's rays and the plentiful minerals and water available to them. Unfortunately, while they did extremely well, they inadvertently created the next big global crisis of atmospheric pollution, leading to the next notable example of taking crisis as opportunity.

Like today's plants that inherited their lifestyle, the photosynthe-sizing archebacteria gave off oxygen as their waste gas. There were, as yet, no oxygen-needy creatures, so the highly corrosive oxygen, after as much of it as possible was absorbed by seas and rocks and soil reddened by its rusting effects, piled up in the atmosphere in highly significant and dangerous quantities. Along with its direct dangers of killing corrosion, this pollution created the ozone layer which caused further diminution of the old sugar and acid food supply requiring the free passage of UV through the atmosphere.

Once again, life responded with a stunning new lifestyle invention — a whole new way of living using oxygen itself to smash food molecules in the most hi-tech biological lifestyle thus far invented — the one we ourselves inherited from them and call 'breathing'. Bacteria that breathed in oxygen gave off the carbon dioxide needed by the photosynthesizers, thereby completing a give and take exchange in which their plant and animal heirs, including us, still engage.

But life has a dynamic way of oscillating between problems and solutions, which seems to keep evolution happening. The 'breathers' needed food molecules to smash while food was becoming scarcer. Solution: they invented electric motors built into their cell membranes, vastly more efficient than human-designed motors up to the present, attaching flagella to them as propellers. These hi-tech breathers drilled their way into big sluggish fermenting bacteria, which I have called 'bubblers'. (Sahtouris 2000). This initiated the era of bacterial colonialism in which the breathers invaded the bubblers for their 'raw material' molecules. Reproducing by division within the bubblers, they literally occupied them as they exploited and drained away their resources, leaving them weakened or dead.

In this primeval Earth world, we can imagine the many conflicts over scarce food and overcrowding that wreaked havoc, yet simultaneously drove innovation. Eventually, in their encounters with each other, archebacteria somehow discovered the advantages of cooperation over competition: *that feeding your enemy is more energy efficient (read: less costly) than killing them off.* All along, in evolving different lifestyles, they had been able to freely trade DNA genes with each other across all the different types in a great World Wide Web of information exchange in which any bacterium had access to the DNA information of any other. Thus they refined a myriad particular body shapes and lifestyles or roles, such as fixing nitrogen or moving by whiplash propulsion or living in mats of millions.

The crowning glory of all their achievements was the evolution of gigantic collectives with highly sophisticated divisions of labour that became the only other type of cell ever to grace the evolutionary scene: the nucleated cells of which we ourselves are composed. This may have begun, as microbiologist Lynn Margulis and others worked it out, when invading breathers felt their bubbler host weakening and took on some 'bluegreens' (photosynthesizers) to make food for the entire colony. The breathers' motors provided transportation by working in unison on the bubbler's cell membrane to drive the colony into sunlight where the bluegreens could work as needed (Margulis 1998).

In such cooperatives, apparently each specialized bacterium donated the DNA it did not need to fulfil its special function into a common gene library that became the new cell's nucleus. To this day our cells and those of plants, animals and fungi, contain the descendants of these archebacteria in the form of mitochondria (breathers) and chloroplasts (bluegreens).

Nucleated cells went through another billion years repeating the cycle of youthful competition and creativity to mature cooperation in the form of multi-celled creatures — the last great leap in evolution — around one billion years ago, bringing us closer to that Cambrian era, when this evolutionary model really took off as described earlier.

The brink of maturity

If indeed the universe evolves within a field of consciousness as I, among increasingly many other scientists, have come to believe, then the most likely single operating principle of such a self-organizing living universe is: anything that *can* happen *will* happen. In such a wide open creative universe, what is of greatest interest to me is what is sustainable — what *lasts* — especially under disruptive conditions. Taking this as a thought experiment, I concluded that the sustainability of any entity depends on its coming into harmony with whatever surrounds it in a mutual give and take that makes it more or less indispensable to the whole in which it is embedded.

Thus it has become clear to me that the very essence of Earth's biological evolution lies in the cycles of maturation from competition to cooperation I have so often described: the mature cooperative phases often driven into existence by crises. Consider how the majority of humans tend to become highly cooperative in times of disaster, surviving predations of the few to create wellbeing for the many.

Species that become sustainable — that survive a really long time — get to their mature collaborative phase while others, stuck in adolescent behaviours that no longer serve them, die out. Humanity now stands on the brink of maturity in the midst of disasters of our own making. Let us take heart from our most ancient Earth ancestors, the archebacteria — the only other creatures of the living Earth to create global disasters through their own behaviour *and* solve them — and see if we can do as well as they did! Let a mature and cooperative global economy be our goal and let us make it as successful, as efficient and resilient, as our own nucleated cells.

In Type I 'pioneer' ecosystems, young species duke it out in hostile competition for territory and resources. Type III 'climax' ecosystems, such as old coral reefs and old growth forests or prairies, on the contrary, are composed of a rich assortment of species each of which cooperatively contributes something valuable to the whole as it consumes its fair share of resources in the efficient energy exchange of the whole system. Mature cooperative efficiency, however, is not enough to make a species or an ecosystem sustainable. Energy efficiency must be balanced by elasticity — resilience to disturbances from within or from without. Ecologists long concerned only with the efficiency now recognize this vital balancing act (see Korhonen and Seager 2008).

When Shell Oil discovered that all their future scenarios led to collapse, and realized that they all lacked the possibility of human transformation, they suddenly developed interest in the latter and began consulting people such as Lynne Twist, founder of the PachaMama Alliance, which has trained thousands of people around the world to Change the Dream of modern civilization by 'Awakening the Dreamers' initiatives. The latest is their 'FourYears.Go' initiative, which may be the best example to date of how only ordinary people can change the world for the better (see www.fouryearsgo.org).

Most ecologists assume that Type I and Type III ecosystems are composed of different types of species, with Type II's being a mix of the Is and IIIs types. Because their basic assumptions about nature include that evolution only happens via genetic accidents and selective adaptation, they cannot entertain notions of intelligent systemic learning or even maturation in nature, however obvious it may appear.

Eshel Ben Jacob, a scientist studying bacterial colonies responding to stress in his Tel Aviv University laboratory for many years now, concluded that bacterial colonies function like group minds able to respond intelligently to stress (see 'Learning from Bacteria about Natural Information Processing' at http://star.tau.ac.il/~eshel/). Before he reached this conclusion, he tried every possible explanation in terms of mindless chemical signalling, 'machine intelligence,' etc., finding them inadequate to describe the creative problem-solving of his bacterial colonies. If even bacteria can demonstrate such intelligent creativity, surely later species evolved from them should as well.

Nature, on the whole, does not fix what isn't broken. It is profoundly conservative when things are working well, and radically creative when they don't. Recall that in Arnold Toynbee's classic study of civilizations that failed, the two critical factors proved to be the extreme concentration of wealth and the failure to change when change was called for (Toynbee 1946).

Resilience permits positive responses to crises, trying out all possible solutions to see what works. Thus life dances between chaos and perfect order without ever losing itself in chaos or getting stuck in rigid order. The dance is improvisational, endlessly weaving old steps into new configurations, new moves or sequences appearing as the dance evolves. It remains to be seen whether our human species will dance its way creatively to true maturity as global family.

Your body economy

Before I move from these lessons of evolution biology into our human way of playing out our own evolution, let me try to inspire awe in you for your own wondrous cells. Consider that the DNA that codes for the proteins you are largely made of is stuffed into the nucleus of each of your invisibly small cells in a two-meter length, along with some protein and water. As you contain some fifty trillion or more cells, putting these two-meter lengths end to end, your DNA would reach so far into space that a jet pilot flying day and night would be flying well over ten thousand years to reach the end of your personal DNA string.

When the human genome project results came out, the scientists expressed surprise at how few genes we actually had, how much 'biological activity' goes on in our genomes, and at bacterial genomes incorporated in ours. Protein-coding genes, including duplicates, account for less than five percent of our genome. Much of the genome is devoted to TEs — transposable elements known since Nobel laureate Barbara McClintock's pioneering work half a century ago that showed TEs not only moving about but doing *so in response to stress from outside the organism*. Her results have been supported by many later researchers (Fox Keller 1983).

Genes contain stored crystalline information or blueprints that must be read, copied and put to use, as they can no more do anything on their own than can the books on library shelves. The vital job of putting genes to use is performed by your proteins, which include countless catalyzing enzymes as well as building block materials. Further, your own feelings, thoughts and mental habits can affect the whole process (Lipton 2005).

The weight of a half century of evidence indicates that evolution does *not* proceed on the basis of selected random mutations. Rather, proteins associated with genomes have the capacity — and no doubt the imperative — to detect and repair such accidental mutations, while making appropriate genes from the well-organized gene banks available as needed to respond to stressful as well as normal requirements and challenges. It seems reasonable to suppose that our human genomic system is behaving as an intelligent hive of activity, part of the vaster hive of activity that is the whole cell including its superbly complex membrane — its interface with its world. This intricate system may even have access to genes or other DNA sequences from external sources such as bacteria, viruses, plasmids, etc. that get by our blood leucocytes and lymph nodes.

Whatever happens in our cells — remember each is as complex as a large human city, so plenty is happening 24/7 — is not determined by genes, but primarily by signals from the cells' environments that activate proteins to do things, which may or may not involve drawing on and copying genetic information (Bhaerman & Lipton 2009).

Each of your cells, along with that DNA library nucleus, has some thirty thousand recycling centres in it just to keep all those proteins you are made of healthy. Each of them is as sophisticated as a chipper machine would be if you could stick a dead or damaged tree into one and get a healthy live tree out the other end! And those exist along with a thousand mitochondrial banks giving out free stored-value ATP credit cards 24/7 with no interest, not even pay-back of what you spent.

There is no more amazing economy to learn from as we design our own future than the bodies in which each and every one of us, regardless of political persuasion, is walking around; bodies in which no organ either exploits the rest for its own benefit or interferes with diversity by trying to make the others be like itself.

Freedom: the human dilemma

We humans have vast freedom of choice compared with other animals. Fish, birds and mammals all have to find mates, establish territories to gain adequate resources and have space to raise their young, but their ways of going about these necessary acquisitions and protecting them show what biologists call 'fixed action patterns', meaning patterns built into them that do not have to be learned. They include ritual courtship and ritual fights that stop short of killing. We humans alone must choose how to get mates, how to govern ourselves, how to negotiate with each other, how to run our economies. We paid for all that freedom of choice by losing the built-in knowledge of those who evolved before us. Whether we use that free choice well remains to be seen.

We also have the great gift of our perceived time, the hindsight and foresight to help us make choices. We can know where we came from, what we have tried in the past; we can project where we will go if we keep doing what we are doing, as well as try out possible scenarios of change in imagination before we commit any of them to practice.

In short, we have the great gift of foresight to help us forestall crises of our own making — and yet, we do not. We have been warned by scientists for decades that our pollution is reaching devastating proportions and that we are using far too many of Earth's resources for her to keep up in replenishing them. Now, we can no longer stop global warming, are running out of oil, and face the predicted disasters brought on by debt money coupled with greed.

We could not be faced with more serious evidence that for all our brash young species' spectacular achievements, we have gone woefully and dramatically astray. It is all very scary ... until we notice that new doors are opening to us with fresh, new choices available, grand new opportunities to build the world of our dreams, even on a hotter planet, even without oil, even with a broken financial economy. We can rouse the proverbial Phoenix from the very ashes of all that no longer works.

The way to go and why we can get there

In creating our global economy as a resource-rapacious, competitive monopoly game based on debt money and powered by fossil fuels, we not only created an unprecedented wealth/poverty divide in the misleading name of democracy, but pushed Earth herself to a tipping point where it becomes clear that we had better begin respecting and more humbly learning from our Big Mama, rather than seeing ourselves as her ever-so-clever masters.

Our choice now is whether to mourn the demise of easy credit, fast food, year-round Christmas glitter shopping malls, and promises of happy retirements, or whether to recognize how our world neighbours paid the price of our conveniences while we ignored the real responsibilities of democracy, letting our wealth be misused, while health care, education and real security eroded under our noses.

If we opt for the latter, we will declare our solidarity with each other around the globe, roll up our sleeves, and do the positive work needed to develop clean energy sources, move coastal cities uphill, reinvent money, green deserts, and cooperate in all our cultural and religious diversity to build a world that works for all, whether or not our governments follow our lead. In the past two years alone over one trillion dollars have been invested in green businesses (see: www. ethicalmarkets.com).

It took little more than a human lifespan or two to get ourselves into the deep trouble we are in. If we truly search out what went wrong, and take advantage of what went right, in another such lifespan we can undo the damage and create a happier lifestyle for all humans and all other surviving species.

While many people find the confluence of current crises so overwhelming that they see little hope for humanity, I continue to be optimistic and excited about the wonderful opportunities at hand for building a thriving future for a number of reasons.

The universe we thought to be non-living, meaningless material running down relentlessly by entropy — comforting ourselves by creating a consumer culture on cut-throat competition so the 'haves' could get what we could and enjoy life as everything fell apart — turns out to be very different. Good news comes from information that science itself has produced. Theoretical physics suggests that ancient consciousness-based Eastern cosmologies are more accurately descriptive of our universe than the Western science story — that the universe is not meaningless matter but rooted in living consciousness, not running down but recreating itself instant by instant. Best of all, we are co-creators in this scheme, not victims of blind and fateful forces.

As I have shown, we can now see that Earth's species can and do learn how inefficient and expensive mutually destructive hostile competition is compared with the rewards of collaboration that is mutually beneficial, as clearly seen in mature ecosystems. Every crisis on our planet created the stress that became an opportunity for further evolution, with Nature on our side in a grand learning process. Our own bodies brilliantly model win-win living economies, as do mature ecosystems such as rainforests and prairies that create endless abundance through sharing and recycling. We have the information, insight, and power required to create a human world every bit as cooperative as these.

The Internet is one of the largest self-organizing living systems on the planet, composed of living people using computers as tools for connection in distributed networks without central control. Thus it provides the practical possibility of its use for global cooperation, information sharing and distributed network governance, even for non-debt currencies.

The King of Bhutan decreed that his economy would be measured in the happiness of his people, rather than in the usual measure of cash flow. It seemed a shockingly radical, if not laughable, idea, yet for nearly half a century, pioneers such as Hazel Henderson have crusaded for quality of life indicators as far more sensible measures of an economy's health than GDP/GNP money measures (Flynn, Lickerman & Henderson 2000).

Even the greatest threat looming over humanity right now is a positive opportunity. Facing the onrushing Hot Age adaptively is far more important than arguing about its precise causes. A positive feedback loop is well underway: the warmer it gets, the more ice melts; the more ice melts, the warmer it gets. 'Proactive, proactive, proactive' must be our call. Think Katrina, or the Asian tsunami, where proactive solutions would have been far cheaper than repairing damage and would have saved so many lives. And remember that some human cultures from ancient times on have lived well and comfortably in deserts.

During the devastating mid-eighties drought in the Ansokia Valley of Ethiopia, John McMillin helped people develop vegetable gardens surrounding fish ponds that produced high protein diets at very low cost in extreme desert conditions. He has since demonstrated this seemingly miraculous desert food production in more than twenty other desert locations (see www.globalregen.com).

I have gained and sustained my optimism as a humble student of our living universe, our living Earth, which clearly shows us the way out of our adolescent crisis into a mature global future. The sooner we create our vision of all we desire for living lifestyles of 100% recyclable and non-toxic elegant simplicity, set our intention to implement it together, and put our individual capacities into collective action, the greater our chances of success. Poverty can be erased in this process, as new win-win economics are implemented and we all thrive.

In short, we humans have all the intelligence and knowledge we need to create clean, sustainable economies that work for everyone, even on a hotter Earth. Now for the confidence, determination and grit to get the job done, and to the discovery that it can even be the most rewarding and enjoyable task we ever took on!

References

Bhaerman, Steve and Lipton, Bruce (2009) *Spontaneous Evolution,* Hay House, Inc.

Fox Keller, Evelyn (1983) *A Feeling for the Organism: The Life and Work of Barbara McClintock,* Henry Holt and Company, NY.

Flynn, P. Lickerman, J. & Henderson, H. (2000) *Calvert-Henderson Quality of Life Indicators,* Calvert Group, Ltd.

Korhonen, Jouni and Seager, Thomas P. (2008) Editorial: 'Beyond eco-efficiency: a resilience perspective', *Business Strategy and Environment,* no. 17, pp. 411–419.

Lipton, Bruce (2005) *The Biology of Belief,* Hay House, Inc.

Margulis, Lynn (1998) *Symbiotic Planet: A New Look At Evolution,* Basic Books, NY.

Sahtouris, Elisabet (2000) *EarthDance: Living Systems in Evolution,* iUniversity Press.

Toynbee, Arnold (1946) *A Study of History,* Oxford University Press.

3. The Greater Copernican Revolution and the Crisis of the Modern World View

RICHARD TARNAS

Richard Tarnas is a professor of philosophy and cultural history at the California Institute of Integral Studies in San Francisco, where he founded the graduate program in Philosophy, Cosmology, and Consciousness. He also teaches archetypal studies and depth psychology at Pacifica Graduate Institute in Santa Barbara. A graduate of Harvard University and Saybrook Institute, and formerly the director of programs and education at Esalen Institute, he is the author of The Passion of the Western Mind, *a history of the Western world view from the ancient Greek to the postmodern that became both a bestseller and a required text in many universities. His most recent book,* Cosmos and Psyche: Intimations of a New World View, *received the Book of the Year Prize from the Scientific and Medical Network. This chapter is an abbreviated excerpt from* Cosmos and Psyche *(Viking, New York, 2006).*

In the course of the past century, the modern world view has seen both its greatest ascendancy and its unexpected breakdown. Every field and discipline, from philosophy, anthropology, and linguistics to physics, ecology, and medicine, has brought forth new data and new perspectives that have challenged long-established assumptions and strategies of the modern mind. This challenge has been considerably magnified and made more urgent by the multitude of concrete consequences produced by those assumptions and strategies, many of them problematic. As of the first decade of the new millennium, almost every defining attitude of the modern world view has been critically reassessed and deconstructed, though often not relinquished, even when failure to do so is costly. The result in our own postmodern time has been a state of extraordinary intellectual ferment and fragmentation, fluidity and uncertainty. Ours is an age between world views, creative yet disoriented, a transitional era when the old cultural vision no longer holds and the new has not yet constellated.

Recently there have been emerging from the deconstructive flux of the postmodern mind the tentative outlines of a new understanding of reality, one very different from the conventional modern view. Impelled by developments in many fields, this shift in intellectual vision has encompassed a wide range of ideas and principles, among which can be identified a few common themes. Perhaps the most conspicuous and pervasive of these can be summed up as a deeper appreciation of both the multidimensional complexity of reality and the plurality of perspectives necessary to approach it. Closely related to this new appreciation, as both cause and effect, is a critical reappraisal of the epistemological limits of the conventional scientific approach to knowledge. This reappraisal includes a more acute sensitivity to the ways in which subject and object are mutually implicated in the act of knowing, a revised understanding of the relationship of whole and part in all phenomena, a new grasp of complex interdependence and subtle order in living systems, and an acknowledgment of the inadequacy of reductionist, mechanistic, and objectivized concepts of nature.

Other major characteristics of this emerging intellectual vision include a deeper understanding of the pivotal role of the imagination in mediating all human experience and knowledge; an increased awareness of the depth, power, and complexity of the unconscious; and a more sophisticated analysis of the nature of symbolic, metaphoric, and archetypal meaning in human life. Behind many of these themes can be seen a rejection of all literalistic and univocal interpretations of reality — of the tendency, as Robert Bellah has put it, to identify 'one conception of reality with reality itself.' (Bellah 1969). Equally fundamental to this shift is a growing recognition of the need for and desirability of a radical opening of the mainstream Western intellectual and cultural tradition to the rich multiplicity of other traditions and perspectives that have evolved both within the West and in other cultures.

Yet this emphatic embrace of pluralism has been balanced by — and to a great extent been in the service of — a profound impulse for reintegration, a widely felt desire to overcome the fragmentation and alienation of the late modern mind. Underlying the variety of its expressions, the most distinctive trait of this new vision has been its concern with the philosophical and psychological reconciliation of numerous long-standing schisms: between human being and nature, self and world, spirit and matter, mind and body, conscious and unconscious, personal and transpersonal, secular and sacred, intellect and soul, science and the humanities, science and religion.

For some time this emerging consensus of convictions and aspirations has seemed to me, as to many others, the most interesting and hopeful intellectual development of our age and perhaps the one most likely to produce a viable successor to the rapidly deteriorating modern world view. Yet from its beginning this new vision or paradigm has confronted a seemingly insurmountable problem. The present world situation could hardly be more ripe for a major paradigm shift, and many thoughtful observers have concluded that such a shift, when it comes, should and very probably will be based on principles resembling those just cited. But to succeed in becoming a broad-based cultural vision, or even to achieve its own implicit program of psychological and intellectual integration, this new outlook has been lacking one essential element, the *sine qua non* of any genuinely comprehensive, internally consistent world view: a coherent cosmology.

The shadow of the Copernican revolution

In retrospect it is evident that the fundamental intellectual turning point of Western civilization was the Copernican revolution, understood in its largest sense. Nothing so effectively bestowed confidence in the supreme power of human reason. Nothing so emphatically and comprehensively affirmed the superiority of the modern Western mind over all others — all other world views, all other eras, all other cultures, all other modes of cognition. Nothing emancipated the modern self from a cosmos of established pregiven meanings more profoundly or more dramatically. It is impossible to think of the modern mind without the Copernican revolution.

Yet the luminosity of that great revolution has cast an extraordinary shadow. The radical displacement of the Earth and humanity from an absolute cosmic centre, the stunning transference of the apparent cosmic order from the observed to the observer, and the eventual pervasive disenchantment of the material universe were all paradigmatic for the modern mind, and these have now come to epitomize humankind's underlying sense of disorientation and alienation. With the heavens no longer a separate divine realm and with the Earth no longer embedded in a circumscribed celestial order of planetary spheres and powers, humanity was simultaneously liberated from and thrust out of the ancient-medieval cosmic womb. The essential nature of reality underwent an immense shift for the Western mind, which now engaged a world possessed of entirely new dimensions, structure, and existential implications.

For all the exalted numinosity of the Copernican birth, the new universe that eventually emerged into the light of common day was a spiritually empty vastness, impersonal, neutral, indifferent to human concerns, governed by random processes devoid of purpose or meaning. At a deep level human consciousness was thereby radically estranged and decentred. It no longer experienced itself as an essential expression and focus of an intrinsically meaningful universe. The Copernican revolution was the modern mind's prototypical act of deconstruction, bringing both a birth and a death. It was the primordial cataclysm of the modern age, a stupendous event which destroyed an entire world and constituted a new one.

Not only the subsequent evolution of modern cosmology, from Newton and Laplace to Einstein and Hubble, but virtually the entire modern intellectual trajectory has sustained and magnified the primary Copernican insight: Descartes, Locke, Hume, Kant, Schopenhauer, Darwin, Marx, Nietzsche, Weber, Freud, Wittgenstein, Russell, Heidegger, Sartre, Camus. From seventeenth-century rationalism and empiricism to twentieth-century existentialism and astrophysics, human consciousness has found itself progressively emancipated yet also progressively relativized, unrooted, inwardly isolated from the spiritually opaque world it seeks to comprehend. The soul knows no home in the modern cosmos. The status of the human being in its cosmic setting is fundamentally problematic — solitary, accidental, ephemeral, inexplicable. The proud uniqueness and autonomy of 'Man' have come at a high price. He is an insignificant speck cast adrift in a vast purposeless cosmos, a stranger in a strange land. Self-reflective human consciousness finds no foundation for itself in the empirical world. Inner and outer, psyche and cosmos, are radically discontinuous, mutually incoherent. The most celebrated of human intellectual achievements, it remains the watershed of human alienation, the epochal symbol of humanity's cosmic estrangement.

Here we face the crux of our present predicament. For it is this post-Copernican cosmological context that continues to frame the current effort to forge a new paradigm of reality, yet that context, utterly at variance with the deep transformations now being urged, thereby confounds them. The cosmological metastructure that implicitly contained and precipitated all the rest is still so solidly established as to be beyond discussion. The physical sciences of the past hundred years have flung open wide the nature of reality, dissolving all the old absolutes, but the Earth still moves — along with, now, everything else, in a postmodern explosion of centreless, free-floating flux. Newton has been transcended but not Copernicus, who has rather been extended in every dimension.

For all the notable strides made in deconstructing the modern mind and moving towards a new vision, whether in science, philosophy, or religion, nothing has come close to questioning the larger Copernican revolution itself, the modern mind's first principle and foundation. The very idea is as inconceivable now as was the idea of a moving Earth before 1500. That most fundamental modern revolution, along with its deepest existential consequences, still prevails, subtly yet globally determining the character of the contemporary mind.

From the cosmological perspective, the various movements now pressing for the creation of a more humanly meaningful and spiritually resonant world have been taking place in an atomistic void. In the absence of some unprecedented development beyond the existential framework defined by the larger Copernican revolution, these less primordial intellectual changes can never be more than brave interpretive exercises in an alien cosmic environment. No amount of revisioning philosophy or psychology, science or religion, can forge a new world view without a radical shift at the cosmological level. As it now stands, our cosmic context does not support the attempted transformation of human vision. No genuine synthesis seems possible. This enormous contradiction that invisibly encompasses the emerging paradigm is precisely what is preventing that paradigm from constituting a coherent and effective world view.

As a long line of thinkers from Pascal to Nietzsche have recognized, the cosmic spaces of meaningless vastness that surround the human world silently oppose and subvert the meaning of the human world itself. In such a context, all human imagination, all religious experience, all moral and spiritual values, can only be seen as idiosyncratic human constructs. Despite the many profound and indispensable changes that have taken place in the contemporary Western mind, the larger cosmological situation continues to sustain and enforce the basic double bind of modern consciousness: Our deepest spiritual and psychological aspirations are fundamentally incoherent with the very nature of the cosmos as revealed by the modern mind. 'Not only are we not at the centre of the cosmos,' wrote Primo Levi, 'but we are alien to it: we are a singularity. The universe is strange to us, we are strange in the universe' (Levi 1985).

The tension of science and spirit in the modern world view

The distinctive pathos and paradox of our cosmological situation reflects a deep historical schism within modern culture and the modern sensibility. For the modern experience of a radical division between inner and outer — of a subjective, personal, and purposeful consciousness that is incongruously embedded in and evolved from an objective universe that is unconscious, impersonal, and purposeless — is precisely represented in the cultural polarity and tension in our history between Romanticism and the Enlightenment. On the one side of this divide, our interior selves hold precious our spiritual intuitions, our moral and aesthetic sensibilities, our devotion to love and beauty, the power of the creative imagination, our music and poetry, our metaphysical reflections and religious experiences, our visionary journeys, our glimpses of an ensouled nature, our inward conviction that the deepest truth can be found within. This interior impulse has been carried in modern culture by Romanticism, understood in its broadest sense — from Rousseau and Goethe, Wordsworth and Emerson all the way through to its spirited renascence, democratized and globalized, in the post-Sixties counterculture. In the Romantic impulse and tradition, the modern soul found profound psychological and spiritual expression.

On the other side of the schism, that soul has dwelled within a universe whose essential nature was fully determined and defined by the Scientific Revolution and Enlightenment. In effect, the objective world has been ruled by the Enlightenment, the subjective world by Romanticism. Together these have constituted the modern world view and the complex modern sensibility. One could say that the modern soul's sustaining allegiance has been to Romanticism, whereas the modern mind's deeper loyalty has been to the Enlightenment. Both live within us, fully yet antithetically. An impossible tension of opposites thereby resides deep in the modern sensibility. Hence the underlying pathos of the modern situation. The biography of the modern soul has taken place completely within a disenchanted Enlightenment cosmos, thereby contextualizing and rendering the entire life and striving of the modern soul as 'merely subjective.' Our spiritual being, our psychology, is contradicted by our cosmology. Our Romanticism is contradicted by our Enlightenment, our inner by our outer.

Behind the Enlightenment/Romanticism division in high culture (mirrored in the academic world by the 'two cultures' of science and the humanities) looms the deeper and more ancient cultural schism between science and religion. In the wake of the Scientific Revolution, many spiritually sensitive individuals have found resources to help them cope with the human condition in the modern cosmological context in ways that, to one extent or another, answer their religious longings and existential needs. Paradoxically, it seems to be this very context, with its absolute erasure of all inherited orders of pregiven cosmic meaning, that has helped make possible in our time an unprecedented freedom, diversity, and authenticity of religious responses to the human condition. These have taken a multitude of forms: the pursuit of the individual spiritual journey drawing on many sources, the personal leap of faith, the life of ethical service and humanitarian compassion, the inward turn (meditation, prayer, monastic withdrawal), involvement with the great mystical traditions and practices from Asia (Hindu, Buddhist, Taoist, Sufi) and from diverse indigenous and shamanic cultures (Native North American, Central and South American, African, Australian, Polynesian, Old European), recovery of various gnostic and esoteric perspectives and practices, the pursuit of psychedelic or entheogenic exploration, devotion to creative artistic expression as a spiritual path, or renewed engagement with revitalized forms of Jewish and Christian traditions, beliefs, and practices.

Yet all these engagements have taken place in a cosmos whose basic parameters have been defined by the determinedly nonspiritual epistemology and ontology of modern science. Because of science's sovereignty over the external aspect of the modern world view, these noble spiritual journeys are pursued in a universe whose essential nature is recognized — whether consciously or subconsciously — to be supremely indifferent to those very quests. These many spiritual paths can and do provide profound meaning, solace, and support, but they have not resolved the fundamental schism of the modern world view. They cannot heal the deep division latent in every modern psyche. The very nature of the *objective* universe turns any spiritual faith and ideals into courageous acts of *subjectivity*, constantly vulnerable to intellectual negation.

Only by strenuously avoiding the reality of this contradiction, and thus engaging in what is in essence a form of psychological compartmentalization and denial, can the modern self find any semblance of wholeness. In such circumstances, an integrated world view, the natural aspiration of every psyche, is unattainable. An inchoate awareness of this underlies the reaction of religious fundamentalists to modernity, their rigid refusal to join the seemingly impossible spiritual adventure of the modern age. But for the more fully embracing and reflective contemporary sensibility, with its multiple commitments and alertness to the larger dialectic of realities in our time, the conflict cannot be dismissed so readily.

The disenchanted cosmos

The problem with this dissociative condition is not merely cognitive dissonance or internal distress. Nor is it only the 'privatization of spirituality' that has become so characteristic of our time. Since the encompassing cosmological context in which all human activity takes place has eliminated any enduring ground of transcendent values — spiritual, moral, aesthetic — the resulting vacuum has empowered the reductive values of the market and the mass media to colonize the collective human imagination and drain it of all depth. If the cosmology is disenchanted, the world is logically seen in predominantly utilitarian ways, and the utilitarian mindset begins to shape all human motivation at the collective level. What might be considered means to larger ends ineluctably become ends in themselves. The drive to achieve ever-greater financial profit, political power, and technological prowess becomes the dominant impulse moving individuals and societies, until these values, despite ritual claims to the contrary, supersede all other aspirations.

In such a context, everything can be appropriated. Nothing is immune. Majestic vistas of nature, great works of art, revered music, eloquent language, the beauty of the human body, distant lands and cultures, extraordinary moments of history, the arousal of deep human emotion: all become advertising tools to manipulate consumer response. For quite literally, in a disenchanted cosmos, nothing is sacred. The soul of the world has been extinguished: ancient trees and forests can then be seen as nothing but potential lumber; mountains nothing but mineral deposits; seashores and deserts are oil reserves; lakes and rivers, engineering tools. Animals are perceived as harvestable commodities, indigenous tribes as obstructing relics of an outmoded past, children's minds as marketing targets. At the all-important cosmological level, the spiritual dimension of the empirical universe has been entirely negated, and with it, any publicly affirmable encompassing ground for moral wisdom and restraint. The short term and the bottom line rule all. Whether in politics, business, or the media, the lowest common denominator of the culture increasingly governs discourse and prescribes the values of the whole. Myopically obsessed with narrow goals and narrow identities, the powerful blind themselves to the larger suffering and crisis of the global community.

In a world where the subject is experienced as living in — and above and against — a world of objects, other peoples and cultures are more readily perceived as simply other objects, inferior in value to oneself, to ignore or exploit for one's own purposes, as are other forms of life, biosystems, the planetary whole. Moreover, the underlying anxiety and disorientation that pervade modern societies in the face of a meaningless cosmos create both a collective psychic numbness and a desperate spiritual hunger, leading to an addictive, insatiable craving for ever more material goods to fill the inner emptiness and producing a manic techno-consumerism that cannibalizes the planet.

Defined in the end by its disenchanted context, the human self too is inevitably disenchanted. Ultimately it becomes, like everything else, a mere object of material forces and efficient causes: a sociobiological pawn, a selfish gene, a meme machine, a biotechnological artifact, an unwitting tool of its own tools. For the cosmology of a civilization both reflects and influences all human activity, motivation, and self-understanding that take place within its parameters. It is the container for everything else.

This, therefore, has become the looming question of our time: What is the ultimate impact of cosmological disenchantment on a civilization? What does it do to the human self, year after year, century after century, to experience existence as a conscious purposeful being in an unconscious purposeless universe? What is the price of a collective belief in absolute cosmic indifference? What are the consequences of this unprecedented cosmological context for the human experiment, indeed, for the entire planet?

It was Friedrich Nietzsche who seems to have recognized most intensely the full implications of the modern development, and experienced in his own being the inescapable plight of the modern sensibility: the Romantic soul at once liberated, displaced, and entrapped within the vast cosmic void of the scientific universe. Using hyper-Copernican imagery to depict the dizzying annihilation of the metaphysical world and death of God wrought by the modern mind, and reflecting that peculiarly tragic combination of self-determining will and inexorable fate, Nietzsche captured the pathos of the late modern existential and spiritual crisis:

What were we doing when we unchained this Earth from its sun? Whither is it moving now? Whither are we moving? Away from all suns? Are we not plunging continually? Backward, sideward, forward, in all directions? Is there still any up or down? Are we not straying as through an infinite nothing? Do we not feel the breath of empty space? Has it not become colder? Is not night continually closing in on us? (Nietzsche 1882)

It is perhaps the very starkness and self-contradictory absurdity of this situation that suggests the possibility of another perspective. The modern mind has long prided itself on its repeated success in overcoming anthropomorphic distortions in its understanding of reality. It has constantly sought to purify its world view from any naïve anthropocentrism and self-fulfilling projections. Each revolution in modern thought from Copernicus onward, each great insight associated with a canonical name in the grand procession — from Bacon and Descartes, Hume and Kant to Darwin, Marx, Nietzsche, Weber, Freud, Wittgenstein, Heidegger, Kuhn, and the entire postmodern turn — has brought forth in its own manner another essential revelation of an unconscious bias that had until then blinded the human mind in its attempts to understand the world. The gist and consequence of this long, incomparably intricate modern and postmodern epistemological development has been to compel us with ever-increasing acuity to recognize how our most fundamental assumptions and principles, so long taken for granted as to fully escape our notice, imperceptibly bring into being the very world we consider unarguably objective.

Beyond the anthropocentric bias

Let us, then, take our strategy of critical self-reflection one crucial and perhaps inevitable step further. Let us apply it to the fundamental governing assumption and starting point of the modern world view — a pervasive assumption that subtly continues to influence the postmodern turn as well — that any meaning and purpose the human mind perceives in the universe does not exist intrinsically in the universe but is constructed and projected on to it by the human mind. Might not this be the final, most global anthropocentric delusion of all? For is it not an extraordinary act of human hubris — literally, a hubris of cosmic proportions — to assume that the exclusive source of *all meaning and purpose in the universe* is ultimately centred in the human mind, which is therefore absolutely unique and special and in this sense superior to the entire cosmos? To presume that the universe utterly lacks what we human beings, the offspring and expression of that universe, conspicuously possess? To assume that the part somehow radically differs from and transcends the whole? To base our entire world view on the *a priori* principle that whenever human beings perceive any patterns of psychological or spiritual significance in the nonhuman world, any signs of interiority and mind, any suggestion of purposefully coherent order and intelligible meaning, these *must* be understood as no more than human constructions and projections, as ultimately rooted in the human mind and *never* in the world?

Perhaps this complete voiding of the cosmos, this absolute privileging of the human, is the ultimate act of anthropocentric projection, the most subtle yet prodigious form of human self-aggrandizement. Perhaps the modern mind has been unconsciously projecting soullessness and mindlessness on a cosmic scale, systematically filtering and eliciting all data according to its self-elevating assumptions at the very moment we believed we were 'cleansing' our minds of 'distortions.' Have we been living in a self-produced bubble of cosmic isolation? Perhaps the very attempt to de-anthropomorphize reality in such an absolute and simplistic manner is itself a supremely anthropocentric act.

I believe that this criticism of the hidden anthropocentrism permeating the modern world view cannot be successfully countered. Only the blinders of our paradigm, as is always the case, have prevented us from recognizing the profound implausibility of its most basic underlying assumption. For as we gaze out now at the immense starry heavens surrounding our precious planet, and as we contemplate the long and richly diverse history of human thinking about the world, must we not consider that in our strangely unique modern commitment to restrict all meaning and purposive intelligence to ourselves, and refusing these to the great cosmos within which we have emerged, we might in fact be drastically underestimating and misperceiving that cosmos — and thus misperceiving, at once overestimating and underestimating, ourselves as well? Perhaps the greater Copernican revolution is in a sense still incomplete, still unfolding. Perhaps a long-hidden form of anthropocentric bias, increasingly destructive in its consequences, can now at last be recognized, thus opening up the possibility of a richer, more complex, more authentic relationship between the human being and the cosmos.

Questions and issues like these compel us to direct our attention with new eyes both outward and inward. Not *only* inward, as we habitually do in our search for meaning, but also outward, as we seldom do because our cosmos has long been regarded as empty of spiritual significance and unable to respond to that search. Yet our gaze outward must be different from before. It must be transformed by a new awareness of the interior: the questions and issues we have confronted here require us to explore yet more deeply the nature of the self that seeks to comprehend the world. They press us to discern yet more clearly how our subjectivity, that tiny peripheral island of meaning in the cosmic vastness, subtly participates in configuring and constellating the entire universe we perceive and know. They compel us to examine that mysterious place where subject and object so intricately and consequentially intersect: the crucial meeting point of cosmology, epistemology, and psychology.

References

Bellah, Robert (1969) 'Between Religion and Social Science,' in *Beyond Belief: Essays on Religion in a Post-Traditional World*, p. 246, Harper & Row, New York, 1970; University of California, Berkeley, 1991.

Levi, Primo (1985) *Other People's Trades*, 'The New Sky,' trans. R. Rosenthal, p. 22, Summit Books, New York,1989.

Nietzsche, Friedrich (1882), *The Gay Science*, trans. Walter Kaufmann, p. 181, Random House, New York, 1974.

Tarnas, Richard (2006) *Cosmos and Psyche: Intimations of a New World View*, Viking, New York.

4. Recapturing the Whole: Brain Hemispheres and the Renewal of Culture

IAIN McGILCHRIST

Iain McGilchrist is a former Consultant Psychiatrist and Clinical Director at the Bethlem Royal & Maudsley Hospital, London, and has researched in neuroimaging at Johns Hopkins Hospital, Baltimore. He taught English at Oxford University, where he was a Fellow of All Souls College. His publications include Against Criticism *(1982) and* The Master and his Emissary *(2009).*

That the brain is deeply divided into two hemispheres is a fact so fundamental that it has been taken for granted, and yet so extraordinary that it cries out for an explanation. For the brain is an organ the whole purpose of which is to make connections. When one realizes that the main function of the bundle of tracts by which the hemispheres are joined, the corpus callosum, is to inhibit, the puzzle is compounded.

In a recently published book, *The Master and his Emissary: The Divided Brain and the Making of the Western World*, I suggest that evolution has carefully preserved the division of the brain into two hemispheres. I argue that, like our bird and animal relatives, we need to be able to apply two different types of attention to the world: a narrowly focussed, precisely targeted attention to what we have already decided is of importance to us, and at the same time the broadest possible, open attention to whatever there may be, without preconception. These two types of attention are so distinct in their nature that they cannot take place in the same 'brain' at the same time — hence the division. In birds and animals, it enables them to be able to feed and stay alive, since it makes it possible for them at the same time to pick out from the background the seed on which it lies, or to lock on to the prey that they are chasing, while at the same time being maximally vigilant for whatever is going on around them, in particular for predators of their own. So it is essential for their survival. And I believe that understanding the significance of this hemispheric divide is essential for our survival, too, for reasons that I shall explain.

Already in animals and birds one gets an idea of the uses of lateralization. Their 'speech' — instrumental utterance — comes from the left hemisphere; if they use tools they tend to do so with their left hemisphere. With their right hemisphere, meanwhile, they recognize and relate to their conspecifics, form bonds, discriminate individuals, and use global or *Gestalt* strategies for identification, rather than categorizing by the presence or absence of certain features, which is how the left hemisphere sees difference. All these differences are in keeping with those to be found later in the human brain.

The defining feature of human brains is their large frontal lobes, which enable us to stand back from the world. This makes it possible to inhibit certain immediate responses, to plan, to organize, and so on. It makes us powerful exploiters of the world and one another, as we are constantly told. But there is another side to the story. It also enables us to see things in perspective, and how they relate to one another, to see the whole picture. It makes us more understanding of the world and more engaged with it and with one another, who, for the first time, we come to see as individual beings like ourselves. It is the ground of empathy.

This gives a new impetus to hemisphere difference, because for the purpose of exploitation and use we need to see something different from what we see when we feel ourselves in connection with the world, and go to meet it with the intention of understanding as much as possible of what we find there. With one hemisphere, the left, we create a sort of simplified but useful map of the world that will makes us efficient at using it. At the same time, with the right hemisphere, we need to be aware of as much as possible of what it is that comes to us from the world outside ourselves, so that we can be open to new understanding. Through it we experience — the live, complex, embodied, world of individual, always unique beings, forever in flux, a net of interdependencies, forming and reforming wholes, a world with which we are deeply connected and which 'presences' to us, as Heidegger would say. In the other we 'experience' our experience in a special way: something that no longer 'presences' but is 're-presented', containing now static, separable, bounded, but essentially fragmented entities, grouped into classes, on which predictions can be based. This kind of attention isolates, fixes and makes each thing explicit by bringing it under the spotlight of attention. In doing so it renders things inert, mechanical, lifeless. But it also enables us for the first time to know, and consequently to learn and to make things. This gives us power.

Beyond this, one could say that one way of attending to the world is whole-perceiving, organically-minded, expectant of newness and interested in whatever lies outside itself; while the other is narrowly focussed, mechanistically-minded, certain of what it already knows and interested in its own purposes. In the right hemisphere world there is what I call 'betweenness', not just the sense of connectedness with the world, but the sense that things come into being 'between' ourselves and whatever else there may be — a sense that is lacking in the left hemisphere world, where there is a separation of subject and object. And the right hemisphere is uncertain, where the left hemisphere is full of a delusive certainty, and is in a state of optimistic denial.

The relationship between the hemispheres

To talk like this makes it sound like the hemispheres are people. But we have to choose between describing them as living, at least 'part people', or as mechanical, without the properties of mind that the brain as a whole clearly has. That to me is a worse distortion. And the fact is that all that I say here is not a figure of speech, but literally, demonstrably true of individuals who have deficits in one or other hemisphere.

My view is that the two hemispheres, with their distinct 'versions' of the world, each have something to offer, but that their relationship is importantly not symmetrical. The right hemisphere both grounds experience at the lowest level and makes sense of it overall at the highest level, while the left hemisphere provides an intermediate level of processing, unpacking the implicit, before it is handed back to the right hemisphere for integration into everything else we know. The trouble is that the left hemisphere's far simpler world is self-consistent, because all the complexity has been sheared off — and this makes the left hemisphere prone to believe it knows everything, when it absolutely does not: it remains ignorant of all that is most important.

The title of the book refers to a story adapted from Nietzsche that goes something like this. A spiritual Master, a wise man who is beloved by his subjects and rules with wisdom, realizes he not only cannot, but must not, be involved in everything that needs to be done on his behalf. So he trusts an emissary to conduct his business in the further reaches of his domain. Unfortunately the emissary begins to believe that he does all the important work, and that his Master is an irksome irrelevance. He usurps the Master, but is so concerned with power and self-aggrandizement that the domain falls into ruin, taking the Master and his emissary with it. Where the Master had realized that he needed the emissary, the emissary did not understand his dependence on the Master.

The relationship between the hemispheres and cultural history

If, as is clearly the case, an emphasis on right or left hemisphere function in an individual results in certain things happening to the way that individual conceives the world, it cannot help being the case that such an emphasis in a group of individuals who share values, concepts, habits of thought — in other words, a culture — will result in the same sort of things happening to the way that culture conceives the world. Since the ways in which we can see the world are constrained by the choices offered us by the two brain hemispheres (though not in an all-or-nothing fashion), then that would *have* to be imaged in the history of both philosophy and culture. Philosophy is a series of attempts to understand the world, and reconcile the paradoxes we encounter in doing so; cultures represent different bodies of beliefs, values and responses to the world, emphasising different aspects of it. How, then, could a clearer understanding of the differences between the two versions of the world offered by our two hemispheres fail to be central to the understanding of either?

If one reviews the history of Western culture with the hemisphere distinction in mind, one sees a pattern emerge. In brief, there is an initial equilibrium in Ancient Greece, with advances in human culture and understanding dependent on the working together of the two hemispheres, which then declines into a more simply left hemisphere construction of the world. Pre-Socratic philosophy, the sense of individual justice, of moral virtue, mythology, mathematics, empirical science, the evolution of drama, music, and poetry rich in narrative, metaphor and humour cede to Plato's analytical philosophy, the codification of laws, military efficiency, the expansion of currency and commerce, science in which theory came to predominate over empirical exploration, and in general the systematization of knowledge. In Rome one sees a similar pattern if one contrasts the Augustan era with the later Empire: there is a poetic as well as historical truth in the fact that the imperial vastness of Roman architecture was made possible by the invention of concrete. The flexibility, empathy, reverence for individuality, and sense of the part to the whole, that one sees initially gives way to a society that is regimented, impersonalized and concerned with power.

And again at the Renaissance, both hemispheres begin by work-ing in tandem — the optimal, indeed necessary, state of affairs. Yet with the Reformation and the Enlightenment, this harmony is lost, and we move into an era of left hemisphere domination. And despite the massively important insights of the intellectual move-ment we call Romanticism, which for a while tried to redress the bal-ance in favour of the more complex understanding supported by the right hemisphere, this bias towards the world of the left hemisphere has been with us ever since. Modernism and post-modernism have presented no challenge to the left hemisphere's view, but have been instead an expression of it.

Our present predicament

What would it look like if the left hemisphere came to be the sole purveyor of our reality? First of all, the whole picture would be unattainable: the world would become a heap of bits. Its only meaning would come through its capacity to be used. More narrowly focussed attention would lead to an increasing specialization and technicalizing of knowledge. This in turn would promote the substitution of information, and information gathering, for knowledge, which comes through experience. Knowledge, in its turn, would seem more 'real' than what one might call wisdom, which would seem too nebulous, something never to be grasped. Knowledge that came through experience, and the practical acquisition of embodied skill, would become suspect, appearing either a threat or simply incomprehensible. It would be replaced by tokens or representations, formal systems to be evidenced by paper qualifications.

There would be a simultaneous increase in both abstraction and reification, whereby the human body itself and we ourselves, as well as the material world, and the works of art we made to understand it, would become simultaneously more conceptual and yet seen as mere things. The world as a whole would become more virtualized, and our experience of it would be increasingly through meta-representations of one kind or another; fewer people would find themselves doing work involving contact with anything in the real, 'lived' world, rather than with plans, strategies, paperwork, management and bureaucratic procedures.

There would be a complete loss of the sense of uniqueness. Increasingly the living would be modelled on the mechanical. This would also have effects on the way the bureaucracies would deal with human situations and with society at large. 'Either/or' would tend to be substituted for matters of degree, and a certain inflexibility would result. There would be a derogation of higher values, and a cynicism about their status. Morality would come to be judged at best on the basis of utilitarian calculation, at worst on the basis of enlightened self-interest.

The impersonal would come to replace the personal. There would be a focus on material things at the expense of the living. Social cohesion, and the bonds between person and person, and just as importantly between person and place, the context in which each person belongs, would be neglected, perhaps actively disrupted, as both inconvenient and incomprehensible to the left hemisphere acting on its own. There would be a depersonalization of the relationships between members of society, and in society's relationship with its members. Exploitation rather than co-operation would be, explicitly or not, the default relationship between human individuals, and between humanity and the rest of the world. Resentment would lead to an emphasis on uniformity and equality, not as just one desirable to be balanced with others, but as the ultimate desirable, transcending all others.

The left hemisphere cannot trust and is prone to paranoia. It needs to feel in control. We would expect government to become obsessed with issues of security above all else, and to seek total control. Reasonableness would be replaced by rationality, and perhaps the very concept of reasonableness might become unintelligible. There would be a complete failure of common sense, since it is intuitive and relies on both hemispheres working together. One would expect a loss of insight, coupled with an unwillingness to take responsibility, and this would reinforce the left hemisphere's tendency to a perhaps dangerously unwarranted optimism. There would be a rise in intolerance and inflexibility, an unwillingness to change track or change one's mind.

We would expect there to be a resentment of, and a deliberate undercutting of the sense of awe or wonder: Weber's 'disenchanted' world. Religion would seem to be mere fantasy. Art would be conceptualized, cerebralized; and beauty ironized out of existence.

As a culture, we would come to discard tacit forms of knowing altogether. There would be a remarkable difficulty in understanding non-explicit meaning, and a downgrading of non-verbal, non-explicit communication. Concomitant with this would be a rise in explicitness, backed up by ever increasing legislation, what de Tocqueville predicted as a 'network of small complicated rules' that would eventually strangle democracy. As it became less possible to rely on a shared and intuitive moral sense, or implicit contracts between individuals, such rules would become ever more burdensome. There would be a loss of tolerance for, and appreciation of the value of, ambiguity. We would tend to be over-explicit in the language we used to approach art and religion, accompanied by a loss of their vital, implicit and metaphorical power.

Making things whole

If we recognize features of our own world in this image of the world 'according to the left hemisphere', what can we do about it? I believe the first step is awareness: without awareness of what is happening, we can do little.

It would be easy to be prescriptive. So, we need to stop seeing ourselves as separate from the world in which we live but as inseparably linked to its wellbeing and to its fate. We should question analyses that are founded only on the values of utility. Where we see the attempt to substitute the simple and explicit for the complex and implicit we should resist. A network of rules is no substitute for trust, and actually helps to erode it. It makes people less reliant on their own and others' implicit sense of morality, and more reliant on an externally enforceable system to specify what is right and wrong. A host of manuals, guidelines and directives do not substitute for skill, and may actually result in loss of skill, as well as loss of morale, which would have come from the exercise of skill. Art that is decodable as a set of concepts or messages that need to be made explicit to make their impact is not art. Art must reach us at a level below the conscious. We need to steer away from the merely clever, and strive to reach something deeper based on skill, commitment and inspiration — though the muses, having been so long neglected, may be in no hurry to respond to our solicitations. In an age where the institutions of religion have lost ground, music and art are far too valuable indices of what lies beyond us for their practitioners to be allowed to go on wallowing in self-congratulatory and self-protective irony, or in sensationalism. We need to have greater respect for the body, too, as not just a *machine à habiter*, but integrally involved in our thinking, our feeling and our spiritual lives.

It would be easy, as I say, to be prescriptive, but whatever it is that allows us to move forward must emerge from a complete change of heart, a new way of seeing things, right hemisphere fashion, not from a set of goals or targets, left hemisphere fashion. My hope is that an understanding of the left and right hemispheres and their two ways of bringing the world into being for us will help us bypass the usual irreconcilable oppositions between faith and science, left-wing and right-wing political views, and so on, and help us to see that our sense of conflicting values is something that cuts across the usual unhelpful polarities. Especially when it is remembered that, while the left hemisphere is oppositional and wants to go it alone, the right hemisphere sees the need for co-operation, and the wisdom that comes from the union of what alone *both* hemispheres can help us to understand.

References

Cutting, John (1990) *The Right Cerebral Hemisphere and Psychiatric Disorders*, Oxford University Press, Oxford.

McGilchrist, Iain (2009) *The Master and his Emissary: the Divided Brain and the Making of the Western World*, Yale University Press, London & New Haven, CT.

Sass, Louis (1992) *Madness and Modernism: Insanity in the Light of Modern Art, Literature and Thought*, Harvard University Press, Cambridge, MA.

5. Reinventing the Human Species: An Evolutionary Crossroads

FRANK PARKINSON

Now retired, Frank Parkinson has taught linguistics and philosophy at universities in the UK, Austria, Canada and Guyana. His special interest is in the impact of evolutionary theory on traditional theology, especially the creation story now emerging from science. He is the author of Jehovah and Hyperspace: Exploring the Future of Science, Religion and Society (2002) *and* Science and Religion at the Crossroads (2009). *He has written widely on contemporary Quakerism and originated the website www. metaeconomics.co.uk*

*Homo sapiens, the first truly free species, is about to decommission natural selection, the force that made us....
Soon we must look deep within ourselves and decide what we wish to become.*
E.O. Wilson, Consilience: The Unity of Knowledge

Setting our evolutionary goal

The crossroads of the title refers to an anticipated future, perhaps nearer than we think, when we must decide whether to remain normally human or go beyond being human. It will be a new exodus, not from slavery in a foreign land, as it was with the Israelites, but from the slavery of a human species imprisoned in a primitive mental and emotional state. It will be a homecoming for those who yearn to be part of a global family and for a world without endless war.

It will not be the first divide in our long evolutionary march from ape to human, and a case could be made that others were greater, such as when our ancestors chose to walk upright or when they invented language. What makes this one different, however, is that if we do not set out now on a course of radical transformation, there is every reason to think that the species will regress to a lower level of morality and to tribal aggressiveness, but now nuclear and on a continental scale. Einstein put it in a memorable nutshell: the First World War was fought with guns, the second with airplanes, the third will be fought with nuclear rockets — and the fourth with stone clubs. In our present state of evolution we seem to be incapable of learning something of critical importance about the continuance of the species, but someone must start the learning process, and small groups must come into existence to promote it. They will begin, without doubt, as networks of individuals who are ready to think the unthinkable, as they realize that all the possibilities of the current social, political and religious paradigms have now been exhausted. At an individual level the challenge is self-transformation, at a social level it is reinventing the species. Both are nice sound bites but both contain all manner of hidden questions. What is this 'self' that is calling for transformation? Into what is it to be transformed, and how and why? What is wrong with the sense of self that I now have and with which I am mostly comfortable? How would I feel if I had this transformed self, how would I see the world, how would I relate to others? How would my new self, emotionally and logically transformed, relate to the traditional creating power of theistic religion? Would it want to do away with such a hypothesis altogether?

The questions are partially answerable, because we have as examples many individuals who have stood out in the past as better than the average, manifestly more compassionate in their feelings, more aesthetically and morally sensitive, more imaginative and coherent in their thought processes, more self-sacrificing — in a word more spiritual. In an evolutionary context such individuals may be considered as biological holotypes, that is to say, isolated specimens which reveal the existence of hitherto unknown species. Crossing the divide will entail the spreading throughout society of the qualities they manifested to the extent that if it were to happen, we could truthfully say that a new kind of human will have appeared. This emergent species would logically take us beyond *Homo sapiens*, the smart ape, who could harness fire, and beyond our present state, *Homo sapiens sapiens*, the very smart ape, who can write poetry and walk on the moon. The new man and woman will certainly have to be smarter in some critical ways, but a new kind of intelligence seems to be called for. It is as if the very very smart ape will cross an evolutionary barrier and change qualitatively, to become recognizably a new human type. We might call it simply *Homo novus*.

Reinventing the species

We have to reinvent the species because it is destroying itself and the planet through greed, ignorance, mindless reproduction and tribal aggressiveness, all of which seem to be getting worse, rather than better. We are now the greatest threat to the existence of our own species. After a couple of centuries or so when material progress and rising literacy promised a utopian future, the vision has turned from dream to nightmare. So much are thinking people oppressed by its approach that a whole new genre of writing has appeared to describe a looming dystopia, exemplified in such novels as *Animal Farm, 1984* and *Brave New World*. Unthinking individuals hope, like children, that everything will be put right by the state or the church, for these are the structures we have largely relied upon in the past to give society its prosperity, justice and moral values, but the reality is that we cannot initiate so radical change as this from the top, since, apart from the fact that radical means 'at the roots,' those in power are those who are committed to maintaining the status quo. Simple logic should enable us to see that radical change can only come from the bottom up, from ordinary men and women who have the courage to be extraordinary. Without doubt those who have been seized by the vision of the 'new human' will at first seem to be as insignificant as the shrews in the age of the dinosaur but it was the small and vulnerable shrew which survived, or so biologists tell us, and was eventually after fifty million years to produce us humans, the new masters of the planet that we now seem bent on destroying.

To talk of crossing the divide as a reinvention of the species will seem at first both pretentious and impossible, since most people would consider the human species to be as fixed as any other, and no more capable of being reinvented than cats or kangaroos. Folk wisdom continues to assure us, despite all the evidence from evolutionary science, that 'human nature never changes.'

From gene to meme

The eminent biologist Ernst Mayr defined species neatly in terms of ability to mate and produce offspring, but we are coming to see now at all levels of biology that it is a very inadequate definition, and especially so as regards the human species. There is reason to think that it is not the persistence of genes so much as cultural memes that is the most relevant factor in defining *Homo sapiens* as a species. The term *meme* was invented by Richard Dawkins, ironically so, since it subverts his famous theory of the selfish gene, and is defined by the Oxford English Dictionary as 'a self-replicating element of culture, passed on by imitation.' Along with our genes, we inherit these memes from the community into which we are born and grow up. One can, for instance, talk about memes in relation to language, politics, religious beliefs, diet, and so on. Their significance is not only that they shape us as humans in a particular way but can be deliberately changed and transmitted across cultural barriers. Memes divide us but can potentially unite us.

Not the least fascinating aspect of viewing evolution from this perspective is that we are able to see clearly how the Western world has been formed by adopting the cultural memes of ancient Greece and Rome, so much so that well into the last century liberal education was to a very large extent devoted to learning the languages, history and mythologies of these two long dead civilizations. A more recent meme that has spread across the world is the classical and romantic music of western Europe. On a less elevated, but hardly less important, level, sporting memes that originated in Britain have also been absorbed into other cultures, so that, for instance, football has become a global passion. Alas, the memes of sporting spirit and fair play have not travelled so well. These brief example are mentioned because there will be a need to both borrow and invent memes of various kind on the other side of the divide. A new kind of human nature cannot arise in a memetic vacuum, so to speak, and almost all the political, scientific and religious memes that silently shape humanity are turning out to be inadequate to our need for fulfilment, if not totally dysfunctional. They support the values of profit-making, the pursuit of power and deceit in business and politics. They work in favour of self-indulgence and against self-transformation.

If such a deliberate change in cultural architecture is to be undertaken, the notion of 'human species' will need to be examined and agreement reached about what is the most significant aspect of being human. We differ from other members of the genus *Homo* (e.g., chimpanzees, baboons and gorillas) in various physical ways, such as the fact that we walk on two legs and are relatively hairless, but the most distinctive thing that sets *Homo sapiens* apart is not morphology but consciousness. If a cow or a cabbage could think and feel like a human, it would be a human. Unfortunately, consciousness is precisely that aspect of reality that science has neglected until very recently, for it was banished from scientific study by Descartes' diktat, as *res cogitans*, thinking stuff that could not be measured. If, however, we are to measure human evolution in terms of *quality of consciousness* — and what other criterion should we use? — the bias of scientific and religious thinking about the human race must now shift to an understanding of what the term 'higher consciousness' means. Only when there is broad agreement about that can we start on the task of bringing it about.

The role of community and prophetic groups

Our me-centred age has largely lost sight of the fact that happiness and fulfilment are vitally connected to living within a community. The primacy of the individual has become so unquestioned that Margaret Thatcher could once say, notoriously, 'You know, there is no such thing as society. There are individual men and women, and there are families.' To be fair to her, this often used quote is taken out of context and her wider point about the negative effects of state 'nannyism' is very valid. Nevertheless, the bare statement serves to sum up a fragmented society in which individual rights almost always come before those of the community. The starkness of her wording serves to highlight the contrasting theory which approaches society as an organism of which each member is an integral part or, to use Dante's powerful image of social entrainment, 'The more souls who resonate together the greater the intensity of their love, for each soul reflects the other like a mirror.'

The moral awareness of the community can only be raised through the conviction of individuals who have greater ethical sensitivity than the norm. Such individuals appear throughout history as prophets to initiate change in conscience, but because they are in advance of their time, they often seem to the ordinary person to be misfits rather than visionaries. It has been said that the individual who is one step ahead of the present is called a genius, but someone who is two steps ahead is a crackpot. There is, presumably, no word in the language to fit someone who is three steps ahead, but that is the kind of logistical philosopher that we need now in a world convulsing with complex problems on the greatest scale. Prophets in general do not change society by influencing the masses, but tend more frequently to awaken a latent moral awareness in a small group who are receptive to their message and who will go on to act as a leaven on society at large. It is no exaggeration, therefore, to say that these 'leaveners' are at least as vital in social evolution as the rare individuals who preach radical change. They not only fulfil a function of bridging and transmission but are an essential part of the prophetic function, for prophets need at least some answering echo from the community around them. If a Jesus, a Socrates or a Newton had been left at birth in some jungle tribe, no one would have ever heard about them. To that extent, then, 'leaveners' are a prophetic community, and the question thus arises as to whether the Scientific and Medical Network is, tacitly or explicitly, a prophetic community, a matrix which nourishes the visionary and amplifies and propagates his or her vision. Certainly, one can say that the founders did not exclude this possibility, for the single constitutional aim of the Network is 'the advancement of learning and religion in any part of the world.'

A new Earth and a new heaven

Two events in the past century have changed normal human consciousness forever. The first is space exploration and the satellite pictures that make us aware that we live on 'island Earth' and thus are members of a global family. Since photos from space were first taken, our understanding of who we are has started to shift, whether or not we are aware of it, for we live now between a tribal and global identity. The problem is that after some 150,000 years of diverging evolution, during which our ancestors multiplied and split into competing groups, we are hard-wired for tribal consciousness. Somehow or other we must now find a way to global convergence, and to do that we must replace the cerebral wiring that keeps us thinking instinctively in tribal ways.

The second shock to our old tribal identity goes even further, for since Edwin Hubble proposed his theory of the expanding universe in the late 1920's, we can look in imagination from the outside, as it were, not only at the Earth but at the whole cosmos. Though Hubble himself did not know it, he was a new Copernicus. His original puzzlement at the galactic redshift can now be seen as a fuse lit under physical science, for it set in train a dynamic cosmology which takes us back to the point when time and space began. The only thing that prevents us from going beyond that point to a 'pre-cosmos' is failure of imagination, an inability to imagine a reality without time but with many, perhaps infinite, dimensions. This is meat and drink for topologists, but hard for the commonsense mind to grasp, and even physicists incline to reject the possibility that such a timeless domain beyond our observation could exist. Among the few who have seen its revolutionary implications is John Wheeler, who once asked the question, 'Should we be prepared to see some day a new structure for the foundations of physics that does away with time?' and shook the conservatives in his audience by answering his own question in the affirmative.

The new cosmology morphs inevitably into cosmogony, a theory of origins, and this makes trouble for traditional religion as well as science, since all religions are founded on a creation story of some kind, which will now have to be abandoned. Some will say, 'Why not just keep the old story as a mythical representation of the emerging new story of science?', and that is not so easy a question to answer as it may at first seem, particularly for Judaeo-Christianity, for there are deep truths in the ancient fictional narrative and these do not translate easily, or at all, into a scientific account. Nevertheless, the Jews have always boasted, 'Our God is a God of truth' (cf. *Deuteronomy* 13:14, and elsewhere) and Christianity in similar fashion has been promoted on the basis that 'the truth will set you free' (*John* 8:32), so now those of the Judaeo-Christian tradition are forced to ask if factual truth is really important to their religion, or are they just kidding themselves. It is crunch time, for when the full implications of the new cosmology are felt, all thinking theists will need to develop a new concept of ultimate reality.

An evolving God

Some fourteen billion years ago our whole vast cosmos was no larger in size than a speck of flour, a fact that calls for an effort of imagination to grasp, but is true nonetheless. An instant before this stage it was, of course, even smaller, but the big question that faces science now is whether or not it all began as a mathematical point, that is to say, a point with no dimensions. If so, simple logic assures us that this is when time and space came into being. The question now arising is, where and how did this timeless, dimensionless point exist and, again, simple logic tells us that it must have been in a timeless hyperspatial realm beyond our senses — and beyond Cartesian science. Should true science, then, venture there, reluctantly or in hot pursuit?

It is probably no exaggeration to say that the spiritual future of our species depends on how this question is answered. Has the universe existed forever or did it happen as a deliberate act of creation? The significance of the question is succinctly expressed in a few lines from Stephen Hawking which throw down the gauntlet to theologians:

> So long as the universe had a beginning, we could suppose it had a creator. But if the universe is really self-contained, having no boundary nor edge, it would have neither beginning nor end: it would simply be. What place then for a creator? (Hawking 1980, p.156–7)

Many are prepared to accept this no-boundary act of faith simply on his authority, but closer examination reveals it to be a pseudo-explanation, essentially sleight of hand in solid geometry, and ignores the really hard question: if the cosmos is expanding, what pre-existing reality is it expanding into? As regards what triggered the expansion, while theistic religions posit a timeless creating agent inaccessible to our normal senses, Hawking puts it down to a 'quantum fluctuation'. This sounds suitably scientific but is hardly more than hand-waving and, ironically, a crypto-religious answer, since it only removes a divine creator in order to replace him (or it) with fairy tale happenstance and a suspiciously Godlike causeless cause.

Hawking poses the scientific challenge, but the religious challenge is of a quite different nature, and strikes to the heart of spirituality — that ambiguous but all-desirable human quality. The religious perspective can be summarized in a quotation from an even more outstanding scientist, Johannes Kepler, writing around 1620:

> There is nothing I want to find out and long to know with greater urgency than this. Can I find God, whom I can almost grasp with my own hands in looking at the universe, also in myself?

His question was to be partially answered thirty years later by the Quakers, who preached a new doctrine of 'that of God within all men,' against which the Blasphemy Act of 1650 was specifically enacted by the English parliament. Then three centuries later came Big Bang cosmology to compound the blasphemy, for if everything that exists in our universe today was once contained in a primeval dot of energy, then the timeline of our self leads back to the moment of creation: we not only have 'God within' but are still in some significant sense 'within God'.

Clearly this divine reality is something far removed from the capricious potentate of the Abrahamic religions. It is, however, not far removed from the Brahman of high Hinduism and to talk of a God within and without is just another way of exploring the Brahman-Atman relationship. While learned theologians may speculate on this relationship, mystics in all traditions, not excluding Jesus, have known it experientially, and in the experience discovered a different sense of self-identity from that of the normal man and woman. The sense of oneness with a higher reality that they knew intuitively is now seen to be more than just compatible with modern science — it fits with a click. Their sense of presence has been recorded and partially described many times, but its acquisition now poses an evolutionary problem, and calls for a new religious meme to make it replicable. Not all by any means are curious to explore this new identity; indeed, it is probably true to say that most religionists would prefer to stick with a familiar God which they can worship or plead with for favours, while most professional scientists are religiously agnostic. For those who seek a different kind of God, however, the new science is on their side.

The new self

The new self is Janus-faced, finding its identity in looking to the deep past and the distant future. The line of advance towards and across the great divide can be roughly plotted as a transformation from self-centred to un-selfish to self-less. This becomes a spiritual progression as it is complemented by an expanding and intensifying empathy. We can be sure that it will not be a rapid advance, since most members of our species have not yet attained even a proper valuation of their individual self. Church-goers, for instance, are on the whole quite comfortable in being referred to as a flock. In fact, the notion of the independent self appeared quite recently in our evolutionary history, a point argued by the psycho-historian Julian Jaynes (Jaynes 1978). Simply put, his argument is that over a period of some centuries around the beginning of Greek civilization our ancestors crossed a threshold that took them irreversibly from the consciousness of the tribal group to the often burdensome self-consciousness of the fully human. For the first time our forebears started to ask, 'Who am I?'

The self-aware and self-determined human appeared only patchily until the full flood of the Enlightenment established it as a cultural meme in after the eighteenth century. Today we take our independent self for granted in the West — indeed, it almost defines 'the West,' but it is easy to forget how scary it must have been for those pioneers who felt compelled to do their own thinking and deny themselves the psychological security of group-thought. Now we are facing a new challenge to our self-identity, which may take a long time to appear clearly and will call at some point in the future for a new Enlightenment. As with our forebears who opted for the free self, it too will take some courage. The challenge will emerge into consciousness in those few individuals who feel themselves to be in the evolutionary stream and already find themselves asking at some level of awareness not 'Who am I?' but 'What can I potentially be?' and 'How can I fulfil that potential?'

An imperative at once religious and practical follows from this, namely, 'What does evolution require of me?' This surely is the unstated implication of E.O. Wilson's phrase 'decommissioning natural selection' quoted at the head of this essay. The answers to these related questions are as yet unclear, but the fact that since Darwin they have come slowly into our consciousness indicates that we as a species are moving towards the evolutionary divide which this essay foresees. Visionary science is now converging with experiential theology, and those who choose to explore the exciting prospect of synthesis will find themselves called to a new identity as co-creators.

References

Hawking, Stephen (1988) *A Brief History of Time*, Bantam, New York & London.

Jaynes, Julian (1976) *The Origin of Consciousness in the Breakdown of the Bicameral Mind*, Houghton Mifflin, New York. (Penguin reprint 2001)

Russell, Peter (2002), *From Science to God: A Physicist's Journey into the Mystery of Consciousness*, New World Library, Novato, California.

Sternglass, Ernest J. (2001) *Before the Big Bang: The Origins of the Universe and the Nature of Matter*, Four Walls Eight Windows, New York and London.

Swimme, Brian (1999) *The Hidden Heart of the Cosmos.* Orbis Books, New York.

Wilczek, Frank & Devine, Betsy (1987) *Longing for the Harmonies: Themes and Variations from Modern Physics*, Norton, New York and London.

Wilson, E.O. (1999) *Consilience: The Unity of Knowledge,* Random House, New York.

6. Restoring Harmony and Connection: Inner and Outer

HRH THE PRINCE OF WALES

Abridged speech by HRH The Prince of Wales at the Foreign Press Association Media Awards, Sheraton Park Lane Hotel, London, November 25, 2008.

There is mounting evidence that our collective perspective is not at all as sure as we once thought it was. Wherever you look the arguments that justify what we call 'progress' are finding it harder and harder to hide the less than glamorous side-effects of all we have achieved. The present crisis in the financial world, known to us all as the 'Credit Crunch', is but one recent graphic example; the environmental crisis that confronts us and is, in fact, a 'Climate Crunch', is another. I wonder, though, whether these crises would have flared so alarmingly had our perspective been somewhat wider when the decisions that have caused the troubles we now face were originally taken?

Also, we live in an age when technological ease has become so much a part of the accustomed way of life that it seems 'natural' to some, and even their right. But what does our comprehensive dependence upon such technology do to our connection with Nature and its patterns? Is it possible that it has loosened our inner moorings and shifted our orientation on to something extraneous to us? Does our increasing dependence upon technology begin to make us believe that we, too, and the world about us, are merely part of some enormous mechanical process?

These are questions that have concerned me for many years, and in considering them I have attempted in various ways to highlight what I see as the limited perspective that supports them. Why? Because there is now a worrying imbalance in the way we are persuaded to see the world. Our perception of Nature, in particular, has become dangerously limited.

Needless to say, when I have spoken of these things I have been shot at from all sides — the natural consequence, I suppose, of having the temerity to challenge the status quo of scientific Modernist rationalism. But undeterred by the barrage of high calibre invective, I would like to explain what lies at the heart of my concern and why I have expended so much of my energy trying to rectify the problem in the areas where it has manifested itself most virulently. I want to do this because the way you see the world, the way you understand why things are the way they are — is, I would suggest, vital to the future of this threatened planet.

Pressures to consume

It was a question from a newspaper correspondent back in the 1930s that drew from Mahatma Gandhi one of his pithiest responses. During his visit to Britain he was asked what he thought of Western Civilization, to which he replied, 'it would be a very good idea'.

Gandhi realized that Humanity has a natural tendency to consume and that if there are no limits on that tendency we can become obsessed simply with satisfying our desires. The desire grows ever more potent as we consume ever more, even though we achieve very little of the actual satisfaction we desire. Is this not so in the Western world today? Despite such high levels of consumption, we hear so many people admitting to feeling deeply dissatisfied. Studies now show this to be the case too. A report by the Children's Society in this country concluded earlier this year that the pressure on children, particularly those from poorer backgrounds, to have the latest designer clothes and computer games is resulting in more and more of them falling into depression. Which reminds me of that wise observation about Gross National Product made by Robert Kennedy forty years ago, that it 'measures everything except that which makes life worthwhile.'

One of the downsides of consumerism, it seems to me, is that it forces us to compromise on issues that should not be compromised. I'm sure there are many people who know that it is wrong to plunder the Earth's treasures as recklessly as we do, but the comprehensive world view which we now inhabit persuades us that such destruction is justified because of the freedom it brings us, not to say the profits. In other words, our tendency to consume is legitimized by a view of the world that puts Humanity at the centre of things, operating with an absolute right over Nature. And that makes it a very dangerous world view indeed.

It is an approach which accepts as the norm a one-sided, entirely 'linear' form of progress and an extremely literalized view of the world. For some reason we have been persuaded that what we see is all we get. It is a view encouraged, I am afraid, by some of the Media, and it concentrates only on the outward parts of creation. It does not look to the whole — so much so that we happily de-construct the world around us, dismissing as unreal anything that cannot be objectively measured and tested. It is, if you like, a world of only visible quantities.

An approach fit for purpose?

The question I would ask you to ponder this evening, then, is whether this predominantly rational, technologically driven and secularist approach to life is actually 'fit for purpose' in the twenty-first century? It is an approach which has been adopted in such a wholesale fashion that I feel many do not even realize that we have lost something very precious — what I might best describe as that intuitive sense of our interconnectedness with Nature — which includes the realm beyond the material.

The movement responsible, in my view, for the imbalance rose to dominance at the start of the twentieth century. As you will know it is often called 'Modernism'. Now, this movement must not be confused with the great social, economic and political advances of the earlier 'modern' age, the many benefits of which endure to this day. The 'Modern-ism' I refer to offered us an unrelenting emphasis upon a material and mechanistic view of the world. To quote from the Victoria and Albert Museum's foreword to its recent exhibition on Modernism, 'Modernists had a Utopian desire to create a better world. They believed in technology as the key means to achieve social improvement and in the machine as a symbol of that aspiration.' Generally speaking, we can say that it focussed its attention upon the parts and not the whole — to the point of deconstructing the world around us — and dismissed as unreal anything that could not be objectively measured and tested. This approach has, of course, brought us obvious benefits. But I would argue, however, there have also been costs to this 'instrumental' relationship with the world which, as we are finding out, are increasingly painful and destructive.

By the arrival of Modernism the West had been held in the sway of a mechanical way of thinking for over two hundred years. An approach set in train by the likes of Descartes with his concept of Man as Machine. The collective view of things had also been shaped by two centuries of what has now become the comprehensive industrialization of life with its linear process of inputs and outputs and with urban perspectives taking precedence over traditional, rural ones. Thus the ground was laid for the arrival of those straight, efficient lines of Modernism with the aim of simplifying and standardizing the world, making things as efficient and as convenient as possible.

This is why, for example, the curved streets of towns became straight matrices and why we have so many buildings grouped into single-use zones, including those for living — most noxious of all, those high rise blocks of flats which, throughout the 1960s and 70s, became the living quarters — indeed ghettos — for thousands of people in every city across Europe and the United States.

Architecture and community

Removed from their communities, people were accommodated in these brand new, convenient, concrete cul-de-sacs in the sky, and lo and behold, when their newness quickly faded those areas all decayed into violent and soul-destroying ghettos with no sense of place, nor any capacity to nurture community. And guess what is happening now in the new cities springing up in China and India? As they doggedly follow the Western pattern of forty years ago people are, once again, compelled by forces beyond their control to leave their farms and their communities to seek housing where they end up living like factory-farmed chickens in those self same, high-rise, soulless, mechanical boxes. Thus are millions more people condemned to the same toxic future.

The reason I have been so exercized about such architecture and such urban design is that the imposition of that simplistic and empty geometry drastically reduces the richness of a complexity that is actually more crucial to health than many seem to realize. Unfortunately, those who drove this twentieth century ideology did not seem to understand (or perhaps they simply ignored) what today's intricate studies of biology and microbiology declare loud and clear — that complexity is actually key to life. The diversity that made up this complexity was bulldozed away in the pursuit of simplicity, of increasing uniform monoculturalism and, above all else, convenience, creating an instant appeal that continues to fuel the conspicuous consumption and throwaway societies we now see everywhere. Just what Gandhi most feared and predicted ...

A crisis in perception

The question is, how has this come to be? I would suggest it is the net result of two important seismic shifts in our perception. First, Modernism fuelled a fundamental disconnection from Nature — from the organic order of things that Nature discloses; from the structure and cyclical process of Nature and from its laws which impose those natural limits Gandhi was at such pains for us to recognize.

As a result, our perception of what we are and where we fit within the scheme of things is fractured. This is why I consider our problems today not to be an environmental crisis *per se* ... nor a financial crisis. They all stem from this fundamental crisis in our perception. By positioning ourselves outside Nature and believing ourselves to be free without limit to manipulate and control her constituent parts, imagining somehow that the whole will not suffer and can take care of itself whatever we do to its separate parts, we have abstracted life altogether to the extent that our urbanized mentality is now out of tune with the key principles underpinning the health of any economy and of all life on Earth. And those principles make up what is known as 'Harmony'.

Biology now shows us that in all living things there is a natural tendency towards Harmony. Organisms self-organize themselves into an order which is remarkably similar at every level of scale, from the molecules in your little finger to those vast eco-systems like the all-important equatorial rainforests. Life seeks and finds balance. This means there is an over-riding coherence to the complexity of life on Earth, at every level of scale — to the extent that we should really see every organism as a complex system of interrelated and interdependent parts. They work together in a coherent way to produce a harmonic whole. And when it is in balance, when there is harmony, the organism is healthy.

But we do not think we need this in our farming, nor in the streets where we live, nor in the way we treat our own health and our immune systems. And so, whether it is the microbe, the ecosystem or the entire environment upon which we all so profoundly depend, the living organism suffers 'dis-ease'. It gets sick.

This is why, for what it is worth, I have been so concerned and outspoken about the way in which industrialized agriculture sees Nature simply as a mechanical process, as if it is supposedly ever capable of producing yet more at no long term cost. When you consider that in one pinch of soil there are more microbes than there are people on the planet you have to ask what irreversible damage do we do to the delicate, complex balance of such a fragile ecosystem as the six inches of top soil that sustains all life on Earth when we subject it to chemicals that are so much part and parcel of the agri-industries of today? The soil's health is our health. And yet we have eroded it and poisoned it and failed to replace lost nutrients to such a degree that a recent worldwide survey for the UN found that in just fifty years we have lost a third of the world's farmable soil. That is hardly a sustainable rate of exploitation. We have done so because we have either ignored or simply forgotten how profoundly 'health' depends upon organisms operating in harmony with their surroundings and within the cyclical rhythms of Nature. This is neither a debating point nor a coincidence. It is a fundamental law of Nature. All organisms depend upon a state of harmony to be healthy.

But this is only half of the story. And I don't want to end without making a brief mention of the other, and in my view, deeply worrying aspect of our separation from what Nature discloses.

Spiritual roots

Implicit in the ideology of 'Modernism' was the notion that we could somehow disconnect ourselves not just from an outward contact with Nature, but from our inner nature too; from the accumulated wisdom of the ages. Thus spiritual practice is nowadays denigrated by many. It is seen to be nothing more than outdated superstition. But, being lovers of words, I am sure you will be as intrigued as I am that 'superstition' actually means something much more profound if you see it as two words. They point to a heightened sense of something within. But what? Could it be that animating source of the harmony inherent in all life? Could it be that intuitive element in our human constitution; that 'sixth sense', perhaps?

It is interesting that the physicist Werner Heisenberg, who gave his name to the Uncertainty Principle in quantum physics, would tell his students not to see the world as being made of matter. It was, he said, made of music. He recognized what Pythagoras knew well, that chaos is ordered by number and that Nature is made up of precise numerical patterns. They express diverse movement, but always within the defining boundaries of Unity.

Is it not worth recalling that every one of the great civilizations right back to ancient times understood this patterning? They depicted what might be called the 'grammar of harmony' in their mythology and through the symbolism that adorns much of their art and architecture. That is because these patterns reflect symbolically the nature of the unseen realm. Such patterns, so familiar to us in every sacred building from the ancient Hindu temples of India to the great Gothic cathedrals of these islands, were seen as key to understanding the subtle structure of awareness, which is the ultimate sacred wonder. Our nature mirrors that sacred wonder. Now, is this superstition or, once again, to do with the fundamental laws of Nature? In cutting ourselves off from Nature we cut ourselves off, more and more, from what we are; from our inner selves, and from what that in-born tutor, our intuition, offers us.

By this stage in the proceedings you may well be asking what on earth I am trying to get at. You may believe that I have some curious and reactionary obsession with returning to a kind of mock medieval, forelock-tugging past. In fact all I am saying is that we simply cannot contend with the global environmental crises we face by relying on clever technological 'fixes' on their own. It is, as the conservationist Aldo Leopold has put it, like fixing the pump without fixing the well. We have to alter our perspective of the world and to begin to realize that Modernism on its own is in fact unfit for purpose in the twenty-first century.

The lessons are all around us. When I went to see the appalling devastation of the tsunami in Sri Lanka I was fascinated — but not surprised — to learn of how the tribal peoples of the tiny Andaman and Nicobar Islands survived. They live in the middle of the Bay of Bengal, 800 miles east of Sri Lanka and 340 miles to the north of Sumatra. They were closest to the epicentre of the earthquake and yet, despite the islands bearing the brunt of the devastation, nearly all their people were saved. And how? By using their instinctive powers of participation. Coastal tribes like the Onge and Jarawa on South and Little Andaman noticed subtle changes in the behaviour of birds and fish. These warning signs are woven explicitly into their folklore — passed down from one generation to another — and so they responded immediately to these warnings.

Participation and harmony

Such people do not observe the world from the outside. They consider themselves to be participants in it; they define life on Earth as 'sacred presence' and they do something if they sense that the balance of things is beginning to fragment. So maybe there are lessons for us here: firstly, that to ignore all the God-given senses, save the rational, may be the quickest way for mankind to head for extinction; and, secondly, that we, too, should consider where our modern day 'folklore' is leading us.

So, what I am suggesting then is a regaining of an active appreciation of the harmony inherent in all life. And that means, shifting our perception; taking a step back and seeing that we are not separate from Nature — we are immersed in it completely, as a fish is in water. But we can only do that by restoring to the mainstream the essence of the lost spiritual dimension. Simply because the real treasure in life lies in our hearts. And yet all Modernist approaches to education educate it out. It is time to restore that sense of the sacred to its rightful place before it really is too late.

I have tried to suggest that the denial of our real relationship with the universal truths through a deep connection with Nature and her laws has engendered a dangerous alienation. In denying or forgetting the invisible 'grammar of harmony' we create cacophony and dissonance. So if we hope to restore the balance, we need to reintegrate in a contemporary way the best parts of this abandoned and ancient understanding of Harmony with the best of modern technology and science, not least by developing the kinds of innovative and more benign forms of technology that work *with* the grain of Nature rather than against it.

You may say that this is impossible, but it seems to me that a good start would be to take that long, hard look at ourselves and, as I suggested, to question very seriously whether the dominant attitude of our day is fit for purpose; whether it really enables us to see things as they truly are. Then, but only then, we may begin to head in the right direction, towards a much more participative, integrated way of living; one that places greater value on coherence and the limits of Nature. And, essentially, sees the world the right way round.

7. Modernity and the Transmodern Shift

OLIVER ROBINSON

Oliver Robinson is Senior Lecturer in Psychology at the University of Greenwich. He has published on the nature and effects of crisis in individual life, and on the parallels between crises and development at the individual and collective level. His interests in philosophy and the history of ideas include idealism, functionalism, the epistemology of science, the nature of the human self / spirit and the nature of modernity. He is a manager of the Scientific and Medical Network.

Before I begin my argument, I must admit to being somewhat wary of the idea that our time is one of seminal crisis, and that we are attempting to usher in a new and better paradigm or era. My wariness stems from the fact that since the second century CE, individuals and groups have proudly claimed that *their* generation heralds the imminent end of the world as we know it, and that a new dawn is nigh. There have been endless failed predictions of judgment day, of the second coming, and the start of a new age. We endlessly replicate the story that the world is fallen as a result of human weakness and greed and that we have the key to its rebirth. Booker, in *The Seven Basic Plots* (2005), has shown that this 'rebirth' plot is a staple of great fiction, while my own research has found the same plotline as a common theme in autobiographical narrative (Robinson & Smith 2009). So if all generations have the propensity to think that theirs is an auspicious and critical juncture in history — a rebirth moment — can we be sure that *ours* genuinely is? We don't have the benefit of historical hindsight with which to judge the significance of our era and its developments, so is there a way that we can assess whether our time has genuine historical relevance? Is a 'New Renaissance' really afoot or are we just telling ourselves a story to give our lives the gloss of significance, as we have been doing for thousands of years?

The best way, I believe, to get some perspective on this question is to consider the antecedent historical context of our time. My research into modernity has helped to convince me that we are living during a time which represents *part of* a shift out of the modern era — a move to a transmodern way of existing. Given that we have been talking about 'postmodern' for some time, this may come as not a particularly novel thesis — but postmodern ideology is not the way the out — it is a critique of modernism's deification of rationality, a parody of modernism, not a movement beyond it. A transmodern worldview is quite different.

Four hundred years ago in England

To highlight the key features of the modern era and its relevance to understanding our contemporary crisis, let's briefly shine a light on England four hundred years ago, several decades before the modern experiment was to begin. England in 1609 was a mainly agrarian society with a population of around three million. After London, Norwich was the second biggest city, with 20,000 people. In London, the average lifespan was 35 years, and in some districts just 25. Infant mortality was around 20%, but in plague years went up to 60%. There was no sewerage system and outbreaks of cholera were frequent. The culture was one of oppressive Protestant religiosity: non-attendance at church services was a punishable offence, Catholicism could not be openly practised and atheism was punishable by torture and death. The monarch was considered divinely appointed and had total power. Society was organized by a rigid caste system — even what you wore was determined by your position in the social hierarchy, and thanks to sumptuary laws you could be fined for wearing garments that were 'above your station'. There was very little freedom of expression — theatres were frequently closed down for 'inflammatory comment' and all printed material was controlled and heavily censored by the king's authorities. Less than 1% of the population was entitled to vote — wealthy male landowners. Literacy was still rare; approximately 70% of men and 90% of women couldn't sign their own name. Arguably, England of four hundred years ago was an environment that had become so socially and environmentally suffocating that the birth of a new era was simply necessitated.

The modern era

The start of the modern era can be traced to the 1640s, the decade during which Britain was plunged into civil war, non-conformist religious groups proliferated and Descartes wrote his *Meditations*. The received divine order of things started collapsing and the apocalyptic Thirty Years War in continental Europe, which had killed almost a third of Western Europe's population, finally came to an end, crushing the prospect of a united Catholic Europe. Auspiciously, Isaac Newton was also born in this decade. This decade was the first spark of a movement that was to eventually affect *every* branch of human endeavour — arts, science, society, religion and politics. Medieval society had been based on faith, duty and the upholding of tradition to maintain the perfections of the past. Modernity challenged these notions with a new subversive worldview based on the following four axioms:

1. The past is *not* a repository of truth that must be clung to at all costs, and the future may contain as yet *unrealized* truth.

2. Tradition, authority and the appeal to precedent are flawed sources of guidance, knowledge and morals, therefore it is right to be sceptical of them.

3. An individual can discover his/her own truth or path by way of employing his/her rational facility and by following the evidence from his/her senses.

4. Individuals should be granted personal liberty to search
   and experiment in the above way.

The implications of these four little precepts are immense. If individuals are not yoked to tradition and can forge their own values and find their own truth, then society must accept constant innovation, revolution and rebellion as established ways are constantly undermined and surmounted. Society will inevitably move towards an individualistic culture when the collective unity of ritual, belief and behaviour that bound pre-modern society together inevitably dissolves as individuals search for their own ways of living. Pluralism is inherent in the modern system, for individuals and groups will find different solutions to social problems and find divergent answers to the big questions, if they are free to explore. A result of releasing rationality from the shackles of dogma is the development of new ways of organizing economic and agricultural life, and corresponding growth in economic activity as both production and demand increase. A further outcome is the rise of nationalism and democracy, as systems of governance based on absolute authority of an aristocracy or an external empire are no longer justifiable to the newly rebellious and empowered modern minds that had internalized the above four axioms. Perhaps the greatest feature of the modern mind is the extraordinary optimism and hope shown in the idea that an individual can improve on the products of history and the great masters of old, whether in science, philosophy or art, and therefore has *total* license to innovate.

Those of a more conservative disposition were terrified by this new desire for continual change and the undermining of traditional hierarchy and authority that came with it, yet the wheels of the Enlightenment had been set in motion and there was no going back. Descartes' dictum to doubt everything was typical of the new modern mind. Philosophers from Voltaire to Rousseau to Kant to Paine extolled the virtues of thinking for oneself and shedding old superstitions. Kant saw the Enlightenment as the process of humanity growing up into a mature form. He wrote:

Enlightenment is man's emergence from his self-imposed immaturity. Immaturity is the inability to use one's own understanding without guidance from another. This immaturity is self-imposed when its cause lies not in lack of understanding, but in lack of resolve and courage to use it without guidance from another. *Sapere Aude*! [dare to know], have courage to use your own understanding! That is the motto of the Enlightenment. (Kant, 1784)

While philosophy was being transformed by the new scope of free rational enquiry, religion was also forced to adapt. Religion based on unquestioning faith and deference to priestly authority did not sit well with the doubt and ceaseless inquiry that modernity had spawned. However, religion is an adaptive beast, and in the first century of the modern era, new 'nonconformist' Protestant sects proliferated in Europe, reflecting (and maybe helping create) the rebelliousness of the modern spirit. Groups such as *The Religious Society of Friends for Truth* (The Quakers) created an approach to religion in which scriptural and priestly authority were ousted in favour of an individual search for truth within oneself that could adapt and change with successive generations. In the experimental furnace of modernity were forged hundreds of new religions and spiritual movements (for a comprehensive survey of modern religions, see Partridge 2006). From movements such as Deism (starting in the eighteenth century), to the Bahai religion (founded in mid-nineteenth century), to the New Thought movement and Theosophical schools of the early twentieth century, to the Westernized Buddhism and Sufism movements that appear in Europe and America after World War Two, to the eco-spiritual groups of the 1960s and 70s, the spiritual impulse has morphed in endless new directions through the modern era. These new religious and spiritual movements were distinct from those with pre-modern roots in that they were more pluralist and tolerant of the other, far less accepting of scripture as a source of authority, and more based on direct experience and mysticism.

Politics also adapted to the pluralism of the times, with multi-party democracy being the inevitable consequence of scepticism of received authority, and of individuals and groups competing for governance based on rational argument. The innovative spirit of modernity spawned industrial, agricultural and technological revolutions. Science became the figurehead of the modern mindset, embodying the virtues of questioning, rationality, continual experiment and a search for new truths. The Royal Society was founded in 1660, and Newton's *Principia* was written six years later (although not published until 1687). Yet there was no rapid shift into a new era — the transformations of modernity took another hundred years of rebellious philosophers, scientific breakthroughs and political revolutions to become a dominant movement that directed society from the centre.

The malaises of modernity

The revolutions and wonders of modernity are legion — it delivered transformations in every sphere of life. But modernity has always been a risky path and has brought all kinds of problems alongside its advances, for in the process of unlocking individual freedoms it brings forth both the best *and* worst sides of human beings into public display. The contemporary philosopher Charles Taylor (1991) distils the problems of modernity down to three. The first of these is the tendency towards narcissistic individualism in modern society and a corresponding loss of a sense of community and social cohesion. The second is the loss of meaning and significance that comes with the dominance of instrumental reason at the expense of intuitive and heart-led modes of knowing and relating. The third is the sense of social alienation and powerlessness that can occur in the face of the complexity and bureaucracy of modern life. Furthermore, modernity has brought war on unparalleled scales of devastation as our capacity to develop weaponry has increased ahead of our maturity and wisdom to deal with international matters peacefully and to move past the xenophobic mentality so characteristic of modern nationalism. Meanwhile the violence between human beings has been matched by the violence towards the natural world enacted in the name of the God of Growth, the deity of capitalism.

Many rightly criticize modernity for these problems, but those who truly despise it and cannot accept its hegemony over the certainties of traditional religious life are fundamentalists. As Karen Armstrong has described in her book *The Battle for God*, fundamentalists are modernity-haters — they pine for pre-modern times of united and insular community, strong faith, and black-and-white morals (Armstrong 2001). Some fundamentalist sects such as the Amish are benign, some have become angry and are not. They detest the ephemera, rational coldness and moral relativism of the modern world. They still hold that Truth and Perfection are in the past, and that the best way of being truthful is maintaining traditions that bind us to that past. Where fundamentalists are deeply mistaken is that the solution to modernity's problems lies in reverting back to a pre-modern social structure. Modernity may be past its sell-by-date, but there is and must be a way *forwards*. An adolescent does not sort out his troubles by reverting back to being a child, he must forge a path into adulthood, and the same is true of society as a whole. Modernity can be construed as a kind of collective adolescence — a transitional time of experimentation, growth and change through which we must pass on our way towards a more balanced socio-cultural adulthood (Robinson 2009). A new phase of human history is required which transcends modernity, taking its many magnificent gains but overcoming its nagging malaises. And this phase is being born around us *right* now — that is what a historical lens shows us.

Towards a transmodern worldview

If we grasp the nature of the modern era and its enduring features, we better understand that we are currently taking faltering steps towards a new phase of human development. Paul Ray, in his article *The Rise of Integral Culture* (1996), is the first person I am aware of to use the term 'transmodern' to describe this emerging worldview. He states that the essence of this paradigmatically new approach to life is a set of values and goals that overcome the endemic malaises of modernity, and that address the requirement for global unity-in-diversity that our pressing environmental and social challenges require.

The evidence for the transmodern shift manifesting around us is found in the ideas and institutions that are addressing modernity's shortcomings in a progressive manner. A characteristic of modernity is its emphasis on *only* rationality as a way of understanding the world and of making moral, social and economic decisions. This raising aloft of logico-mathematical rationality is modernity's greatest achievement and its greatest inherent limitation. There have been countercultural movements throughout modernity that have lauded the spiritual and artistic importance of feelings, such as the Romantic movement of the eighteenth century, but the main modern trajectory has been to keep reason untainted by the subjectivity of emotions. But now there is evidence that the era of untrammeled and dislocated reason is coming to an end. I can first turn to my own discipline, Psychology, to illustrate this. In the 1980s and 1990s several psychologists provided theoretical perspectives that challenged the modern view that 'intelligence' was a purely logico-mathematical and value-free ability to rationalize. Howard Gardner (1983) first upset the establishment by saying that interpersonal abilities, emotional intelligence, and physical abilities such as dance and sport, could all be seen to be important intelligences in their own right. The 'Emotional Intelligence' movement that then started with Mayer and Salovey's work in the 1990s capitalized on the growing idea that there were 'soft' intelligences that should be cultivated to complement the hard intelligences of modern thinking (Salovey & Mayer 1990). These include the ability to handle negative emotions, to cultivate positive ones, to direct one's behaviour purposively and to understand emotions in others. These capacities are much harder to measure than IQ, but they have generated immense interest — Daniel Goleman's popular book *Emotional Intelligence* (1995) has sold millions of copies. Since the year 2000 the shift towards a consideration of wider intelligences has continued with more mainstream psychological research directed towards understanding interpersonal abilities, wisdom, creativity and spiritual development.

The modern idea that rational-analytical-intelligence is sufficient to guide us through life is running out of support in Psychology. It is also being challenged by a renewed engagement with the notion of spirituality, beyond the traditional confines of religion and theology. The spiritual dimension of transmodernism* is evidenced in the diverse literature and organizations that consider ways of reintroducing spirituality into life in a manner that complements rational endeavour rather than compromising it, and that is not

---

* Often referred to using the not-dissimilar term 'transpersonal'.

confined to a particular religion or book. The mystical impulse has survived through modernity in many guises, but it has been inevitably squeezed towards the periphery as rationality has attempted to clear the world of unquantifiable or subjective concerns, while giving the *object* ontological dominance. Modern science posits observable objects and their quantifiable properties as ultimately real, and the world is viewed through the prism of science as a collection of objects governed by laws. However, despite the best efforts of scientists to remove the *subject* from the world, even going so far as to make the word 'I' taboo in scientific articles, it just will not go away. 'I' and the 'you' remain central to our vocabulary and our interactions despite the best attempts of materialist philosophers to reduce the world to a collection of 'its'. The *I* cannot be observed for it is always the observer — it therefore resides outside the province of science, which deals only with observable phenomena. This simple fact has been highlighted by many thinkers including Kant (who referred to the *I* as the transcendental ego), William James (who referred to the *I* as the self-as-subject) and contemporary thinkers such as Peter Russell (2005) and Ken Wilber (2007). Here we find ourselves in the territory of spirituality, for the subject *can* be explored through contemplative or reflective practice. The subject is spirit. In the process of acknowledging one's nature as irreducible subject, a person moves beyond a purely material conception of themselves and the world, not through faith, myth or superstition, but through a realization of their inherent nature. From the exploration of the *I* and the *you*, questions emerge such as: — Are subject and object *necessarily* inseparably and permanently linked? Could the universe *itself* be both subject and object? Am *I* just my body? Could I have a 'relationship' with the universe, or with nature, in the way I have a relationship with human subjects? It is the renewed openness to such questions that is a central part of the transmodern or 'postsecular' shift (King 2009). Such a 'bottom up' approach to spirituality, starting with an exploration of self, is not an alternative to grand theological or cosmological conceptions of Spirit, but is a complementary process that is available to all and highly congruent with the enquiring modern mindset.

Since the 1960s, a chorus of voices from various groups around the world have unified into a movement whose message is to develop more sustainable modes of industrial production and modes of living. It is a non-negotiable truism that perpetual growth on a finite system such as our little planet is impossible, and that we will have to work out how to live in a way that does not worship growth to such an extent. An 'age of equilibrium' (Mumford 1944) has been foreseen by those who are pioneering sustainable solutions, and such a post-growth society will bring revolutions as far-reaching as those brought by the onset of modernity. Our current economic crisis, which is far from over, is an opportunity for us to awaken to the limitations of forced continual growth in national economies and corporate entities. *The Centre for the Advancement of Steady State Economy* is an organization exploring a realistic vision for a balance-based paradigm. Recently, a conference in London was held on the notion of a zero growth economy, hosted by the Quakers. The idea of a post-growth world has been born and will come to be economic orthodoxy one day, unless we are unable to make the transition from our growth-based paradigm and burn out in a frenzy of consumption.

The egoism and self-centredness that characterize modern societies at both the individual and national levels is being tempered by developments since World War II. At the individual level, the growth of the human potential movement, with its emphasis on creativity, openness, simplicity and wholeness as viable ends for the human adult to aspire to, suggest there is hope for a less cut-and-thrust interpersonal world. Nationalism, the social product of modernity, has traditionally been based on purely self-interested activity by nations, with international relations being correspondingly anarchic. A final piece of evidence pointing towards the birth of a transmodern worldview is the gradual dissolution of nationalism as the primary force shaping social relations at the macro-socioeconomic level. The development of transnational organizations such as the UN, which are not based on temporary treaties but on an agreed system of values and frameworks of international law, has provided a stride towards a world in which nations are more accountable and connected. The mutual reliance of nations, facilitated by trade and travel, has led to a world that is less partisan, while the unparalleled rise of electronic communications and virtual communities has led to social groupings and social networks that give no concern to national borders whatsoever. This emergent development of a global community has no precedent in history — it is entirely new, much as the developments at the beginning of modernity had no precedent, and may be part of our generation's contribution to overcoming the tribal them-and-us mentality that has maintained itself through modernity, and so helping create a more united human identity.

Concluding thoughts

I am writing this in 2009. We are in the middle of a recession that occurred off the back of a major crisis in the capitalist system. It seems a seminal time, but we should not fall for the short-termist fallacy that this particular year, and this particular crisis, is the spark of a paradigm shift, and that its fruits will be seen within the next year or two. No — a shift to a transmodern worldview, like the shift into modernity, is a project for an entire century. The thrust of this article has been to emphasize that we are best equipped to see the relevance of any particular time when we view it within the context of historical changes, which inevitably happen slowly. Our forebears only achieved their great shift into modernity thanks to their patient optimism that a new world could be born out of the ashes of the Middle Ages if the individual was empowered to innovate, free of the shackles of the dogma and unthinking tradition. Modernity thus allowed endless differentiation, individualization and novelty. This fragmented age of heady experimentation and expansion is now gradually coming to a close. Around us is being born an era with a new set of challenges — global co-operation, re-integration of the severed strands of modernity, and the search for a more meaningful, re-spiritualized world. That is the transmodern shift, and we are part of it.

References

Armstrong, Karen (2001) *The Battle for God: Fundamentalism in Judaism, Christianity and Islam*, HarperCollins, London.

Booker, Christopher (2005) *The Seven Basic Plots: Why We Tell Stories*, Continuum, London.

Gardner, Howard (1983) *Frames of Mind: The Theory of Multiple Intelligences*, Fontana Books, London.

Goleman, Daniel (1995) *Emotional Intelligence: Why it can matter more than IQ*, Bloomsbury, London.

Kant, Immanuel (1784) *An Answer to the Question: What is Enlightenment?* Retrieved from: http://www.english.upenn.edu/~mgamer/Etexts/kant.html, February 7, 2010.

King, Mike (2009) *Postsecularism: The Hidden Challenge to Extremism*, James Clarke Ltd.

Mumford, Lewis (1944) *The Condition of Man*, Mariner Books, Boston.

Partridge, Christopher (2006), *Encyclopaedia of New Religions: New Religious Movements, Sects and Alternative Spiritualities*, Lion Hudson.

Ray, Paul (1996) 'The Rise of Integral Culture,' *Noetic Sciences Review*, no. 37, pp. 4–16.

Retrieved from: http://www.noetic.org/publications/review/issue37/r37_Ray.html, February 9, 2010.

Robinson, Oliver C. (2009) 'The Not-Yet-Developed World: Exploring the Parallels between Adolescence and Modernity,' *Network Review*, no.98, pp.11–15.

— , & Smith, J. (2009) 'Metaphors and Metamorphoses: Narratives of Identity During Times of Crisis,' in D. Robinson, P. Fisher, T. Yeadon-Lee, S.J. Robinson & , P. Woodcock (eds.) *Narrative, Memory and Identities*, pp. 85–94, University of Huddersfield Press.

Russell, Peter (2005) *From Science to God: A Physicist's Journey into the Mystery of Consciousness*, New World Library.

Salovey, P. & Mayer, J. (1990) 'Emotional Intelligence,' *Imagination, Cognition and Personality*, no. 9, pp.185–211.

Taylor, Charles (1991) *The Ethics of Authenticity*, Harvard University Press.

Wilber, Ken (2007) *Integral Spirituality: A Startling New Role for Religion in the Modern and Postmodern World*, Shambhala, US.

PART 2

Consciousness and Mind in
Science and Medicine

8. Mind and Neurons: Consciousness and the Brain in the Twenty-First Century

LARRY DOSSEY

Larry Dossey MD is a former physician of internal medicine and former Chief of Staff of Medical City Dallas Hospital. He is the author of eleven books dealing with consciousness, spirituality, and healing, including the New York Times *bestseller* Healing Words: The Power of Prayer and the Practice of Medicine *and, most recently,* The Power of Premonitions: How Knowing the Future Can Shape Our Lives. *Dr Dossey is the former co-chairman of the Panel on Mind/Body Interventions, National Center for Complementary and Alternative Medicine, National Institutes of Health. He is the executive editor of the peer-reviewed journal* EXPLORE: The Journal of Science and Healing.

Who are you? What is consciousness? When and where did your mind originate and what will happen to it when you die? There is renewed interest in these ancient questions as a result of recent developments in various areas of science. These findings make possible new images of consciousness that are profoundly different from the strictly materialistic views of the twentieth century. Let's take a look, beginning with a field that has generated enormous excitement in neuroscience.

Mirror neurons

When we say to someone, 'I feel your pain,' recent discoveries suggest that we have the necessary neurological equipment to do just that. And not just pain; other emotions such as shame, embarrassment, lust, guilt, and pride may also be shared between different individuals (Rizzolatti & Sinigaglia 2008). So-called 'mirror neurons' are believed to mediate the sharing. These are neurons that fire both when an animal acts and when the animal observes the same action performed by another (Rizzolatti & Craighero 2004).

Mirror neurons were discovered in the early 1990s by neuroscientists in Parma, Italy, by a team led by Giacomo Rizzolatti, while studying the part of the brain in macaque monkeys that is involved in the planning of bodily movements. The researchers observed that neurons in the F5 region of a macaque's frontal cortex became activated after he grabbed a peanut. They were astonished to see that the same area also became activated when the macaque saw a researcher grab a peanut, even though the monkey was perfectly still. He and his team found the same effect in humans. When people witnessed another individual making hand movements and facial expressions, a part of their frontal cortex that is analogous to the F5 would activate, as if the observing individuals were making the hand movements and facial expressions themselves.

The term 'empathy neurons' is being widely used to refer to mirror neurons. As University of California-Los Angeles neuroscientist Marco Iacoboni explains, '[I]f you see me choke up, in emotional distress from striking out at home plate, mirror neurons in your brain simulate my distress. You automatically have empathy for me. You know how I feel because you literally feel what I am feeling' (Blakeslee 2006).

On the other hand, as we'll see, some experts have serious doubts about whether mirror neurons can explain the *conscious experience* of empathy or any other complex social emotion (Hickok 2009).

Nothing but a pack of neurons?

Many researchers have practically equated mirror-neuron activity with empathy and other social emotions. The implication is that when mirror neurons fire, the firing causes the felt experience of empathy — a bottom-up, brain-to-mind process. We should be cautious in assigning empathy and other manifestations of consciousness to physical structures in the brain, because of the inconvenient truth that no one knows how the physical brain is related to conscious experience. How do intracellular, electrochemical fluxes turn into thought and emotion? Is such a thing even possible? There simply is no obvious connection between the cellular activity of neurons and conscious experience. As the theoretical biologist and complex-systems researcher Stuart Kauffman puts it, 'Nobody has the faintest idea what consciousness is .... I don't have any idea. Nor does anybody else, including the philosophers of mind' (Kauffman 2010). Nobel neurophysiologist Roger Sperry took a similar position, saying, 'Those centremost processes of the brain with which consciousness is presumably associated are simply not understood. They are so far beyond our comprehension at present that no one I know of has been able even to imagine their nature' (Sperry 1995). From the world of modern physics, Nobelist Eugene Wigner agreed, stating, 'We have at present not even the vaguest idea how to connect the physico-chemical processes with the state of mind' (Wigner 1969). And as contemporary physicist Nick Herbert puts it, 'Science's biggest mystery is the nature of consciousness. It is not that we possess bad or imperfect theories of human awareness; we simply have no such theories at all. About all we know about consciousness is that it has something to do with the head, rather than the foot' (Herbert 1987).

In other words, we are profoundly in the dark about *how* an activated neuron is connected with empathy or any other emotion or thought. We don't even know for sure *that* mirror neurons send empathic messages to conscious awareness. For all we know, the neuroscientists may have it backward; i.e., the felt experience of empathy may cause empathy neurons to light up, not the other way round, through what Nobelist Sperry called downward causation. Sperry was emphatic about the importance of the action of consciousness on the physical brain. He said, 'Any model or description [of the brain] that leaves out conscious forces ... is bound to be sadly incomplete and unsatisfactory ... This scheme [downward causation] is one that puts mind back over matter, in a sense, not under or outside or beside it. It is a scheme that idealizes ideas and ideals over physical and chemical interactions, nerve impulse traffic, and DNA' (Sperry 1966).

The profusion of studies using functional magnetic resonance imaging (fMRI) to peer into the workings of the brain have had a bewitching effect on many researchers, prompting them to ignore views such as Sperry's, choosing instead to declare the brain's workings as the initiator and controller of all conscious and unconscious mental activity. For instance, the British neurobiologist Colin Blakemore, after reviewing the use of fMRI in communicating with patients in vegetative states and in probing the unconscious choices of normal individuals, concludes, '[I]ncreasingly neuroscientists are casting doubt on the significance of consciousness. They are revealing that most of what our brains do happens below the privileged arena of awareness, and that conscious states are caused by nerve cells that have already 'made up their minds', rather than conscious intentions which determine what our brains do' (Blakemore 2010). This is another way of saying that our neurons 'tell us so.' The pretzel logic of such statements usually goes unnoticed by those who make them. If Blakemore is right, then his own neurons may well have 'made up their minds' prior to his statement, in which case he is merely saying what his neurons are telling him to say. He has not arrived at his conclusion by careful deliberation and weighing of facts; he is an automaton controlled by his 'pack of neurons,' as neurobiologist Francis Crick put it. For that matter, why should we believe Crick, since, according to his own assertion, 'free will [is] ... nothing but a pack of neurons' (Crick 1995)? If he has no freedom of choice, why take his opinion seriously? In practice, of course, bottom-uppers such as Crick want to have it both ways. Everyone else may be nothing but a pack of neurons, but they are special, able to prevent their own reasoning from being dictated from below. Crick is a crick in the neck of logic.

Voodoo death

The neuron wars have been going on for decades. The flap over mirror neurons is only the latest skirmish in this protracted conflict. An early battle was ignited in the 1940s when legendary Harvard physiologist Walter Cannon published a landmark paper, 'Voodoo Death,' in the prestigious journal *American Anthropologist* (Cannon 1942). Cannon cited evidence from aboriginal cultures strongly suggesting that conscious perception and perceived meaning exert downward causation on the brain and body, occasionally resulting in death. One of his cases was a Maori woman who, on learning that the fruit she had eaten came from a tabooed place, was dead within 24 hours. Cannon's report set off a firestorm of controversy that continues to this day. One critic charged that Cannon's evidence was anecdotal and therefore irrelevant (Lester 1972). Another critic maintained that dehydration through 'confiscation of fluids' was a cause of voodoo death, not some mind-body process. He cited two Australian cases in which the victims were saved by rehydrating them (Eastwell 1982) (and ignored cases such as Cannon's Maori woman; one cannot die within 24 hours from withholding fluids). Cannon did not deny the importance of physical factors; in fact he endorsed them, saying, 'The combination of lack of food and water, anxiety, very rapid pulse and respiration, associated with a shocking experience having persistent effects, would fit well with fatal conditions reported from primitive tribes' (Cannon 1942). The debate is not whether physical factors are involved in voodoo deaths, but whether consciousness plays a significant role in initiating them.

I was involved in a case during my internship in which these issues surfaced. I was caring for a hospitalized African-American man who was dying, but I could not determine why. Every test was normal. One of my colleagues, who had grown up in the Rio Grande Valley in the Texas-Mexico borderland, knew about the activities of *curanderos* and *brujos* firsthand. Acting on a hunch, he interviewed my dying patient and discovered that a fortune-teller had hexed him when he refused to pay her. Convinced he was doomed, he was living out her curse. My colleague and I were convinced the man's death was imminent. As a last resort, we concocted an elaborate de-hexing ceremony that we secretly carried out late one night in near darkness. It frightened the poor man terribly, but it also proved utterly convincing to him. The next morning he awoke with a voracious appetite, perfectly well, and left the hospital shortly thereafter (Dossey 1982).

Hypnosis

No phenomenon in modern psychology presents greater challenges to the bottom-uppers than hypnosis. Reports of top-down phenomena abound, as when a hypnotized subject, when told that a penny placed on her arm is red-hot, erupts in a blister, a second-degree burn. These accounts reveal that the manipulation of meaning can exert physiological changes that are unusual, to put it mildly. As Princeton University psychologist Julian Jaynes explained:

> If I ask you to taste vinegar as champagne, to feel pleasure when I jab a pin in your arm, or to stare into darkness and contract the pupils of your eyes to an imagined light, ... you would find these tasks difficult if not impossible. But if I first put you through the induction procedures of hypnosis you would accomplish all these things at my asking without any effort whatever. (Jaynes 2000)

Hypnosis enables the body to behave in ways that defy ordinary neuronal function. If we are healthy, our neurons instruct our pupils to dilate in darkness, not contract. But under hypnotic suggestion they can abandon their usual function and operate in the opposite direction. This is a severe kink in the materialists' view that our neurons are always in charge — so severe that these events are often dismissed as due to faulty observation or downright fraud.

Many materialists regard hypnosis as the crazy aunt locked away in the attic of psychology, whom the more respectable members of the family avoid lest the insanity prove catching. Thus Jaynes observed:

> Hypnosis is the black sheep of the family of problems which constitute psychology. It wanders in and out of laboratories and carnivals and clinics and village halls like an unwanted anomaly. It never seems to straighten up and resolve itself into the firmer properties of scientific theory. (Jaynes 2000)

Through the centuries, folk healers learned to use downward causation therapeutically. An example is the use of suggestion to cure warts, a technique so prevalent it has been widely accepted in modern psychology. Physician Lewis Thomas, director of research for many years at Memorial Sloan-Kettering Cancer Center, recognized the sensational significance of this phenomenon. Thomas acknowledged that hypnosis sets the process in motion — no one knows how — and that the process downstream is wrapped in even greater mystery. He marveled at the entire event, saying:

> Some intelligence or other knows how to get rid of warts, and this is a disquieting thought. It is also a wonderful problem, in need of solving. Just think what we would know, if we had anything like a clear understanding of what goes on when a wart is hypnotized away. ... Best of all, we would be finding out about a kind of superintelligence that exists in each of us, infinitely smarter and possessed of technical know-how far beyond our present understanding. It would be worth a War on Warts, a Conquest of Warts, a National Institute of Warts and All.
> (Thomas 1995)

Thomas was mainly interested in the cascade of physical reactions occurring in the body following hypnosis, but what of the initiating event — the suggestion, thought, belief — that preceded the subsequent physical reactions?

Another black sheep is the placebo response, one of the most prevalent top-down phenomena known. In the placebo response, what one thinks or expects a therapy to do is so troublesome that researchers spend millions of research dollars trying to rein it in. It's warts all over again. If these unruly black sheep — hypnosis, meaning, belief, suggestion, expectation — would behave themselves, life would be a lot simpler for the bottom-uppers.

Researchers in Sperry's downward-causation camp do not ignore or dismiss the actions of mirror or any other type of neuron; they simply believe the game is more complex than hard-core reductionists realize. But even if the reductionists were correct, and mirror neurons do function as the sole gatekeepers and controllers of our empathic moments by 'telling us so,' that is no guarantee they are functioning for the good of others or ourselves, since one can be empathic toward, say, Hitler, as exemplified by skinhead neo-Nazis, just as one can be empathic toward Gandhi, Nightingale, or Mandela. There is no morality in neurons.

Promissory materialism

As far as we know, neurons don't make consciousness, and mirror neurons don't make empathy. To imply that they do is to descend into what philosopher of science Sir Karl Popper called 'promissory materialism.' This is the notion that one day, not so very long from now, we'll be able to give a completely physical account of consciousness. Lured by periodic advances in brain science, Popper explained satirically, '[W]e shall be talking less and less about experiences, perceptions, thoughts, beliefs, purposes and aims; and more and more about brain processes, about dispositions to behave, and about overt behaviour ... When this stage has been reached, mentalist language will go out of fashion ...' (Popper 1985). Nobel neurophysiologist Sir John Eccles agreed with Popper, saying, '[P]romissory materialism [is] a superstition without a rational foundation. The more we discover about the brain, the more clearly do we distinguish between the brain events and the mental phenomena, and the more wonderful do both the brain events and the mental phenomena become. Promissory materialism is simply a religious belief held by dogmatic materialists ... who confuse their religion with their science. It has all the features of a messianic prophecy ...' (Eccles & Robinson 1985) Mirror-neuron cheerleaders, take note. Empathy neurons are not empathy. Confusing the two involves the fallacies of misplaced concreteness and category mistakes — confusing the map with the territory, the menu with the meal.

Parapsychology

In his book *Parapsychology and the Skeptics*, philosopher Chris Carter's analysis of the role of consciousness in the world is one of the most scholarly critiques to appear in recent years. With withering precision he demolishes two of the perennial, go-to objections of critics of parapsychology — that there are no repeatable, replicated parapsychology (psi) experiments, and that psi experiments cannot be valid because they conflict with the laws of nature. Carter shows that there are thousands of experiments documenting psi, with staggering odds against chance, but that it requires an open mind to recognize them. He concedes that psi is indeed incompatible with the classical, mechanical, Newtonian view of the world, but he shows that psi does not conflict with the modern, quantum-relativistic perspective.

The insertion of psi into the debate about the role of mirror and other neurons is crucial. Neurons cannot account for the operational spectrum of human consciousness as seen in psi. Although there is a growing, vibrant discussion about possible quantum-biological processes in the brain and other biological systems (Garfield 2009; Hameroff & Penrose 2010; Engel *et al* 2007), as far as we know brains are *local* entities, in the sense that their actions are localized or confined to specific points in space, such as individual bodies, and to specific points in time, such as the present. Carter reviews the evidence that consciousness can manifest in ways that are *nonlocal*, ways that are unconstrained by space and time. In other words, *consciousness can do things a brain and its neurons cannot do.*

The implications are profound. If consciousness is *temporally* nonlocal, it is infinite in time, therefore immortal and eternal, because a limited nonlocality is a contradiction in terms; and if consciousness is *spatially* nonlocal, it is omnipresent. Nonlocal consciousness begins to resemble the ancient idea of the soul — some aspect of who we are that has no beginning and no end, and which precedes birth and survives bodily death.

Research documenting psi constitutes devastating evidence that the promissory materialists are off base. The evidence is abundant (Dossey 2009; Jahn 2007; Radin 2006; Kelly et al 2007; Schwartz 2007; Mayer 2007; Powell 2009). It comes from many areas such as, to name only three, computer-based studies demonstrating presentiment or precognition, now replicated in numerous carefully controlled experiments by various investigators around the world; the ability of individuals to influence the output of random-event generators, even when the individual is remotely situated in space and time; and the ability of individuals to 'see' events that are distant in both space and time, often in camera-like detail. Hundreds of controlled experiments attest to these abilities. If the neuronists, bottom-uppers, and promissory materialists admitted this evidence, their case for the primacy of brain stuff would disintegrate. They sense this, and this is why they pursue a scorched-earth policy of denying all evidence to the contrary, and why they generally 'just say no' when confronting evidence such as Carter and others have richly documented. Their denial *must* be total, for if they gave an inch and conceded the validity of a single experiment demonstrating that consciousness manifests nonlocally, their carefully defended neuronal world would collapse.

'Are mirror neurons too cool?'

Following the discovery of mirror neurons, there has been a flurry of enthusiasm to enshrine empathy, altruism, and cooperation as biologically valuable human traits. Empathy and altruism are now 'in,' after being derided for generations by hard-core evolutionary biologists who believe that selfishness is the proper metric for understanding human evolution and behaviour. But now that empathy has its ambassador in the brain in the form of mirror neurons, it's O.K. to talk about the biological value of being nice.

In his essay 'Are Mirror Neurons Too Cool?' science journalist Jonah Lehrer writes, 'Sure, mirror neurons are overhyped, but it's not every day that we get neuroscientific insight into everyday life' (Leher 2006). But how deep are the insights? Mirror neurons appear to contribute nothing that is fundamentally new to our understanding of the essential nature of consciousness. Mirror-neuron activity is a *correlate* of conscious experience — a widely applicable correlate to be sure, but a correlate nonetheless, not some deeply explanatory, unifying discovery where consciousness is concerned. And because 'correlation is not causation,' according to the venerable maxim from experimental science, we cannot say that mirror neurons cause empathy, just as we cannot say that our television sets cause Jay Leno or the World Cup, but are correlated with them. Of course we should applaud any discovery that adds to our knowledge of how the human brain functions. But we should resist the notion that mirror neurons somehow 'explain,' 'make,' or 'cause' empathy or any other expression of human consciousness.

Why the hype?

I suggest that several factors help explain the enthusiasm surrounding the discovery of mirror neurons in human brains. There is a world-wide, growing awareness that it is no longer business as usual for planet Earth and *Homo sapiens*. The litany of the sobering challenges we face is familiar by now to most open-minded people who prize science over polemic and politics; I will not list them here. The discovery of mirror neurons suggests that we have the biological firepower to meet these challenges, because we are geared to care and empathize with one another and the world and its creatures. A caring species is more likely to survive *because* it cares. Just when we thought we are little more than a skin-encapsulated collection of selfish genes, we have stumbled on to the discovery that we are built to be nice. The 'better angels of our nature' is no longer a metaphor; the angels are there, blinking on and off in our brains, in the form of mirror neurons. No wonder there is wild excitement over these tiny brain bits. Their discovery confirms capacities we didn't know we had, or refused to acknowledge, in our macho, winner-take-all world. Everyone seems thrilled. I've seen normally unflappable Buddhists behave giddily, as if mirror neurons are the greatest discovery since the Buddha's Four Noble Truths. The excitement goes beyond the usual gee-whizz reaction when ingenious scientific discoveries are announced, because mirror neurons are about more than science. They are about the virtues of compassion and the promise of human survival, and that's why they're cool.

Homo empathicus

In his important book *The Empathic Civilization: The Race to Global Consciousness in a World in Crisis,* author Jeremy Rifkin compellingly shows that empathy offers our best hope for survival as an endangered species. He says:

> A radical new view of human nature has been slowly emerging
> and gaining momentum, with revolutionary implications for
> the way we understand and organize our economic, social and
> environmental relations in the centuries to come. We have
> discovered *Homo empathicus*. (Rifkin 2009)

Rifkin cites the discovery of mirror neurons as key evidence for this view.

I believe Rifkin is on target about the crucial role of empathy in our future. Without empathy it is difficult to imagine how we can sufficiently cherish one another and safeguard our environment, the only home we have.

At this stage of its development, the main contribution of the mirror-neuron hypothesis is that it is a partial corrective to the view that we humans are overwhelmingly selfish creatures whose sole evolutionary imperative is to survive, reproduce, and perpetuate our genes, at whatever cost to those outside our kinship group. The mirror-neuron hypothesis suggests that we are equipped for empathy, compassion, altruism, and cooperation, in addition to being biologically geared for competition, procreation, and survival.

An empathy manifesto

On Monday, March 4, 1861, Abraham Lincoln took the oath of office as President of the United States and delivered his First Inaugural Address. The situation was grim. Jefferson Davis had been inaugurated as the President of the Confederacy two weeks earlier. Things were so tense that Lincoln had arrived in Washington by a secret route to avoid danger. General Winfield Scott's soldiers guarded his movements.

I have often thought that Lincoln's magnificent words, which were meant to heal broken bonds between North and South, can be applied in a broader context. Lincoln tried to heal political disunion. Today we face a more fundamental kind of disunion, in which we have gradually seceded from a sustainable relationship with the natural world. This rupture cannot endure without horrible consequences. The concluding words that Lincoln spoke to his fellow citizens from the East Portico of the Capitol, we might contritely speak to the greater world that sustains us. We might call it an Empathy Manifesto:

> We are not enemies, but friends. We must not be enemies.
> Though passion may have strained it must not break our bonds
> of affection. The mystic chords of memory ... will yet swell ...
> when again touched, as surely they will be, by the better angels
> of our nature. (Lincoln, 1861)

We are involved in a race toward fully realizing the empathic consciousness that is necessary for our survival. Time is not on our side. So blink and twinkle, you empathy neurons, blink for all you're worth!

References

Blakemore, Colin (2010) 'Do we want brain scanners to read our minds?' Telegraph.co.uk. (http://www.telegraph.co.uk/science/7159464/Do-we-want-brain-scanners-to-read-our-minds.html) February 4, 2010. Accessed Feb. 6, 2010.

Blakeslee, Sandra (2006) 'Cells that read minds,' *The New York Times,* January 10, 2006; (http://www.nytimes.com/2006/01/10/science/10mirr.html?_r=1&pagewanted=all) Accessed January 29, 2010.

Cannon, Walter (1942) 'Voodoo death,' *American Anthropologist*, Vol. 44, pp. 169–81.

Carter, Chris (2007) *Parapsychology and the Skeptics*, Sterlinghouse, Pittsburgh, PA, pp. 112–13.

Dossey, Larry (1982) *Space, Time & Medicine.* Shambhala, Boston, MA, pp. 2–6.

Dossey, Larry (2009) *The Power of Premonitions*, Dutton/Penguin, New York, NY.

Dossey, L, and Hufford, D. B. (2005) 'Are prayer experiments legitimate? Twenty criticisms,' *Explore (NY)* Vol. 1, no. 2, pp. 109–17.

Eastwell, Harry D. (1982) 'Voodoo death and the mechanism for dispatch of the dying in East Arnhem, Australia,' *American Anthropologist*, New Series, Vol. 84, no. 1, pp. 5–18.

Eccles, J. and Robinson, D. N. (1985) *The Wonder of Being Human,* Shambhala, Boston, MA, p. 36.

Engel, G.S., Calhoun, T.R., Read, E.L., Tae-Kyu A, *et al* (2007) 'Evidence for wavelike transfer through quantum coherence in photosynthetic systems,' *Nature*, Vol. 446, pp. 782–86.

Garfield, Michael (2009) 'The spooky world of quantum biology.' From hplus-gazine.com. June 1, 2009 (http://hplusmagazine.com/articles/bio/spooky-world-quantum-biology) Accessed February 10, 2010.

Hameroff, Stuart & Penrose, Roger (2010) 'Conscious events as orchestrated space-time selections.' (http://www.quantumconsciousness.org/penrose-hameroff/consciousevents.html) Accessed February 10, 2010.

Herbert, Nick (1987) *Quantum Reality*, Anchor/Doubleday, New York, p. 249.

Hickok, Gregory (2009) 'Eight problems for the mirror neuron theory of action understanding in monkeys and humans,' *Journal of Cognitive Neuroscience*, Vol. 21, no.7, pp. 1229–43.

Jahn, Robert (2007) 'The pertinence of the Princeton Engineering Anomalies Research (PEAR) laboratory to the pursuit of global health,' *Explore (NY): The Journal of Science and Healing*, Vol. 3, no. 3, pp. 191-345.

Jaynes, Julian (2000) *The Origins of Consciousness in the Breakdown of the Bicameral Mind*, Mariner Books, New York, NY, p. 379.

Kauffman, Stuart (2010) 'God enough.'. Interview of Stuart Kauffman by Steve Paulson. Salon.com. (http://www.salon.com/env/atoms_eden/2008/11/19/stuart_kauffman/index1.html) Accessed January 30, 2010.

Kelly, E.F., Kelly E.W. , Crabtree, A. , Gauld, A., Grosso, M., Greyson, B. (2007) *Irreducible Mind: Toward a Psychology for the 21st Century*, Rowman and Littlefield, Lanham, Maryland.

Lehrer, Jonah (2006) 'Are mirror neurons too cool?' Scienceblogs.com. (http://scienceblogs.com/cortex/2006/07/are_mirror_neurons_too_cool.php) July 24, 2006. Accessed January 31, 2010.

Lester, David (1972) 'Voodoo death: some new thoughts on an old phenomenon,' *American Anthropologist*, New Series, Vol. 74, no. 3, pp. 386-390.

Lincoln, Abraham (1861) Bartleby.com. (http://www.bartleby.com/124/pres31.html) Accessed February 1, 2010.

Mayer, Elizabeth Lloyd (2007) *Extraordinary Knowing: Science, Skepticism, and the Inexplicable Powers of the Human Mind*, Bantam/Random House, New York, NY.

Popper, Karl (1985) Quoted in: Eccles, J. and Robinson D. N. (1985) *The Wonder of Being Human*, p. 36, Shambhala, Boston, MA.

Radin Dean (1997) *The Conscious Universe*, HarperSanFrancisco, California.

—, (2006) *Entangled Minds*, Paraview/Simon & Schuster, New York.

Rifkin, Jeremy (2009) *The Empathic Civilization*, Tarcher, New York.

Rizzolatti, G. and Sinigaglia, C. (2008) *Mirrors in the Brain. How We Share our Actions and Emotions*, Oxford University Press, Oxford, UK.

Rizzolatti, G. and Craighero, L. (2004) 'The mirror-neuron system,' *Annual Review of Neuroscience*, Vol. 27, pp. 169–192.

Schwartz, Stephan (2007) *Opening to the Infinite: The Art and Science of Nonlocal Awareness*, Nemoseen, Buda, Texas.

Sperry, Roger (1966) 'Mind, brain, and humanist values,' *Bulletin of the Atomic Scientists*, Vol. XXII, no. 7, pp. 2–6.

Sperry, Roger (1995) Quoted in: Brian, D. (1995) *Genius Talk: Conversations with Nobel Scientists and Other Luminaries,* Springer, Amsterdam, Netherlands, p. 367.

Thomas, Lewis (1995) *The Medusa and the Snail,* p. 81, Penguin, New York.

Wigner, Eugene (1969) 'Are we machines?' *Proceedings of the American Philosophical Society,* Vol. 113, no. 2, pp. 95–101.

9. New Science, New Earth

CHRIS CLARKE

Chris Clarke was Professor of Applied Mathematics at the University of Southampton, researching Astrophysics, Quantum theory and the physics of the brain, until moving to free-lance work in 2009 to focus on the philosophical and spiritual connections of science. In addition to scientific posts, he has been chair of GreenSpirit (a charity promoting eco-spirituality) and The Scientific and Medical Network. His books include Living in Connection, Ways of Knowing *(edited) and* Weaving the Cosmos *(O-Books, to appear). cclarke@scispirit.com, www.scispirit.com*

Towards a new story

Ken Wilber once referred to our society as 'a world gone slightly mad'. Surely the 'slightly' here must be one of the most ironic of understatements! We humans are presented with almost conclusive evidence that our own actions can either destroy our climate or save it, and the majority are still opting for destruction. We place our economic system in the hands of people so insecure of their own value that they must be paid millions to reassure their egos. Billions of people adhere to religions based on equality, reverence for the world, mutual support and non-aggression; yet this heritage gets reduced to instructions on food and sex ... the list could continue indefinitely.

We have collectively got hold of the wrong end of the stick. Unless this is addressed, unless we start thinking differently, humanity will only blunder from one crisis to the next. Could the force of global warming effect the change, in a way that pleading and preaching cannot? Inevitably our awareness of the Earth as our provider will grow as warming has an increasing affect on our lives, on the weather and on the immediate physical conditions around us. This is a physical awareness, implanted in our bodies when we walk through unaccustomed heat, cold, rains and wind. The Earth starts to confront our whole being as a presence beyond ourselves that has to be acknowledged; it challenges our tendency to focus only on ourselves. Changing the way we think and feel needs this whole-person learning. So let us, in a spirit of hope, explore the direction in which we could be moving, starting by examining the main obstacle to progress.

The question is, why are human beings so extraordinarily creative, and yet we can find it so difficult to change our fundamental mindset? There is a single reason for both these properties of humans, which has been expressed in many different words: from St Paul's spirit and flesh, through Freud's superego and id, to the left brain/right brain split, to the research-based psychological models of Philip Barnard (Teasdale 1995), known as 'Interacting Cognitive Subsystems' or ICS. The message of all these is that we are two-component systems and the two are often at loggerheads. This is, of course, a vast over-simplification, but the ICS version fits the experimental data well and can take us quite a long way. I will call these two components 'rational' and 'relational', terms that will stretch at least to the last two of the examples just listed. The rational side is based on verbal propositions, while the relational is to do with how I conceive and feel my connections with the world around me, including the 'body-spirit knowing' that goes beyond words. On the basis of this sort of model, I propose that the way forward for most people, and the next step if society as a whole is to shift, lies not in attempting to make the two components one (that is to underestimate our anatomical heritage) but in refining both the rational and the relational, respecting their appropriateness in their respective domains, and cultivating the free flow of information and sensation between the two — within the individual and within society.

I began by suggesting that humans had got hold of the wrong end of the stick. We 'get hold of the stick' through a *story* about the world; by which I mean a body of concepts, values, beliefs, emotional associations, etc., supplying both rational and intuitive components held both by society and by the individual. Science influences our collective story because of its official prestige. While it obviously plays a vital role in the rational side of our society, it also feeds into our relational side with a message that the world is logical, controllable, amoral and mechanical. In this chapter I will discuss (with particular reference to physics) how this scientific message is still changing, helping us to get hold of the right end of the stick and change our ways.

The changing face of physics

In this section I will be talking mainly about physics, regarding both its rational and its relational sides. I will be using two concepts which need distinguishing. By *causality* I refer to the chains of connection through which one event causes the next event in what could be quite a 'mechanical' sort of way. (Note that my use of 'causal' here is quite unrelated to that of Wilber). By the active verb *being*, on the other hand (linked with terms like *agency* and *creation*), I refer to acts in which something new is injected into the fabric of the universe. *Causality* is mainly linked with rational knowing, and *being* mainly with relational knowing.

Following a century of quantum theory in physics and maybe half a century of systems theory extending from physics into biology, economics and other sciences, a much more clear and unified picture of causality can now be seen. In the form that quantum mechanics had reached in about 1932 there was a sharp distinction made between the classical 'world' of large things and the quantum 'world' of small things. In each world, considered on its own, causality was rigid: the state of the universe at any one time determined the state of the universe at all other times, past and future. When the two came into contact, however, a special sort of interaction called 'observation' or 'collapse' came into play, the outcome of which was unpredictable. All that could be known about it was the range of possible outcomes and their probabilities. (This was the disturbing feature that Einstein, five years earlier, had sceptically described as God playing dice.)

'Observation' was to be a thorn in the flesh of quantum theoreticians for many years. Von Neumann (1932) thought that observation only involved human beings to the extent that they were a particular sort of large machine, and he showed that it did not matter whether the observation occurred at the level of the measuring apparatus or the level of the human who looked at it. Shortly afterwards, London and Bauer (1939) argued that it was the particular aspect of human consciousness that made the difference, but their view remained a minority opinion. The main point was that, taking the quantum world and the classical world together, causality was no longer deterministic, but had a random element.

Jumping forward to 1996, we find Hans-Dieter Zeh and his collaborators publishing the definitive presentation (Giulini *et al.* 1996) of what some physicists call 'no-collapse quantum theory'. In this there is just one world, described by equations whose mathematical form suggests a deterministic causality. Most of this world is shimmering and unstable; but within it, like the tips of icebergs rising above the surface, are comparatively stable configurations: these form the 'classical world', not seen as separate from the quantum world, but arising from it and part of it. This classical aspect of the world, if looked at separately, has a non-deterministic causality (i.e. it involves random elements).

At this stage quantum theory starts to converge with other branches of science. Much of science, including physics, does not require quantum theory at all, or only requires it in order to provide quantitative corrections to classical (Newtonian) theory. This holds for systems ranging from the solar system to complex chemical reactions involving many different chemicals or biochemical reactions taking place in a cell. By the 1970s these all contributed to the field of 'complex dynamical systems' which showed a similar pattern to no-collapse quantum theory: at its basis may be a deterministic theory, but out of it emerges a richer behaviour that is not deterministic. This *emergence* is now seen by authors such as Stuart Kauffman (2008) as the essence of living creatures, who are agents: sources of new chains of causation. In such systems a new form can unpredictably arise, which in turn brings into being new laws, new patterns of meaning, new mini-worlds (ecosystems) previously undreamed of. Whereas the picture presented by the early developers of Newtonian theory was of a closed, mechanical universe, now, both from systems-theoretic approaches to Newtonian theory and from modern quantum theory, we have a picture of a universe whose causality is open to newness.

The astrophysicist and Templeton Prize winner George Ellis (Ellis *et al.* 2009), coming to this from the quantum mechanical side, argues that what enters in response to this openness is 'top-down causation'. Traditional Newtonian theory and quantum theory used 'bottom-up' causation, starting with the laws governing very small things and deriving from this the behaviour of large things. But we now realize that there is freedom for events at the level of large structures to shape what is happening at the level of the small-scale. The language of quantum theory, originally developed to describe observations, gives a way of understanding how this works. In the case of observations within the old quantum theory there was freedom for the experimenter to decide what sort of quantity was going to be observed (for example, to choose between measuring position and measuring momentum). This set a context, within which the lower level system responded with a particular value for the chosen quantity. Recast in the language of top-down causation, the high level system establishes a pattern of *meaning*, of sensitivities to particular elements in the environment. For example, the *E. Coli* bacterium manifests a sensitivity to nutrients in its environment to which it responds by swimming towards its food, the geologist sub-species of *Homo sapiens* manifests a sensitivity to clues in the landscape indicating underlying faults in the rock. These sensitivities, or patterns of internal meaning, establish contexts which constrain the lower level systems, whose response will be meaningful, though its precise content may be unpredictable.

To take this a little further: when top-down and bottom-up causalities are combined, the lower level systems obey a context dependent logic rather than a classical Aristotelian logic, a logic linked to the radical 'topos logics' developed in recent years (Isham & Butterfield 1998). This gives a rigorous meaning to the popular notion of 'both-and logic'.

But how does the agent — the bacterium or the geologist — decide on one system of meaning, or one context, rather than another? This takes us into 'mystery', meaning that it moves from rational knowing into relational knowing. The web of relationships in which we are held, including internal relationships between parts of our own psyche, enables the emergence of meaning as a truly creative act. As I will allude to later, this is something we can grasp experientially, but much more careful dialogue is needed in order to link it back to physics. Already, however, we have rich ingredients for enabling humanity to start thinking differently.

Telling the new story

Satish Kumar succinctly expressed the quality of the new story that is needed in the title of one of his books: *You are, therefore I am*. That is, we are to replace Descartes' 'I think therefore I am', the old story that enshrines the rational thinking of the isolated ego, by a new story that invites us into ever-expanding I-You relationships, in which we find our true selves. This story is now emerging, as Satish is joined by many other prophetic voices who are also taking part in its telling.

As agents, ones who act, we have responsibility. But my responsibility is not that of choosing between options laid out in advance like tick-boxes on a questionnaire. Once I have insight into what is going on in my mind I can recognize that such choices are no more than a mixture of the random and the mechanical — as also suggested by recent neurological work (Batthyany 2009) following on from that of Libet. Rather than this, I fulfil my responsibility when about to act by entering fully into my web of relationships: within myself, among other humans, within the greater Earth community, with what I sense beyond that. Within this web I can 'seek guidance', as it might be termed in religious traditions. If I hold a clear, sustained intention of being open to an understanding of whatever situation is concerning me, then I usually experience a shift in the *meaning* of the situation in which I find myself. New categories of meaning appear, new relationships between the elements of the situation. From there on, rational analysis can fruitfully take over.

To emphasize what is probably obvious, this concept of top-down causation is based not on fundamental particles but on wholes. (This is the essential insight of systems theory.) Wholeness — being a whole within a greater whole — is a quality that we encounter when we act from the concurrence of our whole being with those others with which we are in relationship. As our surroundings become meaningful for us, giving context and significance to our acts, we feel 'in the flow' and may also feel moved by a love that lifts our entire being into a greater communion.

Subjectivity and consciousness

I have already emphasized the importance of establishing a flow that bridges the relational and the rational while respecting the integrity of each. There is already a vibrant body of experience in this area linked with the concepts of *consciousness*, *subjectivity* and *quality*. These raise major philosophical issues for which there is not space here, but I will try to indicate their connection with the other concepts introduced earlier.

Science aims to deal with *public* knowledge. That is, its data should be such that anyone equipped with suitable training and/or apparatus can verify the data, or could have verified the data at the time when it was available, up to some specified degree of accuracy and reliability. Examples might be an eclipse of the sun, the sorts of charged particles produced by firing high energy protons into a given target, the proportion of the population of the UK with a height under 1.4 metres and so on. In scientific practice this sort of knowledge is expressed verbally and known rationally.

Another category of knowledge is *subjective* knowledge, which is about, or strongly influenced by, a particular personal perspective. For example, it might be my rational (i.e. verbal) analysis of how I think I am affected by past traumas or what I feel on hearing a blackbird singing on a spring morning. Some of this can be made public: the first of these examples is something that I can report verbally to anyone else, so that 'what Chris Clarke thinks about his traumas' is public knowledge — though 'Chris Clarke's traumas' may or may not be. The philosopher Daniel Dennett (1991) has proposed that the only possible science of consciousness, by definition of 'science', has to be restricted to subjective knowledge that is publicly reportable, an approach he calls 'heterophenomenology'.

The blackbird in spring example takes us from the rational into the relational, and into the controversial area of consciousness. It can reasonably be argued that, whereas my rational grasp of my experiences can be reported to others, their relational components can at best only be evoked in others through empathy. Such components are often called 'qualities' (or *qualia,* meaning 'how things are' as opposed to 'what things are') and consciousness is often held to be distinctively to do with this side of experience. This line of argument would imply that on Dennett's definition of 'science' there cannot be a science of consciousness. There are very important public policy issues around this area concerning the welfare of both humans and non-human animals (Wemelsfelder 2001).

If we are to have a robust new story that speaks to our whole experience, we need to make a bridge between our rational knowing, open to public report and easily linked with quantitative science, and our inner relational knowing that can be shared only through a meeting of minds in empathy. Stating, for example, that 'consciousness collapses the wave function' (see Google for instances) is only a clumsy paraphrase of 'then a miracle happens'.

The rational side of physics is based on mathematics while our relational understanding is based on sensed experience, often explored through spiritual practice. When we strive, as we must, to link them we necessarily use ordinary colloquial language for both. This raises a danger of watering down of both rigorous science and spirituality until they become indistinguishable; it can be no substitute for careful and respectful dialogue in order to establish a shared wisdom. A role can be played by mathematics, by the arts which evoke relational knowing through empathy — and particularly by the qualitative academic disciplines that ask of each proposal, who is telling this story, for what reason, on what grounds of tested experience?

The way ahead

When we speak of the 'current crisis' most people think of climate change. But our warming of the Earth through CO_2 emissions is not to be thought of as an isolated mistake — of major impact, but solvable by technology. Rather, it is an indicator of the fundamental unsustainability of our entire way of living. As Jonathon Porritt (2007) reminds us, any way of living which systematically depletes any one of the finite resources on which we depend — our various forms of 'capital' — cannot be continued indefinitely: it is unsustainable. He lists four primary capitals (natural, human, social and manufactured) and one secondary capital, financial, which derives its value from the others. Natural capital, consisting of the planet's resources, taking into account both their quantity and the structure of their distribution, is particularly crucial. Though there are deficiencies in this model (e.g. there is the plus of the available external energy from the sun, and the minus of the whole system becoming unstable well before any capital is exhausted) it provides a simple conceptual indicator of sustainability.

While the model can be elaborated into great complexity, it is crucial to appreciate that the key to living sustainably is not a matter of performing detailed economic calculations, but of opening one's heart to the Earth. Of course, the heart can be wrong, particularly in the distorted psychological state in which we find ourselves today, and so intellect is also needed as a corrective: sustainability ultimately depends on the synergy of intellect and relational knowing.

Relational knowing has withered, so our greatest need is to shift from our obsessive concern with humans and to reconnect in our whole being with the Earth, working with the planet rather than treating it as material to be plundered. But in the light of our new conception of physics, this shift achieves even more than allowing us to live sustainably: it is the first and most important step in our re-engagement with the whole chain of top-down causality of which we ourselves are a part, a step in which we start to discover what it is to be human; that we are agents, whole beings with the capacity to rethink and re-dream our world.

This 'new story' is actually very old! The religious, spiritual and humanistic traditions of society already embody it, at least implicitly, in their various different modes and languages. The opportunity presented by the current crisis is that of bringing these different modes together in a common cause. For the majority of individuals, perhaps, this will be too difficult: when faced with the fear of a threatening future it is too easy either to retreat into addictive behaviour or to cling to the fossilized quasi-rational shell of dogmatic religion. Opening to our true freedom is always a step into the unknown. For an influential minority, however, this step is now being seen as the only right path.

The methods required for connecting our rational and relational parts, which I described above as 'careful and respectful dialogue', have also been with us for some time, particularly as exemplified in the dialogues of David Bohm (1987) and co-operative enquiry practices developed by John Heron (1998). The spirit of dialogue has recently been further extended in meetings promoted by Schumacher College (www.earthlinksall.com/processandpilgrimage/) which incorporate a well grounded input on the side of physics. Organizations such as the Scientific and Medical Network and Learning for Life (engaging with young people) have been putting these principles into action. Now is the time to pursue this approach with urgency, greater depth and wider scope. The Earth calls us to release our presuppositions and seek new actions from a basis in this deeper dialogue. As well as a time of danger, now is a time of great hope for the future.

References

Batthyany, Alexander (2009) 'Mental Causation and Free Will after Libet and Soon: Reclaiming Conscious Agency' in Batthyany, Alexander & Elitzur, Avshalom (eds.) *Irreducibly Conscious: Selected Papers on Consciousness*, Winter, Heidelberg.

Bohm, David (1987) *Unfolding meaning: a weekend of dialogue with David Bohm*, Ark Paperbacks, London.

Dennett, Daniel (1991) *Consciousness Explained*, Allen Lane, New York.

Ellis, George; Murphy, Nancey and O'Connor, Timothy (2009) *Downward Causation and the Neurobiology of Free Will*, Springer, New York.

Giulini, Domenico; Joos, Erich; Kiefer, Claus; Kupsch, Joachim; Stamatescu, Ion-Olimpiu and Zeh, Hans Dieter (1996) *Decoherence and the appearance of a classical world*, Springer-Verlag, Berlin and Heidelberg .

Heron, John (1998) *Sacred Science*, PCCS Books, Ross-on-Wye.

Isham, Chris and Butterfield, C. Jeremy (1998) 'Topos perspective on the Kochen-Specker theorem: I. Quantum states as generalized valuations,' *International Journal of Theoretical Physics*, Vol. 37, pp. 2669–2733.

Kauffman, Stuart A, (2008) *Reinventing the Sacred*, Basic Books, New York.

London, Fritz and Bauer, Edmond, (1939) *La Théorie de L'Observation en Méchanique Quantique*, Hermann, Paris.

Porritt, Jonathon (2007) *Capitalism as if the World Matters*, Earthscan Publications, London.

Teasdale, John D. and Barnard, Philip J. (1995) *Affect, Cognition and Change,* Laurence Erlbaum Associates, London.

von Neumann, Johann (1932) *Mathematische Grundlagen der Quantenmechanik* (Die Grundlehren der Mathematischen Wissenschaften, Band 38) Springer, Berlin.

Wemelsfelder, Françoise (2001) 'The Inside and Outside Aspects of Consciousness: Complementary Approaches to the Study of Animal Emotion,' *Animal Welfare* Vol. 10, pp. 129–39.

10. The Credit Crunch for Materialism and the Possible Renewal of Science

RUPERT SHELDRAKE

Rupert Sheldrake, PhD is a biologist and author of more than 80 papers in scientific journals and ten books, including A New Science of Life *(new edition, 2009). He is Director of the Perrott-Warrick Project for research on unexplained abilities of animals and human. He began his scientific career as a developmental biologist, working at Cambridge University, where he was a Fellow of Clare College. He was also a Research Fellow of the Royal Society. His books include* The Presence of the Past, The Rebirth of Nature, Seven Experiments that Could Change the World, Dogs That Know When Their Owners are Coming Home, *and* The Sense of Being Stared At. *His web site is www.sheldrake.org.*

Credit crunches happen because of too much credit and too many bad debts. Credit is literally belief, from the Latin *credo*, 'I believe.' Once confidence ebbs, the loss of trust is self-reinforcing. The game changes. Something similar is happening with materialism. Since the nineteenth century, its advocates have promised that science will explain everything in terms of physics and chemistry; science will show that there is no God and no purpose in the universe; it will reveal that God is a delusion inside human minds and hence in human brains; and it will prove that brains are nothing but complex machines.

Materialists are sustained by the faith that science will redeem their promises, turning their beliefs into facts. Meanwhile, they live on credit. The philosopher of science Sir Karl Popper described this faith as 'promissory materialism' because it depends on promissory notes for discoveries not yet made (Popper 1977). Despite all the achievements of science and technology, it is facing an unprecedented credit crunch.

In 1963, when I was studying biochemistry at Cambridge I was invited to a series of private meetings with Francis Crick and Sydney Brenner in Brenner's rooms in King's College, along with a few of my classmates. They had just cracked the genetic code. Both were ardent materialists. They explained there were two major unsolved problems in biology: development and consciousness. They had not been solved because the people who worked on them were not molecular biologists — nor very bright. Crick and Brenner were going to find the answers within ten years, or maybe twenty. Brenner would take development, and Crick consciousness. They invited us to join them.

Both tried their best. Brenner was awarded the Nobel Prize in 2002 for his work on the development of the nematode worm *Caenorhabdytis*. Crick corrected the manuscript of his final paper on the brain the day before he died in 2004. At his funeral, his son Michael said that what made him tick was not the desire to be famous, wealthy or popular, but 'to knock the final nail into the coffin of vitalism'. (Ridley 2006, p. 208).

He failed. So did Brenner. The problems of development and consciousness remain unsolved. Many details have been discovered, dozens of genomes have been sequenced, and brain scans are ever more precise. But there is still no proof that life and minds can be explained by physics and chemistry alone.

The fundamental proposition of materialism is that matter is the only reality. Therefore consciousness is nothing but brain activity. However, among researchers in neuroscience and consciousness studies there is no consensus. Leading journals such as *Behavioural and Brain Sciences* and the *Journal of Consciousness Studies* publish many articles that reveal deep problems with the materialist doctrine. For example, Steven Lehar argues that inside our heads there must be a miniaturized virtual-reality full-colour three-dimensional replica of the world. When we look at the sky, the sky is in our heads. Our skulls are beyond the sky. Others, like the psychologist Max Velmans, argue that virtual reality displays are not confined to our brains; they are life-sized, not miniaturized. Our visual perceptions are outside our skulls, just where they seem to be.

The philosopher David Chalmers has called the very existence of subjective experience the 'hard problem' of consciousness because it defies explanation in terms of mechanisms (Chalmers 1998). Even if we understand how eyes and brains respond to red light, for example, the quality of redness is still unaccounted for.

In biology and psychology the credit-rating of materialism is falling fast. Can physics inject new capital? Some materialists prefer to call themselves physicalists, to emphasize that their hopes depend on modern physics, not nineteenth-century theories of matter. But physicalism's credit-rating has been reduced by physics itself, for four reasons. First, some physicists argue that quantum mechanics cannot be formulated without taking into account the minds of observers; hence minds cannot be reduced to physics, because physics presupposes minds. Second, the most ambitious unified theories of physical reality, superstring and M theories, with ten and eleven dimensions respectively, take science into completely new territory. They are a very shaky foundation for materialism, physicalism or any other pre-established belief system. They are pointing somewhere new.

Third, the known kinds of matter and energy constitute only about 4% of the universe. The rest consists of dark matter and dark energy. The nature of 96% of reality is literally obscure. Fourth, the cosmological anthropic principle asserts that if the laws and constants of nature had been slightly different at the moment of the Big Bang, biological life could never have emerged, and hence we would not be here to think about it. So did a divine mind fine-tune the laws and constants in the beginning? Some cosmologists prefer to believe that our universe is one of a vast, and perhaps infinite, number of parallel universes, all with different laws and constants. We just happen to exist in the one that has the right conditions for us. In the eyes of sceptics, the multiverse theory is the ultimate violation of Occam's Razor, the principle that entities should not be multiplied unnecessarily. But even so, it does not succeed in getting rid of God. An infinite God could be the God of an infinite number of universes.

Six steps towards the renewal of science

1. Many scientists and medical professionals are afraid to express their doubts about the materialist ideology to their colleagues because they feel they are a small minority and would be ostracized if their true views were known. What is needed is something like the gay liberation movement, when gays 'came out of the closet'. It will be much easier for scientists and doctors to do so when they realize that their views are secretly shared by many of their colleagues. And to help start this process, it would be good to commission surveys of practising scientists and doctors to find out their attitudes to integral medicine, psychic phenomena, the nature of consciousness, and the existence of a spiritual realm. These surveys will probably show that a large minority, and in some fields even a majority, are not die-hard materialists, and the publication of such finding would embolden people to say what they actually think.

2. The transformation of science and medicine must be a collective process, since science and medicine involve social groups and social norms. This could be helped though workshops or seminars run by skilled group-process facilitators so that scientists and doctors can explore their hopes when they entered their subject, their experience in the practice of it, and ways in which they can re-vision science and medicine together.

3. An exploration of a reformed science education system in schools concerned less with imparting facts and mechanistic doctrines, and more with promoting a direct experience of nature and ability to learn from plants, animals and natural phenomena.

4. Exploration of new ways of funding science which would make it more democratic, more responsive to public interests and free it from the restrictive control of corporations and the government funding agencies. One suggestion is that 1% of public science funding should be used to pay for research that interests the public. People and groups would be asked what questions they would like science to address. It would also be good to re-examine a possible new role of private funding through charitable foundations.

5. An exploration of the career structure in science, which at present usually involves young people doing PhDs, and then a series of low-paid post-doctoral fellowships in other people's laboratories, with little scope for creativity or initiative until they are in their 30s. Could there by better ways of employing the creativity of young researchers?

6. Level playing-field science debates. The culture of debate is sadly lacking in science, and controversial viewpoints are often marginalized through the conservative effects of the peer-review system. A series of public debates on controversial areas of science chaired by a judge or some other impartial figure would bring a breath of fresh air into the culture of science and medicine.

We are facing climate change, great economic uncertainty, and cuts in science funding. Confidence in materialism is draining away. Its leaders, like central bankers, keep printing promissory notes, but it has lost its credibility as the central dogma of science. Many scientists no longer want to be 100% invested in it. Materialism's credit crunch changes everything. As science is liberated from this nineteenth-century ideology, new perspectives and possibilities will open up, not just for science, but for other areas of our culture that are dominated by materialism. And by giving up the pretence that the ultimate answers are already known, the sciences will be freer — and more fun.

References

Chalmers, D. (1998) *The Conscious Mind: In Search of a Fundamental Theory*, Oxford University Press, Oxford.

Popper, K. and Eccles, J.C. (1977) *The Self and Its Brain*, Springer Verlag, Berlin, pp. 96–98.

Ridley, M. (2006) *Francis Crick*, Atlas Books, London, p. 208. .

11. Parapsychology and the New Renaissance

DAVID LUKE

David Luke is Senior Lecturer in Psychology at the University of Greenwich where he teaches an undergraduate course on the Psychology of Exceptional Human Experiences. He is Director of the Ecology, Cosmos and Consciousness lecture series at the October Gallery, Bloomsbury, London and a Research Associate at the Beckley Foundation, Oxford, an organization dedicated to the study of consciousness and its altered states. Currently he serves as President of the Parapsychological Association, the professional international organization for the scientific study of parapsychology.

The scientific study of apparently psychic abilities, currently termed 'parapsychology', has been represented by an official organ since the 1882 formation of the Society for Psychical Research (SPR) in the UK. The SPR came into being only three years after the establishment in Germany of the first psychological laboratory by Wilhelm Wundt, which gave birth to psychology itself as a modern science, so has accompanied psychology as a discipline since its infancy. In the last 125 years or so there's been a very small, but steady, chipping away at the block of our empirical understanding of telepathy, precognition and clairvoyance (collectively termed 'psi'). Regrettably, this sculpted work in progress has been mostly either ridiculously ignored by the vast majority of more mainstream scientists, or ignorantly ridiculed by a few others, despite parapsychology being one of the most rigorously executed branches of social science.

Science over scientism

This stagnant situation seemingly arises because most mainstream scientists commonly subscribe to what has been called 'scientism'. This is the view that science has ontological supremacy in the explanation of reality, and further assumes that all processes can be reduced down to mechanical explanations governed only by physical laws, an outdated position known as materialist reductionism. Such adherence to scientism also limits the kinds of questions that scientists are supposed to ask: Psychic ability, defying a physical explanation, is presumed to be delusional and so only those questions concerning why people should be gullible enough to believe in it can legitimately be asked. However, parapsychology, as a scientific discipline, has been brave enough not to make such materialist assumptions by upholding the dictum that science is just a method, not a position or a belief system, thereby keeping a door open for the genuine existence of consciousness, and even spirit. Nevertheless, much to the alarm of many of its opponents in the mainstream, parapsychology has long since used modern methods and technologies to devise experiments that increasingly point toward humans as genuinely psychic beings, currently constituting something like a new renaissance in our understanding of consciousness.

Psychic technologies

Considering such recent advances, had it not been for the introduction of psychophysiological monitoring technology, such as electroencephalograph (EEG) brain mapping equipment, psychical research might otherwise have languished in the repetitive and boring loops of card-guessing experiments so popular a few decades ago.

Oddly enough, however, the man renowned for naming the EEG, Hans Berger, developed this technology early in the twentieth century for measuring electromagnetic (EM) fluctuations in the brain because he (incorrectly) thought that these EM emissions might be the carrier waves responsible for psychic transmissions between brains. Marconi had earlier thought the same of EM when he invented the telegraph, though we now know better. Berger himself had changed career from astronomy to psychology to study the neurophysiological processes of psi after his distant sister had an accurate vision of him involved in a near-fatal accident. Somewhat poetically then, Berger's EEG, after disappearing as a tool of psi research but flourishing in neuroscience, has wholeheartedly been brought back into the field of parapsychology. This time though, the EEG is being used to find telepathic thought transmissions in a slightly different way, by demonstrating that distant brains can seemingly communicate without the owners of those brains being conscious of it, but not through the medium of electromagnetism as Berger once thought.

What many people may not be aware of is that much of the recent research in parapsychology adumbrates psi as a genuine, albeit subtle and largely unconscious phenomenon. To illustrate, using brain-mapping technology such as EEG, a person in one room has their brain monitored while a person in a distant room has their brain randomly stimulated, usually through visual stimulation, such as a flash of bright lights. These visual stimulations are known to reliably cause easily observable reactions in the brain of the person directly perceiving them. What is not generally known is that these stimulations can also be observed somewhat more subtly in the brains of a distant person sealed in another room, well out of sight of the flashes (Kittenis *et al.* 2004). Some successful experiments even found this effect to occur in the visual cortex, the brain region where the effect might be expected if their brains were being stimulated directly. The same effect was also found using functional magnetic resonance imaging (fMRI) technology — even localizing the spot in the brain where the effect was detected — and so these findings, repeated with different technologies, cannot be easily explained away as an artefact of the brain imaging technique (Richards *et al.* 2005). However, the effect tends to be observable only with pairs of people who have some kind of emotional bond, such as with friends and lovers, with some indication that twins do particularly well. Complete strangers, curiously enough, tend not to exhibit this distant brain synchronization effect, which seems to imply that those people who are emotionally bonded are also somehow distantly cerebrally bonded too. The implications of this for world peace alone would seem staggering.

Other psychophysiological advances are also being exploited. Using sensors that detect minute fluctuations in skin perspiration by measuring skin conductance, called electrodermal activity (EDA), an accurate gauge of general physiological arousal can be obtained. Parapsychological research with EDA shows that people may also be unconsciously responsive to the psychophysiological interaction, intention or influence of other people. In a series of experiments designed to test the feasibility of direct psychic healing or intercessory prayer, a participant — the receiver — has their EDA monitored in one room and relayed to another room by computer. In the other room another participant, the 'agent', monitors the receiver's EDA and attempts to influence the receiver's physiology at randomly determined intervals. As you might now expect, there is good evidence from these experiments to suggest that, in line with the agents' intention, some kind of interaction or possible influence is occurring between the physiology of these distant pairs (Schmidt *et al.* 2004). This is something parapsychologists call 'direct mental interaction between living systems', or DMILS.

The unconscious psychic reservoir

As with the distant brain correlation experiments these changes in the receivers' physiology appear to go consciously undetected, and collectively these experiments seemingly indicate that our physiology supersedes our cognition in the reception of psychic information, interaction or influence. One interpretation of this is that we may all be continuously psychic, albeit subtly, and yet we remain consciously unaware of the fact, even though our body apparently reacts on our behalf. This unconscious knowledge makes economic sense in evolutionary terms because otherwise our awareness of psychic information would have to compete with our other cognitive systems for our attention and might become conflated or lost. Alternatively, *unconscious* psi information would prevent our conscious awareness from becoming overloaded by a potentially infinite amount of direct psi information. So it would be advantageous if psi worked directly through our physiological systems, enabling us to act unconsciously on this information where necessary, and perhaps stopping us from having accidents or helping us to have useful synchronicities at times.

There certainly seems to be very good evidence for the fact that anyone can perform well in a laboratory psi tests and yet most people only have one or two conscious psi experiences in their lives, usually through dreams, and usually only when the information is *really* needed, such as with the death or sudden crisis of a distant loved one. This then suggests that, mostly, we are not really consciously aware of our own exceptional abilities but that crisis can facilitate an awareness of our psychic connection to others. Given the current ontological crisis in science and its general denial of spirit and even consciousness, the scientific discipline would similarly seem ready to behold psi experiences, hopefully as part of an integrated psychology that incorporates both empirical and experiential approaches to realizing human potential.

Looking now at the legacy of psi research, fastidiously investigated for many years, there appears to be compelling evidence for the existence of psychic abilities (Radin 2006), yet this would hardly surprise most people on the street. Surveys typically reveal that the majority of people believe in the authenticity of one or more paranormal process (Moore 2005). This widespread belief and evidence for psychic abilities is all well and good but the question remains of whether or not these abilities are readily accessible and can be learnt, and whether we can develop these skills for our purposes and our growth as a species.

Rebranding psi: making the paranormal normal

You might disagree that the development of psychic techniques is something we all aspire to — there's certainly an element of ingrained fear in potentially accessing our 'latent omniscience', as Emerson (1883 p.177) called it — but our current technology argues for itself.

If we had no desire for telepathy (the ability to communicate remotely with anyone anywhere) we would never have become so obsessed with mobile phones or even bothered inventing them. The Internet too, in part at least, attempts to satisfy our need for clairvoyance, to readily know anything there is to know, and so cyberspace can be seen as modern man's grasping to clutch the Akashic Records, the supposed cosmic catalogue of all events in time. It may be no surprise then to find, although it's a little-known fact, that the television, the radio and the telephone were all born of the desire to augment psychic abilities (Goff 2005). The three Victorian fathers of these inventions, Guglielmo Marconi, Alexander Graham Bell and John Logie Baird, had all shared a serious interest in the spirit mediumship movement, Spiritualism, and had expected to develop technologies for improved psychic communication with the deceased.

But is all this hardware just filling a gap we can't bridge with our own 'wetware' — the human nervous system and the mind — or is it just a means of demonstrating what is possible through technology until our lapsed imagination catches up and we hone the flaccid muscles of our psyches? We might then consider modern telecommunications and information technology as a kind of rebranding exercise of psychic abilities to prepare us for using our dormant psychic skills. An exercise to help us fake it till we make it, by showing us what a readily available telepathy and clairvoyance would be like, but without the tariffs, the gadgets, and the electromagnetic radiation blasting invisibly out of the phone masts. I know one parapsychologist who, prior to working in this field, developed a biofeedback system which enables completely paralysed people to control a computer merely with their brain waves, thereby using technology to mimic psychokinesis (the direct control over matter by mind). Is all this technology just a warm up for the next stage? Certainly, Rupert Sheldrake's research with telephone telepathy — the widespread experience of knowing who is calling when the telephone rings — seems to suggest that the *technology* of telepathy hasn't reduced the direct experience of it (Sheldrake & Smart 2003). One of the most consistent and robust findings in parapsychology is that psi can be demonstrated best in the laboratory by those who believe it to be real. Perhaps Bell's desires for psychic communication and his important patent were just a stepping stone to bring the experience of telepathy to virtually everybody, thereby enabling the critical mass of belief in such experiences required to ensure the following development of the paranormal analogue of the experience, that is, real telepathy. Perhaps widespread telepathy and the transcendence of the technology to augment it are only round the corner in evolutionary terms. Perhaps.

Reasons to be hopeful

One thing is for sure: an aggressive adherence to scientism currently prevents most scientists from asking some of the most important questions about the nature of reality being probed by parapsychologists, such as: What is consciousness? What are its limits and how do we access its full potential? Nevertheless, after 125 years of subsisting as a part-time, desperately under-funded and wholly peripheral science, parapsychology has still managed to make some concerted headway studying the outer reaches of human ability. It was once estimated that the total person-hours accrued in the lifetime of the field has only amounted to the equivalent of two months' research in conventional psychology in the United States alone (Schouten 1993). Imagine what progress might ensue if parapsychology were widely accepted as a valid research field and funded with more than a handful of loose change.

Thankfully, this crisis of rejection is also parapsychology's opportunity because although a lack of funding and ostracism by the mainstream prevents many potential researchers from investigating psi, this restriction also acts as a talent filter that favours only the most tenacious, committed, creative and independent-minded researchers (Roe 2009). Such persistence has paid off, particularly here in the UK where in the last few decades a total of 84 researchers have completed or are completing PhDs on parapsychological topics — mostly thanks to the efforts of the late Professor Robert Morris at Edinburgh University — with 24 of these proceeding to obtain permanent academic positions (Carr 2008). Such a diaspora has led to the current situation where sixteen university departments are actively engaged in teaching and/or researching parapsychology. This raises the question of whether we are witnessing a renewed scientific interest in parapsychology as part of a New Renaissance. If this is so, parapsychology may help to counter the hegemony of scientism as arbiter of research and of reality, leading us on a path to a truly public understanding of the psychology and science at the core of our being. Anticipating such a manoeuvre, telepathy might become more widely accepted and the ensuing degree of psychic transparency implied might lead to an era of unprecedented honesty, loyalty and positive regard for our fellow humans, and perhaps even other species too. If this is the dawning of a New Renaissance then we had better seize the day.

References

Carr, Bernard (2008) 'Past and present UK parapsychological students,' *Paranormal Review*, no. 48, pp. 18–20.

Emerson, E.W. (ed.) (1883) *Ralph Waldo Emerson: Lectures and Biographical Sketches*, Houghton, Boston.

Goff, Hannah (2005) *Science and the séance*, retrieved from: http://news.bbc.co.uk/1/hi/magazine/4185356.stm, 10th February 2010.

Kittenis, M., Caryl, P.G. & Stevens, P. (2004) 'Distant psychophysiological interaction effects between related and unrelated participants.' In S. Schmidt (ed.), *The Parapsychological Association 47th Annual Convention: Proceedings of Presented Papers, Vienna*, pp. 67–76.

Moore, D.W. (2005) *Three in Four Americans Believe in Paranormal: Little change from similar results in 2001*, The Gallup Organization, Princeton.

Radin, D. (2006) *Entangled Minds: Extrasensory Experiences in a Quantum Reality*, Pocket Books, New York.

Richards, T.L., Kozak, L., Johnson, C. & Standish, L.J. (2005) 'Replicable functional magnetic resonance imaging evidence of correlated brain signals between physically isolated subjects,' *Journal of Alternative and Complementary Medicine*, no.11, pp. 955–63.

Roe, C. (2009) 'Personal reflections on Utrecht II,' In C. Roe (ed.), *Proceedings of an International Conference: Utrecht II: Charting the Futures of Parapsychology*, pp. 533–58, Parapsychology Foundation, New York.

Schouten, S. (1993) 'Are we making progress?' In L. Coly & J. McMahon (eds.) *Psi Research Methodology: A Re-examination*, pp. 295–322, Parapsychology Foundation, New York.

Schmidt, S., Schneider, R., Utts, J. & Walach, H. (2004) 'Distant intentionality and the feeling of being stared at — Two meta-analyses,' *British Journal of Psychology*, no. 95, pp. 235–47.

Sheldrake, R. & Smart, P. (2003) 'Videotaped experiments on telephone telepathy,' *Journal of Parapsychology*, no. 67, pp. 187–206.

12. Any Dream Won't Do: Changing our Minds about Consciousness

PAUL DEVEREUX

Paul Devereux is a founding editor of the academic publication, Time & Mind — The Journal of Archaeology, Consciousness and Culture *(Berg), a research affiliate with the Royal College of Art, and a Senior Research Fellow of the International Consciousness Research Laboratories (ICRL), Princeton. He has written many articles for general publications and a string of peer-reviewed papers, plus twenty-six books since 1979, including* Re-Visioning the Earth *(Fireside/Simon & Schuster, 1996),* The Sacred Place *(Cassell, 2000), and* Spirit Roads *(Anova, 2007). His latest book, due 2010, is* Sacred Geography *(Octopus/Gaia). See pdevereux@onetel.com*

There is an uneasy sense growing in Western culture that we are in the grip of an 'all-embracing and growing crisis' as some commentators have described it (Robinson *et al.* 2009). Despite this, most people would be hard pressed to actually define what the crisis is.

Like a babushka doll

Is it an ecological, environmental crisis? We hear much about the threat of global climate change, and there were those who thought that the major Copenhagen climate change conference in 2009 (Conference of the Parties — COP 15, 2009) would end up producing binding international agreement, but more realistic observers knew the conference would fail, and for a variety of reasons — too many vested interests and inadequate political will being only two of them.

An obstacle to arriving at a sustainable plan for human existence on this planet of ours is the unrestrained and directionless growth economy model by which we live. 'The Market' is talked about as if it is a force of nature rather than an artefact of human nature. It is used to excuse every form of institutionalized greed — whether corporate and financial sector 'bonus cultures', environmental rapacity, unfair international trade policies, geopolitical wars, and an ever-growing divide between rich and poor — even within Western societies, let alone globally. 'The Market' has no mind and no morals, it is a powerful beast that exists on reflexes and instincts — not for nothing do we have metaphors like 'bull' and 'bear' markets. Like a dangerous animal it needs containing and training, a measure of regulation and moral direction it eschews. Instead, it has been left to run amok like a bull in a china shop. Many people became aware of this only in the recent financial meltdown, which encouraged predictions that the end of capitalism was nigh. But we can see the old habits of greed and inhumanity gradually re-asserting themselves. Nothing has truly changed. The levers that would need to be pulled in order to redefine the prevailing economic model lie rusting deep within the socio-political strata of the 'all-embracing' crisis.

Politics is by definition one of those strata. Yet large sections of Western populations are profoundly disillusioned with their politicians. Where is the grand political vision? Where is the 'thinking outside the box'? Instead, there is just tinkering inside the box, a parading of short-term measures trying to prop up the existing, ailing economic model, with too many politicians looking after their own interests in the process.

Total cynicism about politicians is to some extent unfair, but those who might kindle a vision are pretty much extinguished by ingrained political and social systems and vested interests. Even though some political parties now talk of a 'green economy' it is only a healthier-sounding recipe for keeping the economic status quo. No, politics as a lever for real, deep change remains rusted in the off position.

The social stratum holds no greater promise, the way things stand. While there are still brave, bright strands within it, the overall tendency is for things to deteriorate. More wealth is falling into the hands of fewer people. Education is patchy around the world, even within Western societies where politicians forever try to interfere. Universities are increasingly pressurized to act like businesses and to provide fodder for 'The Market'. The print media are becoming more compliant with their political and corporate masters, with increasing numbers of journalists being laid off and those left standing having to deal with so much they too often have to skip thoroughness and analysis with the consequence that there is less investigative journalism and more homogeneity of received opinion and worldview (Davies 2008). Television is faring no better, pumping out an excess of 'reality' programming and other mind-numbing offerings. There are still excellent programmes, but the overall deterioration in mainstream media is there for all to see.

Even the World Wide Web is a double-edged sword. It is a wonderful research tool, but a serious user of the Web has to know how to research, how to evaluate the provenance of information and bloggers' opinions — a skill that many users of the Web do not truly possess. As a consequence, the Web has also become a global rubbish tip of misinformation.

There is also another problem engendered by online and digital media in general — a fragmentation of understanding. People, especially a majority of young people (although not them alone), are at risk of losing the 'robust framework' of the information they take in from the Web (Greenfield 2006). Context and connections are being lost, and information is confused with knowledge. This is not merely a cognitive problem, it is also a neurophysiological matter, for people immersed in the digital age are apparently showing changes in the firing patterns between their brain cells (Greenfield 2003 2006). Teachers and others for some time now have been commenting on the short attention span of students, one of the effects of these changes. Further, people are increasingly 'not present', walking and talking on their mobile phones, or texting or twittering, or listening to MP3 players wired into their ears, semi-oblivious of their surroundings. It is all a far cry from the mynah birds on Aldous Huxley's utopian island of Pala that were trained to croak at passers-by, 'Here and Now, boys ... Attention' to re-mind them (Huxley 1964).

In general, people in developed Western societies are finding the pace of their world becoming remorselessly faster, leaving ever-diminishing time for depth of understanding or quiet reflection. That increased speed is driven by the computer, with the workings of society being fashioned after and enslaved to the algorithms of computer programming.

The human soul cries out for accommodation within this brave new world, yet the spiritual end of the socio-political stratum is also in crisis. At one extreme there is religious fundamentalism, especially Christian and Islamic, and though it also permeates other religions to some extent, these two versions are particularly inimical because they infect politics, leading to terrorism (by both state and individual instigators), wars, and the curtailment of personal freedoms by state powers within societies. At the other extreme there are many people who evince a type of spiritual grazing, in which they sample many spiritual traditions without living them, or seek solace in New Age pastiche versions of them and becoming prey to fads and even cults. In between these extremes is a mass of people variously clinging to rote, formal religions, or professing atheism or agnosticism. Overall, the spiritual domain is fragmented.

To a neutral observer, it seems that while formal religions can offer comfort and *communitas* for those who need it, and also inspire great art and music, they are on the whole divisive. How many religions can be the one, true way? All manner of horrors are committed in the name of religion. They do not seem to be the tools humanity needs to get out of its crisis, any more than is the denial of any form of spirituality.

The crisis, then, is actually a set of nested symptoms, like a babushka or Russian doll. The treatment of one of the nested symptoms won't cure the disease. Such treatment is to be applauded, it may make the patient feel more comfortable, but it won't get to the root of the all-embracing crisis, which is the worldview that has spawned it. What is that worldview, and what is a worldview anyway?

Weltanschauung

A worldview, a *Weltanschauung*, is 'a particular philosophy or view of life; a conception of the world' the dictionary tells us. When a particular worldview becomes the established, mainstream consensus of a culture, it determines how the societies beneath that cultural umbrella behave in and act on the world, and how they perceive reality.

The worldview adopted and maintained by the mainstream culture of the West is essentially an overarching materialist paradigm that forms a reductionist-positivist plank on which everything rests. Despite the counsel of its mystics, and the more recent findings of some branches of its science, our culture considers matter to be primary. Its worldview does not explain exactly how life and consciousness (the 'inside' of external objectivity) comes about. It argues that the complexity of interactions in the brain produces consciousness, like sparkles glinting off the facets of a jewel, but it doesn't actually explain how collections of atoms and molecules morph into larger systems that can think, that can love, that can sing, that can create. It is a crucial explanatory gap that is crossed as quickly and quietly as possible in the philosophy of the West, like a conjuror's sleight of hand.

Because it considers matter to be inert, the way the West considers the material world is conditioned, and it treats the environment — the land, natural resources, the non-human biosphere — accordingly. Worldviews affect behaviour and have consequences. So it is the underlying question about the nature of consciousness that forms the base on which the grim babushka doll stands. And that is where any answers to resolving the all-embracing crisis in an all-embracing way need to be sought.

Worldviews in collision

The Western worldview is enormously powerful, developing technologies that make it extremely portable, so it has been able to project itself into far corners of the world, shouldering out other worldviews, other perceptions of reality. The only formal eyes and ears that Western culture has in other, older cultures belong to anthropologists. They study and often live with such societies, some of which hold different worldviews to our own and so have different realities. Occasionally, some anthropologists encounter these other tribal realities and report on them. Let us listen to just a few.

Griman

Anthropologist Marianne George lived among the Barok people of New Ireland Province, Papua New Guinea, for a total of twenty months during four periods between 1979 and 1985. Early during her first stay, Kalerian, the 85-year-old 'big woman' or village elder 'adopted' George as her sister. Early one morning, two of Kalerian's sons, Alek and Bustaman, came to George's hut while she was boiling water for tea.

'Did you understand her?' Alek demanded. George was nonplussed. 'Who?'

'My mother was talking to you last night,' Alek answered, watching the anthropologist closely.

'I did not talk to her last night,' a confused George replied.

'Do you not remember? When she came to see you in the night?' Alek persisted. 'In Tokpisin we call this *griman* — dreaming.'

George then recalled that she did indeed have a dream the previous night in which Kalerian directed her to do something about a problem. With a deep ontological shock, George realized these boys must have witnessed her dream. How had Kalerian got into her dream, and how was it that Alek and Bustaman had shared the dream? The sons patiently explained that Kalerian had come to them too in their dreams and instructed them to visit George in the morning.

'Do you always do this, communicate with people — visit people — in their dreams at night?' George wanted to know. The sons indicated it was what 'big people' could do, and that it could happen over long distances as well as within the village.

Over the course of her time with the Barok, George was involved in several other instances of *griman*. She mulled over these extraordinary experiences for about a decade before deciding to 'go public' with them in an academic anthropological journal. 'Positivist science continues to resist the acceptance of transpersonal experiences as data,' she comments. 'And researchers who report such experiences open themselves to being treated as pariahs.' (George 1995). She now believes that the Barok (and other native) models in which dreaming can create reality are at least as valid as the Western model that insists reality creates dreams.

An inconvenient blob

A particularly famous (or infamous) encounter with other worldview reality involved anthropologist Edith Turner, the widow of the eminent anthropologist Victor Turner and editor of the academic journal, *Anthropology and Humanism*. In 1985, she was invited by the Ndembu people of Zambia to participate in a healing ritual under the leadership of an experienced native healer known as Singleton. In the ritual, the healer aims to remove a dead hunter's tooth (*ihamba*) from a patient. The tooth, it is believed, wanders around inside the sick person's body causing pain.

The patient was a middle-aged woman called Meru. Various ritual preparations were undertaken, and the curing procedure began. This included the cutting of small slits in Meru's back, and then the placing of cupping horns over the incisions.

'Come out!' Singleton yelled repeatedly to the *ihamba* spirit inside Meru's body at the point where the cups were held by suction. Eventually, the woman's body began to shake violently, and Singleton was able to identify the *ihamba* spirit as being that of the old ancestral hunter, Kashinakaji. Turner sensed a tangible feeling of breakthrough. Singleton pressed the woman's quivering back. Suddenly, with an entranced expression on her face, she raised her arm. 'I saw with my own eyes a giant thing emerging out of the flesh of her back,' Turner reported. 'It was a large gray blob about six inches across, opaque and something between solid and smoke. The gray thing was actually out there, visible, and you could see Singleton's hands working and scrabbling on the back.'

Singleton transferred the blob-like thing to a tin. As he checked to ensure that everything had come out of Meru there was a flash of lightning and a clap of thunder that exploded overhead. Meru sat up panting but radiant. Everyone watching the procedure shouted and jumped with excitement as it became clear the woman was healed. Later, Singleton showed Turner the *ihamba* 'tooth' he claimed he had extracted from Meru's body, but it was an old tooth, a molar, not the peculiar object Turner had seen emerge from Meru's flesh.

'It was a small experience, but one which demanded a reorganization of the way I did anthropology,' Turner later wrote (Turner 1994).

Better than field radio

The use of mind-altering plants often figures in anthropologists' accounts of transpersonal events when in the field with tribal peoples. A classic case involved Kenneth Kensinger, who spent time living with the Cashinahua tribe in the Peruvian Amazon. He noted the fairly common occurrence of apparent remote perception ('clairvoyance') by many of those who took part in ritual sessions using the mind-altering brew, ayahuasca. On one notable occasion, six out of nine men who had taken part in an ayahuasca session told Kensinger that his *chai* (his maternal grandfather) had just died. It was not until two days later that the anthropologist was informed by field radio of the death (Kensinger 1973).

Numerous such accounts are lodged in the anthropological archives (Devereux 2007). They are not the products of fringe parapsychologists, sensation seekers, the anecdotal claims of untrained people, or the folklore of rural indigenous societies — they are the sober accounts of experiences undergone by validated Western scholars, given at some risk to professional standing. The trouble is, their home culture is incapable of taking those reports on board because its own worldview gets in the way, and such reports are almost totally ignored. They nevertheless tell us that worldviews can create realities, and that we should not assume ours is the only one. More importantly, though, *they indicate that it can be modified*. This is the most valuable wisdom we can receive from the elders.

Reactions

So we return to our grim babushka doll, our all-embracing crisis. The varied reactions to it are fascinating. On the one hand, there are people responding practically in the fields of environmental activism, in attempts to deepen the process of education, drawing out and encouraging the enthusiasm and hope that young people naturally represent, and in many other spheres that impinge upon aspects of the crisis. On the other hand, there are those who are in denial, claiming that there is no climate change threat, for example, or who seek some form of alien or divine intervention, be it via fundamentalism, the Rapture, or New Age fabrications such as extra-terrestrial contact or the supposed 2012 apocalypse, which they believe to be predicted in the Mayan calendar.

Then there are those masses of people who haven't even thought or cared about the crisis and when suddenly presented with it recoil and become depressed (an understandable reaction). This has been remarkably evidenced in the public response to the hugely successful 2010 film, *Avatar* (Piazza 2010). This depicts a paradisal planet, Pandora, inhabited by its indigenous beings, the Na'vi, who live in harmony with their natural world. But corporate powers from Earth, which is dying due to the predations of the self-same industrial-military complex, seek to mine Pandora for its rare minerals. It is a simplistic parable regarding our actual situation but made especially powerful because it is immersive — in 3D sound and vision with exceptional computer graphic imagery. It has had a strong effect on audiences, as these examples from the *Avatar Forums* website illustrate:

> 'Watching the wonderful world of Pandora and all the Na'vi
> made me want to be one of them ... I even contemplate suicide ...'
> 'When I woke up this morning after watching *Avatar* for the
> first time yesterday, the world seemed ... gray. It was like my
> whole life, everything I've done and worked for, lost its meaning
> ... I live in a dying world.'
> 'It's so hard I can't force myself to think that ... living like the
> Na'vi will never happen.'

The film is an example of how some people in the media, James Cameron in this case, are attempting to raise awareness.

Finally, there are those who react by focussing on the basis of the crisis — the need to correct a worldview in which consciousness is seen simply as an epiphenomenon of matter. Until that is addressed, the grim babushka doll cannot be fully disassembled. Debates and theories about the nature of consciousness abound, and conferences on consciousness are legion. While it is good that this is happening, it is all too easy to think that these debates and conferences have a bigger impact than they do, for they operate in a relatively small world (how often do delegates find themselves meeting one another at different events, for instance?) when compared to the vast and powerful culture in which it is embedded. It will take more to shift the foundations of the West's essentially materialist worldview.

Ride a black swan

One way is to start at the ground floor — parapsychology. It isn't spirituality, it isn't mysticism, but it is a portal to understanding consciousness as something greater than a mere epiphenomenon of complex material interactions.

Parapsychologists study the anomalies of consciousness, events that are popularly referred to as 'paranormal' (yes, the sort of things the anthropologists sometimes experience in tribal societies) — telepathy, precognition, remote perception ('clairvoyance') and so forth, sometimes referred to collectively as 'psi phenomena' or simply 'psi'. There are a number of British and a few Continental European universities that have parapsychology departments or units, though often under some other name (such as 'anomalistic human experiences'). In the United States, parapsychological research has tended to be funded by benefactors, many of whom are dying off or changing their interests, leaving psi research there in some danger of waning — though there is still some vigorous research taking place.

It has been calculated that the total expenditure on psi research over the last half century is equivalent to about two months' expenditure on mainstream psychology in the United States. Despite this, a strong body of evidence for the existence of psi has been established (Radin 1997). But cultural orthodoxy simply will not countenance the validity of parapsychological research. Perhaps because too much is at stake — if it was openly accepted that psi did exist, then the materialist plank the Western worldview is based upon would be severely strained, leading to the need for a replacement, one in which consciousness holds a very different place.

Things are currently at something of an impasse. There are rustlings of interest in psi by even 'hard' scientists, but it is on an individual basis. Orthodoxy in the collective still won't budge. It often will not even look at the evidence, and positive results of experiments are typically dismissed as being due to flaws in methodology. Academic parapsychologists continue to churn out their questionnaires and statistical analyses, but no one outside their own community is taking any notice; it's like a turning wheel that isn't touching the ground. All the while, of course, a great many human beings have experiences that can't be explained by the prevailing materialist paradigm, the worldview. But the orthodoxy dismisses such experiences as mere anecdotes, delusions of the Great Unwashed. So people who have these experiences have nowhere to bring their tales — there is no serious mainstream cultural forum. At best, they are picked up by the media who want to use them for sensationalist purposes at Hallowe'en or midwinter, or for ridicule.

This impasse is actually a little-noticed aspect of the crisis. To break through, something a little different is needed. That is why the present writer is deeply involved with others in creating a freshly-angled effort called the Black Swan project. If it can be backed by the required resources (being sought at the time of this writing) the project hopes to link very specific, targeted psi research with a strong socio-political engagement, so that the implications of positive results will be forced into the mainstream, orthodox arena to instigate an open, cultural discussion. It will be a different, less passive way of handling psi research.

Why 'Black Swan'? Well, in the first century AD a Roman writer used the phrase 'a rare bird in the lands, and very like a black swan', meaning that as such a swan did not exist nor did the supposed matter being discussed. Subsequently, the term 'black swan' acted as a metaphor for that which was impossible. But in the seventeenth century, a Dutch explorer made the first sighting by a European of a black swan in Australia. The Black Swan project aims to be like that explorer, only its 'black swan' is the nature of the human mind. Its objective is to bring that bird back, just as eventually happened with the news of the Australian black swan.

As things stand right now, though, the impasse continues. To paraphrase the Lloyd Webber/Tim Rice song (Lloyd Webber and Rice 1968), the world is waiting, but it is still hesitating. The hour is late, but perhaps the urgency of the situation will galvanize us into the necessary actions. And just any dream won't do.

References

Davies, Nick (2008) *Flat Earth News*, Chatto & Windus, London.

Devereux, Paul (2007) 'The Moveable Feast,' in *Mind Before Matter*, Trish Pfeiffer, John Mack and Paul Devereux (eds.), O Books, Winchester.

George, Marianne (1995) 'Dreams, Reality, and the Desire and Intent of Dreamers as Experienced by a Fieldworker,' *Anthropology of Consciousness*, Vol. 6, no. 3.

Greenfield, Susan (2003) *Tomorrow's People: How 21st-Century Technology is Changing the Way We Think and Feel*, Penguin, London.

—, (2006) 'Education: Science and Technology,' *Hansard* (Column 1219), House of Lords, London.

Huxley, Aldous (1962) *Island*, Penguin, Harmondsworth (1964 edn.).

Kensinger, Kenneth (1973) 'Banisteriopsis Usage among the Peruvian Cashinahua,' in *Hallucinogens and Shamanism*, Michael J. Harner (ed.), Oxford University Press, New York.

Lloyd Webber, Andrew and Rice, Tim (1968) 'Any Dream Will Do,' in *Joseph and the Amazing Technicolor Dreamcoat*.

Piazza, Jo (2010) 'Audiences Experience "Avatar' Blues",' CNN.com, 11 January. (http://edition.cnn.com/2010/SHOWBIZ/Movies/01/11/avatar.movie. blues/index.html)

Radin, Dean (1997) *The Conscious Universe*, HarperOne, New York.

Turner, Edith (1994) 'A Visible Spirit Form in Zambia,' in *Being Changed*, David E. Young and Jean-Guy Goulet (eds.), Broadview Press, Peterborough, Ontario.

13. Thinking about Thought

F. DAVID PEAT

F. David Peat carried out research in theoretical physics at the National Research Council of Ottawa before turning to writing. As a result of a sabbatical spent at Birkbeck College in 1971 Peat began an interaction with David Bohm which lasted until Bohm's death. He has also engaged in dialogue circles with Native Americans and between artists and scientists. He works at The Pari Center for New Learning, in Tuscany.

This volume of the Scientific and Medical Network invites us to consider the nature of the present crises we face and to consider ways in which we could move forward to a New Renaissance.

How is it that we find ourselves in this present condition? Is there a particular question we must seek to address? Could it be that in our current approach to the environment, society, economics and to the structure of our various institutions we have lost touch with our deepest roots? Is all of this perhaps a fault of our particular globalized society? Some inevitable accident of history? Or, perhaps, something inherent in the human species itself?

And has it always been this way, or is our present crisis a new and different phenomenon? We have all heard stories of societies that have traditionally lived close to the land and remained in harmony with nature and the seasons. Many Native American groups speak of 'all my relations', extending their direct relationship from members of the tribe into the plant and animal world, the rocks and rivers, and the energies of the earth and sky. They teach that everything is in balance, so that when something is taken from nature something else must be given back. In this manner they are able to live in a sustainable way with the land around them. When it comes to making a decision they consider the impact this will have on the seventh generation to come after them. (A related idea has been put forward by Stuart Brand and his Clock of the Long Now, that the sorts of decisions we are taking today will affect life and the planet thousands and tens of thousands of years into the future. Time scales should not be thought of in terms of a few tens of rotations of the Earth around the sun but rather in the precession of the solar system through the galaxy.)

This view of harmony with nature, one which we shall question later in this essay, would have been shared by Europeans in the first part of the Middle Ages, a time before human beings began to abstract themselves from nature by means of the power of thought. The great change that began in the thirteenth century occurred when humans learned how to magnify thought and to treat the world as an object to be controlled and manipulated within the mind, and its future behaviour predicted. And, with the rise of science, this world was seen to be largely mechanical, obeying Newton's fixed laws. Eventually such mechanistic and hierarchical thinking would be applied to society, the environment and the even human body. Machines can be subject to analysis, and obey predetermined patterns of behaviour. They can be repaired or replaced if they do not conform to a desired pattern. But what are the consequences when such thinking is applied to individuals and society?

This was a period associated with such things as the discovery of double entry book keeping which, combined with the adoption of Arabic numerals enabled merchants to have an overview of the state of their businesses and calculate the value of investments in the future. Other developments in the same period included the refinement of philosophical arguments via strict logical steps, as demonstrated by Aquinas.

Just what is natural?

At the start of this essay I considered those groups that lived 'close to nature' and learned from the natural world. But just what is nature, and what is natural? In fact the behaviour of the natural world ranges from the gentle and sustaining to the violent and threatening. Leaving aside geological change and the fluctuation of the sun's output there is the perfectly natural mutation of viruses that brought about the Black Death, plague and an influenza epidemic that wiped out more people than did the First World War.

On the other hand, the natural world teaches us that when matter or energy flows into a region that region will self-organize and show great stability and inner complexity. Trapping and circulating the energy of the sun produces the rainforests that support a wide variety of plant, insect and animal life. Rainforests also teach us that diversity and even competition are the keys to long term sustainability. If we substitute the flow of money for the flow of energy then we have an economic system that has self-organized and will support a vast inner complexity of suppliers and buyers. But compromise its nest of feedback loops and the entire economic system may collapse.

And so if we are to live in harmony with nature does that mean that we will also see, within the human race, the same range of behaviours from gentle sustainability to violent change? It is certainly true that humans have been the agents of destruction, sometimes unwittingly and at other times deliberately. There is circumstantial evidence, for example, that links the discovery of the Clovis spear to the extinction of animal species. There is a strong argument that when animals, carried on the first vessels to fish off the east coast of North American, escaped they spread viruses to which the human population had no resistance. The result was an extinction of as many as 90% of the indigenous human population.

Of course that was an unwitting disaster, but the same excuse could not be made for those who introduced the Nile Perch into Lake Victoria and resulted in what has been termed 'the greatest mass vertebrate extinction in recorded history' as well as causing deep disruption in the lives of the people in that area. Officials were warned what could happen when an alien species is introduced into a closed ecosystem but took no notice. It had happened before, when a handful of rabbits were introduced into Australia for weekend shooting. But is this just the insensitivity of a modern industrial society that has lost its sense of the Earth? Not so, look for example at Wordsworth's Lake District. It is an artificial landscape created by the Neolithic farmers who burned down the trees. Nature did the rest through soil erosion. There are other examples of environmental change where people did not really understand the consequences of what they were doing. Take the dustbowl of the Great Plains of North America: a direct consequence of soil erosion when the deeply rooted buffalo grass was replaced by wheat. And after all, who needs buffalo grass when the buffalo were made virtually extinct by the large-scale buffalo hunts of the nineteenth century. And if the buffalo could be sacrificed in the past to economic necessity of farming, then why not the rainforests today?

Thought

While 'living in harmony with nature' would seem to be a good strategy it may not always work, after all, as we have seen, nature itself is not always 'harmonious'. It is just nature. Admittedly human beings are part of nature but they also possess a power that could almost be considered 'un natural', and that is the enormous power of thought to model and so dominate the world. Thought can create the world in its own image. It has always been able to do this but, as I pointed out earlier, this power was considerably amplified starting in the thirteenth century and, with all the power of modern science and technology it now extends its reach from the subatomic micro world on into outer space.

Thought is an ideal tool when it comes to mechanical systems which can be analyzed, repaired or replaced. But what if this same mode of thinking is applied to society and the environment? The inherent danger in such an approach is that we overlook the deep inner complexities, the subtle internal relationships and the networks of sensitivities. Our dominant logic is that everything must be going to plan; and these plans are created by thought. If things do not work out in this way we must step in and correct them. There are times when such intervention can be effective, but there are also others when it can be aggressive. After all, the language we use at times contains violent overtones, for we wish to wage 'war on drugs', 'war on want', 'war on terrorism'. We 'shoot down ideas' and when people are ill doctors apply aggressive medical treatments sometimes using 'magic bullets' to 'battle' disease.

As we have seen, the self-organized systems of nature, such as a rainforest, are both complex and flexible. They can repair themselves and are able, to a certain extent, to adjust to external change. But the systems we create in the image of thought are not always so desirable. Some can be rigid, hierarchical and rule bound. In short, so many of them do not seem to be appropriate to the rapidly changing world in which we find ourselves. Moreover we often fail to listen to what these systems are trying to tell us. For far too long the insights of chaos theory have warned us that our modern economic systems, ones in which very large sums are globally traded at the click of a mouse, must be inherently unstable and in danger of chaotic breakdown. Now an economic crisis has hit and it may only be the first of many. Certainly all this can be patched up with economic band aids but what is really needed is a longer term solution, and this means a radical change in thought. We need to develop the ability to put thought in its proper place — not to continue to abstract the world but to learn to listen to the world, to allow thought to become more creative, more flexible and more adjustable. We need to understand, and not in a mere intellectual sense, that we are part of a living cosmos. We must come to honour what the physicist Pauli predicted: that the time has come for the 'resurrection of spirit in matter', a spirit that had been banned centuries ago by Descartes and the rise of materialistic science, and to confront what he felt was the key issue facing us: the lack of soul in the modern scientific conception of the world.

The trickster

In this essay I am suggesting that if we are to face the crises of our modern world we need to go far beyond new plans and super sized band-aids to something truly radical. That it is not a matter of changing our institutions but of the very nature of thought that creates them. But how is such a radical change of direction possible? Are we asking for thought to change its mode of thinking? How can this be done?

Some years ago I was invited to participate in Banff, Alberta, at meetings to discuss Native Canadian self government and Native justice. While the first half of these meetings was devoted to talks by representatives of the Canadian government and Elders of the First Nations, the second was an exercise to create, for example, a justice system. Inevitably there would be several hours of discussion and the exploration of ideas but as the day continued someone would point out that a new approach to justice, or to self government, could not be created in the abstract. What was needed was an origin story, the account of how a particular people came to be, and how they came into relationship with the land. It would only be then, with the story of origin that people could move forward. By analogy I think we in the West need to learn from our own origin stories, and reconnect to the great myths. It is only with the help of the wisdom contained with these archetypal accounts that we can be bring about change.

One of our myths is that of Prometheus who defied Zeus by bringing fire to humans. Fire was a great gift to the human race, but it also contains the seeds of destruction, as we saw during the twentieth century when superpowers began to stockpile nuclear weapons to such an extent that a nuclear war would bring about major extinctions and a nuclear winter. In addition to fire Prometheus also brought the human race the arts of civilization, including writing, mathematics, agriculture, medicine, and science. (Of course if he had been the subject of a Chinese myth he would also have brought the art of the kitchen!)

In part the crisis our planet faces today is the result of Prometheus's gifts — agriculture has been transformed into large scale agribusiness, yet it does not have the ability to feed the world. What's more what was once hailed as a triumph for humanity, the Green Revolution, is now viewed critically. Medicine had brought many triumphs but also the science of genetic modification with all its moral, ethical and agricultural implications. And what of science?

Science today has enormous power. It has extended beyond its original seventeenth century roots in Europe to become the international yardstick against which all other knowledge systems are to be measured. In turn , these knowledge systems are generally found wanting as mere stories or myths. But this is to do a great disservice to other traditions and cultures, and to suggest that science has nothing to learn from them so that there would be little point in science engaging in an open dialogue with such traditions. Science attempts to confirm its prime position by claiming that, above all, it is totally objective and value free. Indeed, some scientists would even argue that discussions about the ethical issues around genetic engineering, for example, should not be the province of science but should be left to politicians and philosophers to debate. Science prefers to occupy the high ground and not to dirty its hands with moral and ethical discussion.

But just how true is this objectivity, this culturally uncontaminated knowledge? It is certainly the case that measurements made in a laboratory should be independent of the experimenter's belief system. It does not matter if a prediction of the second law of thermodynamics is tested by a Hindu in Delhi, a Buddhist in Peking, or an atheist in New York; the results will be the same. But what of the theory itself? Here the story is less clear-cut. Following the French Revolution, French engineers realized that they had fallen behind the British who had made considerable advances during their Industrial Revolution. And so engineers such as Sadi Carnot set up to build ever more efficient machines, but soon found out that there was a limit to efficiency and that was set not by deficiencies of human ingenuity but by nature itself. Understanding this limit provided one of the paths to the formulation of the second law of thermodynamics. And thus, while measurements of theoretical predictions may be objective, scientific theories themselves are certainly not. Likewise the questions asked by science are very much the product of a particular culture and world view. They are questions about what we consider important about the world, and about how we view the world. In turn these questions lead to scientific theories and, as Einstein pointed out to the young Heisenberg, it is the theories themselves that suggest the observables, not the other way around.

The implications of thermodynamics were taken even further. Helmholtz had applied its insights to living organisms in what he termed 'psychodynamics'. It was a small additional step for Sigmund Freud, following in Helmholtz's footsteps, to apply notions of energy flows and blocks and even 'inertia' to the understanding of the human mind and its relationship to the unconscious. And thus even the psychoanalytic understanding of human behaviour itself was to flow in a natural way from certain cultural assumptions as to how we see the world.

I believe that we must recapture the power of the mythic level if we are to change these ways of thinking and this means facing the story of Prometheus's gifts. We have seen that these gifts are two-faced. And when we revisit Prometheus we realize that he is in fact the two-faced trickster figure. Could it be that the trickster is our conduit to the sacred? He is the one who can mock authority and transcend the laws and rules of society. The trickster always surprises us. He can both make us laugh or terrify us.

The trickster can remind us of life's paradoxes and multiplicity; of the essential duality of the world. If we are to change our current attitude towards the world, if we are to change our institutions, if we are to put thought in its proper place, then we must accept the trickster as both crisis and opportunity. Good intentions and keen intelligence are certainly needed if we are to survive, but I believe that we need to go beyond the limitations of our own individuality, and collectivity, and reconnect with the deep, and sometimes mythic, forces of the world.

References

Brand, Stuart (2000) *Clock of the Long Now: Time and Responsibility: The Ideas behind the World's Slowest Computer*, Basic Books, New York.

Crosby, Alfred W., (1997) *The Measurement of Reality: Quantification and Western Society 1250–1600*, Cambridge University Press, Cambridge, UK.

Jacobs, Jane (2000) *The Nature of Economies*, Random House, New York

Peat, F. David (2005) *Blackfoot Physics: A Journey into the Native American Universe*, Weiser, Newburyport, MA.

—, (2008) *Gentle Action: Bringing Creative Change to a Turbulent World*, Pari Publishing, Pari, Italy.

PART 3

Spirituality and New

Understandings of the Sacred

14. Who Are We and Why Are We Here?

ANNE BARING

*Anne Baring (b. 1931) MA Oxon. is a retired Jungian analyst —
author and co-author of seven books including* The Myth of the
Goddess; Evolution of an Image *(1992),* The Mystic Vision *(1994),* The
Divine Feminine *(1996) and* Soul Power: an Agenda for a Conscious
Humanity *(2009). Her work is devoted to the recognition that we live in
an ensouled world and to the restoration of the lost sense of communion
between us and the invisible dimension of the universe that is the source
or ground of all that we call 'life'. She lives near Winchester, England.
Website: www.annebaring.com*

If other more advanced forms of planetary life were observing events
on this planet and our calamitous effect on it, I wonder what they
would think of the various beliefs which influence our behaviour?
Early in the twentieth century the French artist Odilon Redon painted
a picture of the Cyclops. Its single eye gazes down on the flower-
strewn expanse where a naked woman lies in a brilliantly luminous
landscape. To me, the image of the Cyclops reflects the constriction as
well as the inflation of the modern human mind which, ignorant of the
vast dimensions of planetary and cosmic life on which it rests and out
of which it has evolved, believes itself to be in control of nature and its
own nature. It evokes the much-quoted words of Blake: 'May God us
keep from the single vision and Newton's sleep.'

Yet the painting also communicates a tremendous sadness, the sadness of a one-eyed consciousness that is cut off from its ground, that has no relationship with soul and with nature — personified in this painting by the woman lying on a flower-strewn ground. The rational or literal secular eye stands lonely and supreme, alienated from the landscape of the soul.

Over the last few centuries but more pervasively during the last fifty years, a secular worldview or belief system has infiltrated every aspect of the modern world, dominating the media, the arts, science and philosophy as well as economic, political and educational agendas. It views life through an increasingly utilitarian and materialistic mindset, seeing no goal for humanity beyond the survival of our ever-increasing numbers. By excluding, rejecting and deriding so much, particularly in relation to the great spiritual and cultural achievements of the past and the unanswered questions of the human condition, it drastically restricts our understanding of ourselves and our place in the cosmos.

Yet science itself has opened up an immense and thrilling panorama of the universe in whose life our lives are embedded: geologists and biologists have pieced together the story of the Earth's evolution; cosmologists have defined the incredible story of the birth, expansion and extent of the visible universe, although this is continually being revised in the light of new discoveries; particle physicists are penetrating the mysteries of the sub-atomic world; geneticists are making new discoveries related to the genetic code and applying them to healing the terrible diseases which still afflict us; neuroscientists are making phenomenal discoveries about the human brain. All this can be described as a stupendous revelation but there is no unifying vision of our purpose on this planet which could engage the whole of humanity and take us beyond the single vision of Newton's sleep.

The secular worldview

Modern secular culture has exalted man as the supreme agent of his own triumphant scientific and technological progress but it has also reduced him to the level of a biological mechanism, subject to the programming of his genetic inheritance. It has created a society that believes in nothing beyond the myth of technological progress and the omnipotent power of science and the human mind. It has done away with any ethical foundation for values. It does not question the premises which direct its conclusions nor does it look at the effects of its impoverished beliefs on children growing up in an addicted and superficial culture. In sum, we live in an unconscious civilization, as the Canadian philosopher John Ralston Saul describes it in his book of that title (Saul 1995).

The dominant belief of secular culture is the Neo-Darwinian one that life on this planet has evolved by natural selection and that we are simply the product of our biological genes and our interaction with our environment. Life has come into being by chance; its biological evolution is controlled by chance. It has neither meaning nor purpose. Matter is primary and gives rise to mind as a secondary phenomenon. Consciousness is therefore a by-product of the brain. This belief system tells us that we are the products of mindless forces operating on inanimate matter: atoms are lifeless particles, floating in a dead universe. There is no such thing as free will, nor any meaning to our lives because we are nothing more than a random assembly of nerve cells. We exist to improve the material conditions of our lives, to work, consume and enjoy what we can accumulate in the way of wealth or material things. When we die, that is the end of us. A paranoid need for technological surveillance and ever-extended control is part and parcel of this soul-less scenario.

So are we the random creation of a mechanical, mindless universe as scientific materialism proclaims, or do we participate in the life of a living universe that animates and orchestrates its evolution from within its own cosmic, planetary and biological processes? How can we answer this question until we understand what consciousness is and the whole evolutionary development of the kind of consciousness we now have? We can only truly comprehend our history and ourselves through the lens of human consciousness. This lens may not as yet be capable of giving us the full picture, however much empirical scientific knowledge we may have.

It may be that our vision is clouded by something comparable to a giant cataract or restricted to single vision in the manner of Redon's Cyclops. This hypothesis is supported by a remarkable book published in 2009 called *The Master and His Emissary: The Divided Brain and the Making of the Western World.* (McGilchrist 2009) Its author,

Iain McGilchrist, suggests that there is not a balanced relationship between the right and left hemispheres of our brain because of the rigid control and censorship exercised by the left hemisphere over the more holistic relational consciousness of the right hemisphere. If the insights of this book could reach enough people with the ability to grasp its implications, there might be a chance that, understanding a fundamental problem at the root of our malaise, we could take steps to restore balance to the relationship between the two hemispheres of our brain and, eventually, balance to our culture.

All the knowledge we have gained about the evolution of our species, including the consciousness aspect, does not admit that our present concept of reality might be limited to the view created by our literal-minded left hemisphere alone, disregarding the more subtle and comprehensive vision of the right. Nor does it acknowledge the presence and influence of what Jung called the 'root and rhizome of the soul' — all the multi-layered memories of our entire evolutionary experience that we carry within our cellular memory. This complex patterning of species memory, incrementally expanding and increasing over thousands of millennia has contributed to the evolution of planetary life, the evolution of our species and, finally, the evolution of human consciousness itself. We are the only species on this planet that can speak, write, reflect, discover, create and communicate with each other in words and gestures and give expression to our imagination and our skills in beautiful artefacts, exquisite musical forms and brilliant technological inventions such as the Hubble telescope. How have we come to believe that this entire creative panorama has no meaning?

The roots of our beliefs and our alienation from nature

Our current worldview rests on the premise of our separation from and mastery of nature, where nature is treated as object with ourselves as controlling subject. I think this belief has its distant roots in a concept of God imagined and defined as something above and beyond nature, a creator separate and distinct from the created order and from ourselves. Western civilization, despite its phenomenal achievements, developed on the foundation of a fundamental split between spirit and nature, creator and creation. This split effectively removed the presence of spirit from the phenomenal world and opened the way to its ultimate exploitation. It directed our gaze upwards to the sky, away from the Earth. Developing patriarchal societies grew up in the shadow of an image of deity that was utterly different from that which prevailed in an earlier phase when the image of the Great Mother embraced both the life of the cosmos and the life of the Earth. Only now are we brought face to face with the effects of this split in the devastation we have wrought upon the Earth. In his last book, *Man and His Symbols,* Jung comments on the effects of our alienation from nature:

> As scientific understanding has grown, so our world has become dehumanized. Man feels himself isolated in the cosmos, because he is no longer involved in nature, and has lost his emotional 'unconscious identity' with natural phenomena. No voices now speak to man from stones, plants, and animals, nor does he speak to them believing they can hear. His contact with nature has gone, and with it has gone the profound emotional energy that this symbolic connection supplied. (Jung 1994, p. 95)

The following story illustrates how long atrophied faculties once connected us with the life of nature. Next to the Potala Palace in Lhasa there is a temple called the Lukhang or 'Temple of the Serpent Spirits' that the present Dalai Lama describes as one of the hidden jewels of Tibetan civilization. This temple was the private chamber of the Dalai Lamas — the place where they retired for deep meditation. Miraculously it has not been destroyed by the Chinese invasion of Tibet. The walls of the upper floor are decorated with extraordinary paintings describing the Tantric practices of the Dzogchen path to the direct experience of reality — the path practised by the Dalai Lamas for centuries. Only these murals depict the practices that were otherwise transmitted orally, and poetically referred to as 'The Whispered Lineage.'

Prior to the Chinese invasion of Tibet on one day each year, the Lukhang was open to pilgrims who crossed the lake to the temple to make offerings to and invoke the blessing of the water spirits believed to reside beneath the lake. This ritual went back to a time when the Potala Palace was being built and a deep pit had been excavated to provide mortar for the palace walls. Legend says that a female water spirit or Naga came to the Fifth Dalai Lama (1617–1682) during his meditations and warned him that the work on the Palace was destroying the Nagas' ancestral home. The Dalai Lama promised that he would build and dedicate a temple to the spirits of the lake which had formed over the desecrated land so that their presence would be recognized and honoured (Baker 2000, pp.12–16).

This story illustrates how people in shamanic cultures respected the hidden entities believed to be the guardians of the Earth's life. They saw the visible world embedded in an invisible one: nature immersed in the matrix of spirit. People once knew that the spirit entities they saw in dream and vision manifest and express the deepest wisdom of nature. These serpent-spirits were respected as the guardians of spiritual knowledge and no man or woman could gain access to the highest wisdom without receiving their help.

I believe that the roots of our alienation from nature also lie in the disastrous influence on western civilization of the literal interpretation of the Myth of the Fall. In the Book of Genesis we find the story of our expulsion from a divine world and our exile to a world of sin, suffering, and death that was brought into being by a woman — Eve — who listened to a serpent and disobeyed the command of God (Genesis 3). A virulent misogyny developed out of this myth as well as the belief — imprinted through the influence of St Augustine in the late fourth century — that the whole human race was mired in original sin (transmitted through the sexual act) and that only some were predestined to be saved.

Possibly because of the many negative beliefs arising from this myth, the patriarchal religions placed the emphasis of their teaching on transcending the world, transcending the body, controlling and subjugating the instincts. The body and its ways of knowing were superseded by the emphasis on mind and spirit. We were told that we live in a fallen world, saturated with sin, that was not impregnated with the radiance of spirit. Gradually, through a complex interweaving of religious teaching and scientific beliefs, the mind assumed a position of dominance over the body and man a position of dominance over nature and woman. Once science began to dissociate itself from religion, matter lost any residual numinosity which it had retained. Since it was now viewed as 'dead' and devoid of spirit it could be rendered the servant of man with impunity. Yet the very fascination of science with matter can be seen as a necessary compensation to the former unbalanced emphasis of religion on spirit.

Now, it seems as if science is being led to rethink its basic premises. In his book *Why Us?* James Le Fanu writes:

> We are left to stare into the abyss of our radical ignorance about virtually every aspect of the history of life: the mysterious creative evolutionary force which from the beginning has elaborated ever more complex forms of organization from the simplest elements of matter; the inscrutable origins of the primordial cell with its capacity to bring into being every form of life that has ever existed; the sudden dramatic emergence of new forms of life from the Cambrian explosion onwards; the mechanism of those transitions from fish to reptile, to mammals, to birds, each stage initiating a further 'explosion' of millions of new and unique species ... The substantial point remains that science has quite inadvertently broken the stranglehold of the materialist view on western thought.
> (Le Fanu 2009, p. 255)

A time of choice

We are living in a tremendously significant time: a time of choice, a time of stupendous scientific discoveries which are enlarging our view of the universe, shattering the vessel of our concepts about the nature of reality. Yet the delicate organism of life on our planet and the survival of our species are threatened as never before by an ethos that still seeks to maintain dominance and control of nature. This ethos reflects a ruthless desire to conquer and master nature for our own purposes, shows no respect for the Earth and disregards the perils of our present interference with the intricate web of relationships upon which life on this planet depends. We are an integral part of this great web of life, and are dependent upon it for our survival yet we are blindly extinguishing species at an alarming rate.

Thomas Berry, in his book, *The Dream of the Earth*, writes that this supremely important time is asking us for perhaps the most complete reversal of our values that has taken place since the Neolithic era. Our commerce, industry and economics are, he says, grounded in the devastation of the Earth. Yet, in the rising tide of ecological awareness, we can recognize that the universe is calling to us, awakening us through the influence of the deepest elements in our nature, through our genetic coding (Berry 1988, pp.159, 215).

But our values and behaviour won't change unless we change our beliefs. Acting together under the inspiration of a new vision of our role on this planet, we may, through the transformation of our understanding, be able to extricate ourselves from an outworn worldview and begin to replace the deficient values that have long controlled our culture with new values based on respect for the Earth. This, as Berry rightly says, is the alchemical Great Work that is now in progress as increasing numbers of people awaken to the values which express our responsibility towards life, each other and the planet as a whole.

It may be that the new epoch we are entering will see the creation of a new concept of God or Spirit, a new understanding of the extraordinary intelligence of nature, and how two or more dimensions of reality interact with each other. This new understanding may help to modify the deeply entrenched belief that spirit and nature are separate and distinct and may eventually restore to us our lost sense of relationship with a sacred Earth and a conscious universe.

Over the course of many centuries, we have developed a formidable intellect, a formidable science, a formidable technology. But what of the soul — source of our deepest instincts and feelings? What of our visions, dreams and hopes for the future as well as our unhealed wounds and the suffering generated by our cruelty and lack of compassion towards each other? What of our need for relationship with an unrecognized dimension of reality? The pressing need for the soul's recognition has brought us to this time of choice. It is as if mortal danger is forcing us to take a great leap in our evolution that we might never have made were we not driven by the extremity of circumstance. Because our capacity for destruction, both military and ecological, is so much greater today than it was fifty years ago, and will be still greater tomorrow, we have perhaps only decades in which to heal the Wasteland we have brought into being through our ignorance of the interdependence of all aspects, all forms, of life.

The threat of climate change appears to be the catalyst which is forging a profound shift in our values. Instead of treating our planetary home as the endless supplier of all our needs, without consideration for its needs, we are having to rethink beliefs and attitudes which have influenced our behaviour for millennia — beliefs and attitudes which are deeply rooted in our religious traditions as well as in the secular beliefs of modern science.

Once again, as in the early centuries of the Christian era, it seems as if new bottles are needed to hold the wine of a new understanding of reality, a new worldview. What is the emerging vision of our time which could offer a template for a conscious humanity? I believe it is a vision which takes us beyond an outworn image of deity and offers us a new concept of spirit as a unifying energy field — a limitless sea of being — as well as the creative consciousness or organizing intelligence within that sea or field, and a new concept of ourselves as belonging to and participating in that incandescent ground of consciousness.

It is a vision which recognizes the sacredness and indissoluble unity of this great cosmic web of life and imposes on us the responsibility of becoming far more sensitive to the effects of our beliefs and our actions. It invites our recognition of the needs of the planet and the life it sustains as primary, with ourselves as the conscious servants of those needs. Above all, it is a vision which asks that we relinquish our addiction to weapons, war and the pursuit of power; that we become more aware of the dark shadow cast by this addiction which threatens us with ever more barbarism, bloodshed and suffering.

From this perspective, the crisis of our times is not only an ecological and political crisis but a spiritual crisis. The answers we seek cannot come from the limited left-hemispheric consciousness which currently rules the world but could grow from a deeper understanding born of the union of mind and soul, helping us to see that all life is one, that each one of us participates in the life of a cosmic entity of immeasurable dimensions. The urgent need for this psychic balance, this deeper intelligence and insight, this wholeness, could help us to recover a perspective on life that has been increasingly lost until we have come to live without it — and without even noticing it has gone — recognizing the existence of no dimension of reality beyond the parameters set by the human mind. It is a dangerous time because it involves transforming entrenched belief systems and archaic survival habits of behaviour that are rooted in fear and ignorance, as well as the greed and desire for power that are born of these. But it is also an immense opportunity for evolutionary advance, if only we can understand what is happening and why.

After so many billion years of evolution, it is surely unacceptable that the beauty and marvel of the Earth should be ravaged by us through the destructive power of our weapons, our insatiable greed and the misapplication of our science and technology. It is inconceivable that our extraordinary species, which has taken so many billion years to evolve, should destroy itself and lay waste to the Earth through ignorance of the divinity in which we dwell and which dwells in us. For a rapidly increasing number of us, there is the possibility of choosing whether to continue in the patterns of the past or to create new patterns, living and acting from a different relationship with life, committing ourselves to the immense effort of consciousness we need to make to understand and serve its mystery.

References

Baker, Ian A. (2000) *The Dalai Lama's Secret Temple*, Thames and Hudson, London, pp. 12–16, .

Berry, Thomas (1988) *The Dream of the Earth*, Sierra Books, San Francisco, pp. 159, 215.

Jung, Carl G. (1964) *Man and His Symbols*, Aldus Books, London, p. 95.

Le Fanu, James (2009) *Why Us? How Science Rediscovered the Mystery of Ourselves*, Harper Press.

McGilchrist, Iain (2009) *The Master and His Emissary: The Divided Brain and The Making of the Western World*, Yale University Press, New York and London.

Saul, John Ralston (1995, 1998) *The Unconscious Civilization*, House of Anansi Press, Canada; Penguin Books, London.

15. The Spiritual Imperative: Elegant Simplicity is the Way to Discover Spirituality

SATISH KUMAR

Satish Kumar, a former Jain monk, walked 8000 miles from India to Europe then to the United States and Japan in the name of peace and nuclear disarmament. He has been the Editor of Resurgence Magazine since 1973, and is one of the longest serving editors in the UK. He is a founder of the Small School in Hartland and of Schumacher College in Dartington. Satish is a champion of spiritual ecology and has a written a number of books including No Destination: An autobiography of an Earth Pilgrim; You Are Therefore I Am; Spiritual Compass *and* Earth Pilgrim. *For further information visit www.resurgence.org The following is an abridged text of Satish Kumar's Schumacher Lecture given on October 30, 2004, in Bristol. www.schumacher.org.uk*

Matter and spirit are two sides of the same coin. What we measure is matter, what we feel is spirit. Matter represents quantity, spirit is about quality. Spirit manifests itself through matter; matter comes to life through spirit. Spirit brings meaning to matter, matter gives form to spirit. Without spirit, matter lacks life. We are human body and human spirit at the same time. A tree too has body and spirit; even rocks which appear to be dead contain their spirit. There is no dichotomy, no dualism, no separation between matter and spirit.

The problem is not matter but materialism. Similarly there is no problem with spirit, but spiritualism is problematic. The moment we encapsulate an idea or a thought into an 'ism' we lay the foundations of dualistic thought. The universe is uni-verse, one song, one poem, one verse. It contains infinite forms which dance together in harmony, sing together in concert, balance each other in gravity, transform each other in evolution and yet the universe maintains its wholeness and its implicate order. Dark and light, above and below, left and right, words and meaning, matter and spirit complement each other, comfortable in mutual embrace. Where is the contradiction? Where is the conflict?

Life feeds life, matter feeds matter, spirit feeds spirit. Life feeds matter, matter feeds life and spirit feeds both matter and life. There is total reciprocity. This is the oriental world view, an ancient world view, a world view found in the tribal traditions of pre-industrial cultures where nature and spirit, Earth and heaven, sun and moon are in eternal reciprocity and harmony.

Modern dualistic cultures see nature red in tooth and claw, the strongest and fittest surviving, the weak and meek disappearing, conflict and competition as the only true reality. From this world view emerges the notion of a split between mind and matter. Once mind and matter are split then debate ensues as to whether mind is superior to matter or matter is superior to mind.

This world view of split, rift, conflict, competition, separation and dualism has also given birth to the idea of separation between the human world and the natural world. Once that separation is established, humans consider themselves to be the superior species, engaged in controlling and manipulating nature for their use. In this view of the world, nature exists for human benefit, to be owned and possessed and if nature is protected and conserved then the purpose is only for human benefit. The natural world — plants, animals, rivers, oceans, mountains and the skies — are denuded of spirit. If spirit exists at all, then it is limited to human spirit. But even that is doubtful. In this world view humans too are considered to be nothing more than a formation of material, molecules, genes and elements. Mind is considered to be a function of the brain, and the brain is an organ in the head and no more.

This notion of spiritless existence can be described as materialism.

All is matter; land, forests, food, water, labour, literature and art are commodities to be bought and sold in the marketplace — the world market, the stockmarket, the so called 'free' market. This is a market of competitive advantage, a cut throat market, a market where survival of the fittest is the greatest imperative: the strong competing with the weak and winning the biggest share of the market for themselves.

The religion of materialism and the culture of consumerism which have been promoted by Western civilization have blocked the flow of joy and beauty. Once Mahatma Gandhi was asked, 'Mr Gandhi, what do you think of Western civilization?' He replied: 'It would be a good idea.' Yes, it would be a good idea because any society discarding spiritual values and fighting for material goods, going to war to control oil, producing nuclear weapons to maintain its political power cannot be called a civilization. The modern, consumerist culture built on unfair, unjust and unsustainable economic institutions cannot be considered to be civilized. The true mark of civilization is to maintain a balance between material progress and spiritual integrity. How can we consider ourselves to be civilized when we don't know how to live with each other in harmony and how to live on the Earth without destroying it? We have developed technologies to reach the moon but not the wisdom to live with our neighbours, nor mechanisms to share food and water with our fellow human beings. A civilization without a spiritual foundation is no civilization at all.

The way we treat animals is a clear example of our lack of civilization. Cows, pigs and chickens live as prisoners in factory farms. Mice, monkeys and rabbits are treated as slaves as if they feel no pain; all for human greed and human arrogance. Western civilization seems to believe that all life is expendable in the service of human desire. Racism, nationalism, sexism and ageism have been challenged and to some extent eradicated but humanism still rules our minds. As a result we consider the human species to be superior to all other species. This humanism is a kind of speciesism. If we are to strive for civilization we will have to change our philosophy, our world-view and our behaviour. We will have to enter into a new paradigm where all beings are interbeings, interdependent, interrelated and interspecies.

Spirit in religion

Sometimes the words spirituality and religion are confused, but spirituality and religion are not the same thing. Politics should be free from the constraints of religion but should not be free of spiritual values. The word religion comes from the Latin root *religio* which means to bind together with the string of certain beliefs. A group of people come together, share a belief system, stick together and support each other. Thus religion binds you. Whereas the root meaning of spirit is associated with breath, with air. We can all be free spirits and breathe freely. Spirituality transcends beliefs. The spirit moves, inspires, touches our hearts and refreshes our souls.

When a room has been left closed, doors and windows shut and curtains drawn, the air in the room becomes stale. When we enter the room after a few days we find it stuffy so we open the doors and windows to bring in fresh air. In the same way when minds are closed for too long we need a radical avatar, a prophet, to open the windows so that our stuffy minds and stale thoughts are aired again. A Buddha, a Jesus, a Gandhi, a Mother Teresa, a Rumi, a Hildegard of Bingen appear and blow away the cobwebs of closed minds. Of course we don't need to wait for such prophets, we can be our own prophets, unlock our own hearts and minds and allow the fresh air of compassion, of generosity, of divinity, of sacredness to blow through our lives.

Religious groups and traditions have an important role to play. They initiate us into a discipline of thought and practice, they provide us with a framework; they offer us a sense of community, of solidarity, of support. A tender seedling needs a pot and a stick to support it in the early stages of its development or even the enclosure of a nursery to protect it from frost and cold winds. But when it is strong enough it needs to be planted out in the open so that it is able to develop its own roots and become a fully mature tree. Likewise religious orders act as nurseries for seeking souls. But in the end each one of us has to establish our own roots and find divinity in our own way.

There are many good religions, many good philosophies and many good traditions. We should accept all of them and accept that different religious traditions meet the need of different people at different times, in different places and in different contexts. This spirit of generosity, inclusivity and recognition is a spiritual quality. Whenever religious orders lose this quality, they become no more than mere sects protecting their vested interests.

At present the institutionalized religions have fallen into this trap. For them the maintenance of institutions has become more important than helping their members to grow, to develop and discover their own free spirit. When religious orders get caught in maintaining their properties and their reputation they lose their spirituality and then they, too, become like a business without spirit. As it is necessary to restore spirit in business and in politics we also need to restore spirit in religion. This may seem a strange proposition because the very *raison d'être* of every religion is to seek spirit and to establish universal love. The reality is otherwise. Religions have done much good but also they have done much harm and we can see all around us that tensions between Christians, Muslims, Hindus and Jews are major causes of conflicts, wars and disharmony.

The rivalry among religions would cease if they realize that religious faiths are like rivers flowing into the same great ocean of spirituality. Even though the various rivers with their different names give nourishment to different regions and different peoples they all provide the same quality of refreshment. There is no conflict among the rivers. Why then should there be conflict among the religions? Their theology or belief system may differ but the spirituality is the same. It is this spirituality which is paramount. Respect for a diversity of beliefs is a spiritual imperative.

Spirituality and science

Often it is believed that science and spirituality are like oil and water. They cannot mix. This is a mistaken notion. Science needs spirituality and spirituality needs science. When science forsakes the restraints of moral, ethical and spiritual dimensions and strives to achieve everything that is achievable, experimenting with everything irrespective of consequences then science leads to the technologies of nuclear weapons, genetic engineering, human and animal cloning and poisonous products which pollute soil, water and air. It is dangerous to give science *carte blanche* to dominate human minds and to subjugate the natural world. Contemporary science has acquired such status of superiority that it is presently commanding the total adherence of industry, business, education and politics. Some of its experiments have become so crude and cruel that it reaches beyond the constraints of civilization. Ethical, moral and spiritual values are essential to moderate the power of science.

As science needs spirituality, spirituality also needs science. Without a certain amount of rational, analytical and intellectual skills spirituality can easily turn into sectarian and selfish pursuit. I was a monk for nine years pursuing my own purification and salvation. I saw the world as a trap and spirituality as a way of liberation from the world. Then I came across the writings of Mahatma Gandhi. He said that there is no dualism between the world and the spirit. Spirituality is not confined to monastic orders or caves in the mountains. Spirituality is in everyday life; from the growing of food to cooking, eating, washing up, sweeping the floor, building the house, making clothes and caring for neighbours. We must bring spirituality into all parts of our lives, into politics, into business, into agriculture and into education. That was such an inspiring insight that I decided to leave the monastic order and return to the world of everyday life.

Three practical steps towards spirituality

Trust

So let us explore a few areas of spirituality. First and foremost among them is removal of fear and cultivation of trust. If we look deeply we will realize that many of our psychological difficulties stem from fear. A sense of insecurity, the ambition to be successful, the desire to prove ourselves, efforts to impress others, craving for power over others and to be in control, addiction to shopping, consuming and possessing, all are ultimately related to fear. This personal fear expands into social insecurity and political insecurity. So the first step towards spiritual renewal is to look at the phenomena of fear in our lives and realize that much of this fear is aggravated by more fear. Fear breeds fear and fear is led by fear. We go to great lengths to build psychological and physical defences but they only increase our fear. Even when we have nuclear weapons to protect us we are not free from fear.

Moreover, history has proved that nuclear weapons are no defence and bring no security. The attack on the Twin Towers of the World Trade Centre in New York proved that ultimately all defences are futile. The attackers can attack with a knife or a razor blade so where is the justification for spending so much effort, time and resources in building nuclear warheads when they bring no defence and no security? Western societies seem to be obsessed with safety and security and go to great lengths to ensure themselves against all eventualities. Such obsession has a paralyzing effect.

The first step into the spiritual sphere is to understand fear and cultivate trust. Trust yourself. You are as good as you are. You embody the divine spark, the creative impulse, the power of imagination which will always be with you and will protect you. Trust others; they are in the same boat as you. They long for love as much as you do. Only in relationships with others will you blossom. You are because others are and others are because you are. We all exist, flourish, blossom and mature in this mutuality, reciprocity and unity. Give love and love will be reciprocated. Give fear and fear will be reciprocated. Sow one seed of thistle and you will get hundreds of thorny thistles. Sow one seed of Camellia and you will get hundreds of Camellia flowers. You will reap what you sow, this is the old wisdom. And yet we have not learnt it.

Then trust the process of the universe. The sun is there to nourish all life. Water is there to quench the thirst; the soil is there to grow food. Trees are there to bear fruit. The moment a baby is born the mother's breast is filled with milk. The process of the universe is embedded in the life support system of mutuality. Hundreds of millions of species; lions, elephants, snakes, butterflies, all are fed, watered, sheltered and taken care of by the mysterious process of the universe — trust it. As St Julian of Norwich said: 'All shall be well, all manner of things shall be well.'

Participation

The second spiritual quality is participation. Participate in the magical process of life. Life is a miracle, we cannot explain it nor can we know it in full but we can actively and consciously participate in it without trying to control it, manipulate it and subjugate it.

Participation is easy and simple. We have been given two wonderful hands to cultivate the soil and grow our food. Working with the soil in the garden meets the need of the body as much as the need of the mind. Industrial farming has taken away our birthright to participate in the cultivation of food. Large-scale mechanized and industrialized farming is born of our desire to dominate. Small-scale, natural, local farming, still better, gardening, is a way of participation with the rhythms of the seasons. England should be gardened not farmed. Animals should be freed from the prisons of factory farms. Growing food is one example of the principal of participations. Baking bread, cooking food, sharing the meal with family, friends and guests are as much spiritual activities as they are social and economic activities. The culture of fast food has deprived us of the fundamental activity of participation in the daily ritual and practice of physical and spiritual nourishment. It is wonderful that people all over Europe are inspired by the Italian movement of Slow Food. Slow Food is spiritual food. Fast food is fearful food.

Slowness is a spiritual quality. If we wish to restore our spirituality we have to slow down. Paradoxically only when we go slower can we go further. Doing less, consuming less, producing less will enable us to be more, to celebrate more, and to enjoy more. Time is what makes things perfect. Give yourself time to make things and give yourself time to rest. Take your time to do as well as to be. It is in the dance of doing and being that spirituality is to be found.

Once the Emperor of Persia asked his Sufi Master: 'Please advise me, what should I be doing to renew my soul, revive my spirit, and refresh my mind so that I can be happy in myself and effective in my work?' The Sufi Master replied: 'My Lord, sleep as long as you can!' The Emperor was surprised and amazed to hear this answer and said: 'Sleep? I have little time to sleep. I have justice to perform, laws to enact, ambassadors to receive and armies to command. How can I sleep when I have so much to do?' The Sufi Master replied: 'My Lord, the longer you sleep the less you will oppress!' The Emperor was speechless; he saw the point of the Sufi sage. Even though the sage was blunt, he was right.

Western countries are in a similar position to the Emperor of Persia. The longer we work, the more we consume: we drive cars, fly in planes, burn electricity, go shopping and produce waste. The faster we do these activities the more damage we inflict on the environment, on the poor and on our own peace of mind. So true participation is to live and work in harmony with ourselves, with our fellow human beings and with the natural world. Participation is not about speed and efficiency; rather it is about harmony, balance and appropriateness of action.

Gratitude

The third spiritual quality is a sense of gratitude. In our Western culture we complain about everything. If it is raining then we say: 'Isn't it awful weather, so wet and cold'. When it is sunny we complain: 'Isn't it hot, so hot!' The media is full of complaints and criticism. Debates in the parliament are mostly concentrated on the negative aspects of government policies. The opposition blames the government and the government complains about the opposition. The national culture of blaming and complaining permeates throughout, even in our family life and in our work place. Because of the dominance of a culture of condemnation we learn to condemn ourselves too. 'I am not good enough,' is a widespread feeling. Whatever we do we don't appreciate it. We think we should be doing something different, something else, something better. Then whatever other people do we don't learn to appreciate it either. 'I had a terrible childhood,' we complain. 'My school was awful,' we reflect. 'I'm never appreciated by my colleagues,' we grumble, and this kind of criticism goes on and on.

In order to develop spiritually we need to balance our critical faculty with the faculty of appreciation and gratitude. We need to train ourselves to turn our minds to recognize the gifts we have received from our ancestors, our parents, our teachers, our colleagues and our society in general. We also need to express our thankfulness for the gifts of the Earth. What a wonderful Gaian system it is, that we are part of. It regulates climate, it organizes the seasons and provides abundance of nourishment, beauty and sensual pleasures to all creatures. When we are in awe and wonder at the workings of the sacred Earth we can feel nothing but blessed and grateful. When food is served we are filled with a sense of gratitude. We thank the cook and the gardener but also we thank the soil and the rain and the sunshine. We even express our gratitude to the earthworms who have been working day and night to keep the soil friable and fertile. However green a gardener's fingers are, without the worms there will be no food. So in praise we say, 'Long live the worms,' and further we join the poet Gerard Manley Hopkins and say, 'Long live the wet and the wilderness yet.' It is the beauty of the wild which feeds our soul while the fruit of the Earth feeds the body.

The generosity and unconditional love of the Earth for all its creatures is boundless. We plant one small seed of an apple in the ground. That tiny seed results in a tree within a few years and produces thousands and thousands of apples year after year. And all that from a tiny pip, sometimes self-sown. When in the autumn apples ripen with their fragrant, juicy, crisp flesh we eat to our heart's content. The tree knows no discrimination, it asks no questions. Poor or rich, saint or sinner, fool or philosopher, wasp or bird, one and all can receive the fruit freely. What else can we feel for the tree but gratitude? And from our gratitude flows humility as arrogance comes from complaining and criticism. When we are critical of nature we come to the conclusion that nature is not good enough: it is imperfect and unreliable. Nature needs our technology and engineering so we go to great lengths to improve on it but we end up destroying it. With a sense of gratitude we go with the grain of nature, we work in harmony with it and we appreciate its miraculous qualities.

Regaining the perennial wisdom

There is no dualism and separation between matter and spirit. Spirit is held within matter and matter within spirit but we have separated them and have made spirit a private matter and have allowed matter alone to dominate our public life. We need to heal this rift urgently. Without such healing the material world, the Earth itself will continue to suffer catastrophic consequences and spiritual insights and wisdom will continue to be seen as idealistic, esoteric and otherworldly practices totally irrelevant to our everyday existence.

When we are able to heal this rift we will be able to instill spirit in business, in commerce and in the economy. We will be able to create a politics which works for all. Our religions will not be divisive; on the contrary they will become a source of healing and resolving conflicts.

The movement for environmental sustainability and social justice will inspire rather than agitate and, personally, human beings will be at ease with themselves and with the world around them. The marriage of matter and spirit, of business and spirit, of politics and spirit, of religion and spirit and of activism and spirit is the greatest union required in our time.

People are hungry for spiritual nourishment; this hunger cannot be satisfied by material means. Therefore, the great work we have in our hands is to create space and time for people to discover their spirituality as well as the spirituality of others.

It should not be necessary for me to make a case for spiritual space but because in the last few hundred years Western culture has been in denial of spirit and has been busy elevating the status of matter, so our society and culture has lost its balance and wholeness. In order to restore this balance I have emphasized the importance of spirit. In an ideal world people would recognize that spirit is always implicit in matter. Traditionally that is how it was. People took pilgrimages to holy mountains and sacred rivers, life was considered sacred and inviolable. We recognized the metaphysical dimension of trees. The speaking tree, the tree of knowledge and the tree of life express the implicit spiritual quality of the tree. Regaining this perennial wisdom is life's greatest imperative.

16. Beyond The Material: The New Renaissance and Agnostic Spirituality

MAX PAYNE

Max Payne was formerly a lecturer in philosophy at Sheffield Hallam University. He was originally trained as a scientist but spent his academic career in philosophy. His main interests are the philosophy of science, the philosophy of religion, and theoretical and practical politics. He has written many book reviews and articles on the intersection of science and religion and is co-author, with the late Dr Peter Leggett, of A Forgotten Truth.

A New Renaissance means a totally transformed vision of what human knowledge is, and what its present limits are. The meaning of this transformation can be given by an analogy with our knowledge of the electromagnetic spectrum. Until the end of the nineteenth century scientific understanding was confined to what could be seen in visible light. Then with the discovery of the infra-red, the ultra-violet, radio waves and X-rays the whole spectrum was widened out so that visible light was seen as only a narrow slice across a far wider range of vibrations. Using the whole spectrum twentieth century science has expanded the frontiers of human knowledge to the limits of the universe and the ultimate recesses of the atom. In the same way the twenty-first century may come to realize that ordinary human consciousness is but a narrow slice across inner reality. The result has to be a healthy humility at the limits of our knowledge and the beginning of a profound agnostic spirituality.

The twentieth century has been an age of unparalleled progress in scientific knowledge. An exponential expansion of understanding based on the achievements of the seventeenth, eighteenth and nineteenth centuries, has given us relativity, quantum theory, the decoding of the inner structure of the atom, and the vision of a vast universe exploding from a Big Bang fourteen billion years ago. The blueprint of life has been deciphered in DNA. In turn this knowledge has had vast and unprecedented technological consequences which have transformed the lives of ordinary people planetwide. Faraday's experiments in electromagnetism have given us refrigerators and lighting, television and radio. We have nuclear power, but live under the shadow of the atom bomb. The world is united by instant communication through telephone, e-mail and television. Rapid transit by jet plane makes the other side of the world next door. The life expectancy in the poorest nations of sub-Saharan Africa is now higher than that of the richest nations of Western Europe one hundred years ago. This success of our material knowledge has had the inevitable consequence of the triumph of a materialistic worldview. However nothing fails like success, and the materialistic worldview makes assumptions that are not merely dubious, but profoundly and dangerously wrong. It assumes that science can explain everything, and that the present material world picture given by modern science is all the reality that there is.

Qualification is required. The materialistic worldview is a not a majority view of the world's population. In one sense, with the exception of a few ascetic hermits, all of mankind, in all cultures, at all periods of history, have been materialistic. They have been preoccupied with the eminently material problems of finding food, shelter and security for themselves and their family, and then, if they have sufficient leisure and wealth, they have indulged their surplus energies in amusements, sports, and the enjoyment of the arts. All eminently material activities. But they have also acknowledged that their lives, and their deaths, had an overarching meaning and purpose beyond mere material satisfaction. That meaning has usually been given by the rules and customs of an ancestral religion. For most of the seven billion people on Earth today, that is still true. The secular post-Christian materialist worldview of Western Europe is unique not only in time, but also in place. Even in the wealthiest and most advanced Western nation, the USA, a large minority deny Darwinian evolution on religious grounds. Islamic nations are becoming more self confident in their religion, and fundamentalists of all religions are becoming more extreme. But it is the triumph of modern science that has produced the world in which we live, and it is the secular materialism of the West that has the cultural initiative.

The argument about a New Renaissance therefore addresses a small élite. That élite is not necessarily composed of those with a long string of academic qualifications, or who occupy positions of power in politics, finance or commerce. The élite that matter are the minority who think, and are self-aware of the society which they live in. It was an élite minority who created the modern world. It is another such group who alone are capable of pointing forward towards a new vision for the twenty-first century.

Einstein's Theory of Relativity seeks that description which is true for all possible observers. A traveller in a railway train sees the poles alongside the track whizzing past and thinks himself to be still, an observer by the track sees the poles as still, but the train and its passengers as moving. Astronomers on Earth record a distant galaxy to be receding from us at a large fraction of the speed of light. Any intelligent form of life on that galaxy will presume that they are the still point, and that it is we who are nearing the speed of light on our movement away from them. Relativity seeks that description which explains and unites all these apparently contradictory observations. In doing so it unites space and time, reveals the exchange rate between matter and energy which is the secret of atomic power, and shows that commonsense experience is but a limited reflection of a deeper reality. The search for the New Renaissance must go through the same process. It is necessary for each seeker of a new vision to state quite honestly how they see the cultural crisis of our times from their perspective.

The materialist quandary

The central problem of the West is the materialism at the heart of the high culture. The highest knowledge we have is the world picture of science, and if we ask the fundamental question: 'What is a human being?' in that world picture, then the answer is that man is a material object, and therefore all thought and consciousness is the product of the electrical and chemical operations of the physical brain. The thrill of love, the delight of music, the thrust of ambition, the cool calculation of thought are all nothing but the passage of electrons through the synapses of the cerebral cortex. The picture can be blurred and made more complex by adding that human beings are also animals, and therefore we inherit evolutionary traits from our distant ancestors, but animals are material objects as well, and the evolutionary drive, whether for competition or for altruism, is ultimately merely a material energy.

If human beings are nothing but material objects, and consciousness is nothing but an illusion, then it follows that they will be motivated by material desires alone. Mass advertising and the crude hedonism of much of popular culture work on that principle. Many people are still inspired by the altruistic commands of Christianity or the Enlightenment ideals of social responsibility, but equally, for many, these are like light from a dead star, reaching us through cultural space from a source that, for them, is already extinguished. Life for the majority is comfortable and prosperous, indeed more comfortable and more prosperous than any preceding generation, but there is a growing underclass in the inner cities on the fringe of society that is alienated from the mainstream of society, living outside its norms and values. They are like the cancer cells in an otherwise healthy body. They only give the occasional ache but they presage a condition which is serious and may be terminal.

A definitive version of Reductionist Materialism has been given with brutal clarity by Francis Crick, the co-discoverer of DNA:

> You, your joys and your sorrows, your memories and your ambitions, your sense of personal identity and free will, are in fact no more than the behaviour of a vast assembly of nerve cells and associated molecules. (Crick 1994, p. 3)

This purports to be a scientific statement, or at least a statement that makes clear the consequences of science. In fact it is a dogmatic declaration of faith which is practically unprovable, theoretically impossible, and logically contradictory. It is obvious that there is a connection between our thoughts and the activity of the brain, but the readings of the most powerful brain scanner are many magnitudes cruder than the subtlety of the thoughts which provoke the measurements. It may be possible to deduce that a subject is not telling the truth, but it is not possible to tell exactly what they are lying about. An area associated with mathematical calculation may be shown to be active, but the scanner cannot tell whether the subject is making 2+2=4 or 5, or solving Gödel's theorem. But it might be objected that though it is not possible to reduce mind to matter at the present, in principle, in the future, with the further advance of science, it will be possible. A new generation of brain scanners will be able to pinpoint the brain structure associated with every thought. Mind will then be finally reduced to matter.

If mind can be totally reduced to matter, then the point of reduction must lie in the properties of the smallest and most ultimate sub-atomic particles, and in particular with the behaviour of the electrons, neutrinos and gluons which reside in the outer shells of the atom or which pass through them. There are billions of cells in the human brain, each cell is composed of many complex molecules containing many atoms, and each atom is made up of many sub-atomic particles of energy. It is impossible to conceive any scanning machine which in practice could determine the exact position and movement of all these countless billions of particles. Not only is it impossible in practice to imagine such a machine, such a machine is theoretically impossible. Heisenberg's Indeterminacy Principle prohibits the exact measurement of the position and the momentum of a sub-atomic particle at the same time. This has been applied by physicists to the behaviour of single electrons under precise laboratory conditions. It would certainly apply to the billions of particles making up the human cortex. It is impossible to imagine a one-to-one exact description of any brain state fitting any state of mind.

The holes in materialism

Not only do we not know what matter really is, we do not know what mind really is either. The Behaviourists and Linguistic Analysts such as Gilbert Ryle denied the existence of the mind, but they thought they knew exactly what it was they asserted did not exist. Everyone knows what it is to have a self-aware mind; even those who deny that they have one. But consciousness is something wider than ego-centred human rationality. Psychoanalysis and hypnosis reveal an infra-red to consciousness outside the narrow visible spectrum of rationality. Genius, great intuitive creativity and mystical experience reveal ultra-violet and X-ray frequencies beyond and above the normal. These days the better class of biologist recognizes that animals possess an inner consciousness. Chimpanzees and crows can show considerable constructive intelligence. Pet owners and farmers have always known that their animals have an inner awareness, but the stories of Beatrix Potter give us no clue to what is there. We do not know what it is like on the inside to be a bat, or a cat, or a member of a flock of migrating birds, let alone a honey bee or an amoeba. We do not know if, or in what degree, consciousness goes down as far as life.

The paranormal puts further problems about the nature and range of consciousness. Such phenomena as telepathy, psychokinesis, and post-mortem appearances all suggest that consciousness is something independent of matter. Rare, and unreliable, as the evidence for the paranormal is, enough has been attested to by men and women of unimpeachable integrity and academic standing to show that these fringes of human experience exist. But the paranormal has been ruled out of court by orthodox science. It quite simply appears to be the case that the paranormal contradicts the whole of modern scientific knowledge as we know it. There just is no way in which telepathy or psychic phenomena could happen in terms of the four fundamental forces of nature. And if it is the case that it is a choice between the vast understanding of the universe that science gives us, and a few rare and uncertain events, then there is no contest. Even those who have had paranormal experiences first hand may doubt the reality of what they have witnessed.

However there is a 'double bluff' argument. Granting for a moment that mind is just totally the by-product of matter, we nevertheless know from modern cosmology that matter consists of 95% 'dark matter' whose properties are not at the moment understood. Such 'dark matter' could provide a possible physical mechanism for every form of paranormal phenomena that has been recorded. 'Dark matter'

193

does not, of course, validate the paranormal, it simply shows that it does not contradict the total consensus worldview of modern science. Once that inhibition is removed, then the massive evidence for the paranormal can no longer be ignored. In the face of this evidence the hypothesis that mind is totally the by-product of the physical brain is no longer easily tenable.

There is a last logical objection to Reductionist Materialism. If all thoughts are just ultimately physical brain structures, then one set of thoughts is as good as another set of thoughts, both are just brain states. Brain states are not right or wrong, they just are. The Reductionist's arguments are just a brain state, and the counter argument of some Idealist is also just a brain state, and neither is right nor wrong. If we assert that: 'Ah, but the Reductionist's brain state corresponds to the reality of things, while the Idealist's is mistaken', then this is a higher order judgment passed by a conscious mind upon its observation of a physical state. It is not logically possible to explain away the operations of a conscious mind in any other way than in terms of the inner logic of consciousness itself. Mind is irreducible.

What this means is a profound metaphysical question. Does it imply a reverse reductionism in which matter is merely an illusion produced by the activity of a higher spiritual consciousness, as the Vedanta would have it? Or do we simply accept that consciousness is just a dimension of a multi-dimensional reality which includes space and time as well? Either way any form of materialism is discounted.

If Materialist Reductionism is no longer scientifically, philosophically, or logically valid then this is the hinge upon which the New Renaissance turns. None of the achievements of modern science are contradicted, indeed we can hope that it will continue its triumphant advance, but the reality of things studied in science, has been opened up. If mind is no longer seen as the epiphenomenal side effect of the physical brain, then what are its dimensions, what is its possible range? How does it fit alongside the vastness of the physical cosmos? The whole perspective of what it is to be a man or a woman alters. We are no longer merely physical beings guided by our appetites and desires, and imprisoned by our genes and our evolutionary history. We are a consciousness in a physical body, but something more than its physical instrument. We are not consumers, or voters, or objects of desire or hatred, we are full human beings with a full inner self.

This perception alone subverts the sleazy, easy, hedonistic permissive morality of the late twentieth century.

Towards an agnostic spirituality

This shift of perception carries further. The most valuable inner experiences are the self-transcending ones; the times when we are lifted out of our normal ego-centred awareness into something higher such as the sheer power and beauty of high art, or an achingly altruistic compassionate love for suffering humanity. Rarely, and occasionally, we may feel the presence of a power greater than ourselves, though public opinion polls reveal at least 40% have such an experience at least one in a lifetime.

What is that description which is true for all religious positions? Above all what is the evidence from the rare incandescent mystics, saints, prophets and incarnations that have advanced beyond ego-centred normality into the transcendent realms of consciousness ? They have sensed love, power, and an awesome otherness, which is paradoxically also an intimate immanent nearness. These overwhelming experiences have condensed and crystallized down into words, scriptures, rituals, religions, dogmas and teachings.

Religious beliefs seem obvious fundamental truths to believers on the inside, but appear highly questionable from the outside. The sceptic might doubt whether God's final and definitive revelation was preached in the Arabian desert, or whether some well intentioned old gentleman really is God's vice-regent on Earth, or if some obscure tribe from a semi-arid region of the Eastern Mediterranean really did have a special covenant with God. It is less than obvious to the outsider that turning a prayer wheel or making the precisely exact ritual offering to the statue of a many-armed Hindu God will actually ensure a happier rebirth in the next life. God, whatever God is, is that creative purpose and power which is behind the manifestation of the myriad galaxies in this universe, and perhaps an infinite number of other universes.

The relativistic description of the religious dimension leads to a form of spiritual agnosticism. All material knowledge is simply a ground state of a far vaster reality which we can hardly comprehend.

The first consequence of spiritual agnosticism is therefore humility. The thought that a few equations written up on a blackboard could be a 'theory of everything' vanishes. With the distinguished exception of Gautama Buddha, many great religious teachers have erected vast metaphysical cloud castles to explain the spiritual mystery that surrounds human existence. There is the verbal complexity of the Christian creeds: the Second Person of the Trinity was 'begotten not created'. What on earth do those words mean? Esoteric doctrines talk of seven planes of existence which are but sub-planes of the first of seven vaster cosmic planes. The Mahayana has nirvana upon mahaparanirvana. But no one can actually *know* these things in terms of any meaningful definition of verifiable knowledge. The ultimate Reality is incommensurate with the human intellect. There are too many paradoxical opposites to be reconciled. God is nearer to us than our jugular vein, and yet is also the THAT which is the creative origin of universe upon universe. The shelves of the theology section of any library groan with the weight of the books attempting to solve the problem of suffering, and none of them succeed. God is the God of love, and yet there is the appalling suffering generations of men, women and children have endured through famine, disease, and the cruelty of other men. To that is added the suffering of all sentient life through biological evolution red in tooth and claw, and with the disappearance of whole species in mass extinctions. If all this is justified by the final emergence of human freedom, then God is not a God of love, but a cosmic Stalin who breaks a lot of eggs to achieve his final omelette. The term 'God' is far too anthropomorphic to be any use to describing what is beyond. The only answer is agnostic humility. There is a spiritual beyond which we cannot fully comprehend. There is evidence that individual consciousness survives death, but despite the confident, dogmatic and conflicting pronouncements of the great religions, we do not know what that survival means. The only response is awe, worship according to whatever ritual stirs our hearts, and humility at the limits of human knowledge.

If agnostic spirituality is to spearhead the New Renaissance, what does this mean? Historically spirituality has pointed human action in two opposite directions. Eastern religion has the tradition of the world-denying yogi squatting cross-legged in the Himalayas, and original apostolic Christianity was world negating: *'Take no thought for the morrow'*. Yet, despite an ascetic monastic tradition, Christian civilization in Europe has been highly activist, and the Hindu *Bhagavad Gita* reconciles an exalted vision of the Divine with an ethic of action and duty in this world. Evolution is a key concept in the modern world, and the evolutionary doctrines of Henri Bergson, Sri Aurobindo, and Teilhard de Chardin all visualize divine nisus operating into this world and universe, and returning it all to Itself. The pursuit of spiritual enlightenment, and practical positive action for good, are both two human sides of the same cosmic process. This was also the opinion of Origen, one of the greatest of the early Christian theologians. Without drawing too many blank cheques on metaphysical speculation, it is possible to see how agnostic spirituality can give meaning and purpose to human existence. We are droplets of a higher power, and at our highest are capable of more than we at present know.

Agnostic spirituality resolves the conflict of religions with a wise tolerance which sees beyond the conflicts of dogma and ritual. It provides a vision of the meaning and purpose of human life which can be a justification for sensible political action on a global scale. It can also provide the climate for a cultural Renaissance. The triumph of science and technology in the twentieth century is one of greatest achievements of humanity in the whole of its history, but much of the rest of twentieth century culture is a desolate blind alley which will be left behind by the advance of human civilization. A New Renaissance offers the promise of arts and music which will seek a beauty which embodies the most delicate sensibilities and highest aspirations of the human spirit. Philosophy will once again search for the deepest understanding of goodness and truth. Agnostic spirituality demands humility and offers hope.

References

Crick, Francis (1994) *The Astonishing Hypothesis*, Simon and Schuster.
Fenwick, Peter & Fenwick, Elizabeth (1996) *The Truth in the Light*, Headline.
Hick, John (1980) *God has Many Names*, Macmillan.
Leggett, Peter & Payne, Max G. (1985) *A Forgotten Truth*, Pilgrim Books.
Lorimer David (ed.) (1998), *The Spirit of Science*, Floris Books, Edinburgh.

Montefiore, Hugh (2002) *The Paranormal,* Upfront.
Ravindra, Ravi (2000) *Yoga and the Teaching of Krishna,* Theosophical
  Publishing.
Sri Aurobindo (1955) *The Life Divine,* Ashram Press.
Ward, Keith (1991) *A Vision to Pursue,* SCM Press.

17. From Sacred Ecology to Sacred Health

HENRYK SKOLIMOWSKI

Henryk Skolimowski received his D.Phil. from Oxford in 1964. He is the creator of eco-philosophy and director of the Eco-philosophy Center. He is Professor Emeritus at the University of Michigan and Professor of Ecological Philosophy at the University of Lodz in Poland. He has lived and fought and survived all kinds of vicissitudes in various not so friendly regimes in order to emerge as a champion of Light and a New Renaissance, which he cherishes as guides and values to live by and for.

Ecology is a Sacred Light of Consciousness — nowadays dimmed by the noxious fumes of industrial waste. Ecology is the fire, the fire to burn and transform; to burn the wastes and poisons; and to transform deserts into oases of beauty. Ecology is a call to action — the call to our consciousness to awaken and to understand who we are. Ecology is the call to justice and equitability. Ecology is this prism, which enables us to see clearly justice and compassion — in this world full of strife and injustice. Those who try to avoid ecology, or bypass it, are trying to avoid their inner selves — for the sake of expedience, comfort and easy life. Ecology does not invite you to an easy life, but to the reflective and frugal life.

Frugality is a precondition of inner beauty. Frugality is grace without waste. The choices are clear and inevitable. Either you settle for comfort, while keeping your conscience at bay; or you embrace ecology, responsibility and frugality — while paying tribute to your inner self.

Spirituality

The inner self is not a trifle but the most powerful engine of action amidst compassion, love and palpable justice. The time of verbal declarations is over. We must bring justice to the real world — even if we ourselves have to become more frugal in the process. Yet we are reluctant to become frugal. We want to leave the world just as it is. We are afraid of losing our privileged position. We are afraid to think that we might have to change. But we must change. We are changed already by knowing that we have to change. There is no return to our cushioned lives. There is no return to looking at the world through a veil.

The bell is tolling. It is tolling for you and me. A true concern for ourselves is a true concern for others. Are we capable of that concern? Are we capable of reaching this inner core of ourselves, which we sometimes call spirituality and sometimes we call altruism? True spirituality always unfolds towards altruism. Altruism ultimately merges with spirituality. Is your inner sanctum large and generous enough?

We are not talking about abstract theological schemes. We are talking about spirituality in the real world. In this context, ecology bows to us again. Not as a form of technology for cleaning the sewers, but as a form of spirituality. Ecology is this form of awareness and corresponding forms of action, which enable us to think about the word as a sanctuary. Cleaning the world and ourselves is not a hygienic process but a divine one. Ecology and spirituality embrace each other, and co-define each other in our times.

An in-depth comprehension of ecology is reverence in action, is a deep identification with the beauty of life pulsating through the universe until we become it. Thus understanding becomes empathy. Empathy becomes universal reverence. This reverence is a form of spirituality. In our times the ecological and the spiritual become one.

In our personal lives, ecology means healthy food, but also following clean, right and impeccable ways, which lead to sanctity. Ecology in its essential sense means connectedness, cooperation, symbiosis and holism. And holism itself is holy.

Our health and the insanity of the civilization

How can we be healthy while our civilization is not? Once we have stated this dilemma clearly, we have an altogether different perspective on our health and on our wellness. As a civilization, we are a sick people, with depression growing, with male fertility disastrously shrinking, with allergies abounding, with human happiness and human meaning dwindling and evaporating. Occasional spectacular breakthroughs in medicine, mending this gene or that troublesome illness, help us a little, because they are directed to the human body as an isolated atom, while at the core of our problems are our strained relationships with the Cosmos and with ourselves.

We must be quite clear that the problem is holistic and that it entails all the fields that connect us with living nature and the Cosmos. Whoever ignores this holistic picture of our health and tries to see it through the telescope of individual human atoms and specific medicines — which alleviate the symptoms only — is on a wrong trail.

In this holistic context, hope is more important than drugs; love is more important than shrinks; the sense of the grandeur of the Universe is more important than the knowledge of chemistry of drugs. The most potent medicine that exists in the cosmos is to be in love with the Cosmos, to be in love with nature, to be in love with each other, to be in love with the miracle of life.

The divinely inspired Plato has claimed that health is a consummated love affair of the organs of the body. This is quite superb. It goes a long way, but actually only that far. We have to extend this definition in our times to include our consummated love affair with the biotic community around us. And here is the rub. In order to have a consummated love affair with nature we have to remove the toxins — also from human minds and hearts and from human relationships — because only then will the conditions be right to pursue health as a positive proposition, as an enhancement of the radiance of human life.

I mentioned earlier that human health is not an attribute of an individual static human body. It is a *process of maintaining a dynamic harmony*. This dynamic harmony, through which we seek to maintain our positive health, will not come by itself. There are too many traps and dangers, which we must avoid. To maintain this dynamic harmony requires a painstaking effort. In a nutshell: *the pursuit of positive health is a form of spiritual practice*. The more clearly we state this the better. After all, we are all sanctuaries. To maintain well your own sanctuary is a spiritual practice.

And here again, Ecology makes a re-appearance. Yes, Ecology means health. The most important things it advocates are congruent with the pursuits of right health and right spirituality. In our polluted world, health should above all mean the purification of all the structures imposed on us by the merciless technology — because the subtotal of all these poisons is the cause of the sickness of our civilization. But my aim here is not to talk about sickness. It is to celebrate the radiant health of the human and of the world — in their natural conditions of existence.

What kind of courage must we have?

What kind of consciousness, what kind of courage and lucidity must we possess to dream about the New Renaissance, and even more so — to be it? Courage is of the essence to do anything new, and especially to do anything creative. Courage is essential to living well. Without courage we stumble, we hide in little mole holes and inadvertently become cowards. Courage and creativity go hand in hand. They are both divine gifts because they are so exceptional and unexpected. They are the invisible resources to go on, to transcend, to seek larger horizons. These resources are within us. But to begin with, we have to have the courage to bring them to the surface and then use them wisely. *We have to have the courage of our courage.*

This has never been truer than in the present times. We have made our life manageable; and on the surface of it secure, but at the cost of living in a stressful and not so healthy environment. In recent times, however, this apparent security is gone. The whole seemingly safe edifice has crumbled. And we have to face our reality. We cannot hide in mole holes.

We have to reinvent ourselves — with courage, boldness and imagination. But we cannot do it individually, while protecting our bruised individual egos. We must do it jointly, while creating a much larger reality, which will demonstrate that the Earth is fair and the people compassionate. In our shaky and precarious situation, dreaming about the New Renaissance is not an escape but a bold act of transcendence. Where else can we go, but to much larger horizons? We can try to rebuild our present civilization, but for what purposes? To recreate the existing injustices, to maintain polluted environments, and to suffer the inhuman and alienating institutions?

No, our civilization has run its course. It has delivered what it could. At present, it is delivering cancers, financial crashes (amidst great human suffering) and an over-technicized hell on Earth. Yes, there is a price to be paid for everything. There is a price for material progress. And we have paid it. Enough is enough. The time has now arrived to promote *human* and *spiritual* progress. The bargain we have struck with the God *Mechanos* has made us naked and shivering in disbelief how much we have been duped. The idea of the New Renaissance that we have been dreaming over the last years is no longer a fairy dream, but a kind of compelling invitation to do what is necessary and beautiful — on behalf of the whole biotic community, including all human beings. We must think large and inclusively, and not only think of what is good for the civilization of white man. We must be aware that although we shall be working on behalf of all others, we ourselves shall carry the main burden of responsibility.

Let us look at the New Renaissance in positive terms. We are all familiar with the achievements of the Classical Renaissance and still admire its inspirations. The Renaissance has shown that it is possible for people to liberate themselves from most constraining, intimidating and humiliating conditions — and emerge in freedom, dignity, exuberance and creativity. The Renaissance has shown us what creativity, freedom, independence and imagination truly mean, and how indispensable they are for a meaningful life and building a new life. The Renaissance has shown us that change in the structure of consciousness is possible — from submission and dogma to freedom and creativity. This example could serve us well in our struggle against the tyranny of mechanistic consciousness, which tries overtly and covertly to control us, to intimidate us, to make us appendages to the system.

Eugene Ionesco claimed that revolution signifies a change in the state of consciousness. Within the midst of such a revolution, we are at present. And we must accomplish this revolution, even if in the long run it will be called evolution. Evolution has its gambits of which revolutions are not aware. To put it simply, we must break the tethers of mechanistic thinking and all the muzzling it brings about. We need to overcome the slimy consciousness of consumerism, which so often clings to us. And we need to do it in the name of freedom, creativity and imagination for which we long. In our fierce struggle the classical Renaissance is such a worthy model. We are living in a peculiar age of history. Perhaps at a particular kind of time that happens once in every few hundred years. We are living at a time of crisis. Out of the scattered pieces, there emerges an outline of a new consciousness, and also an outline of the new human.

The dawn of the new human is on the horizon.

References

Skolimowski, Henryk (1981) *Eco-philosophy: Designing New Tactics for Living,* London, Marion Boyars; (1994) *The Participatory Mind,* London, Penguin Arkana; (2005) *Philosophy for a New Civilization,* Gyan, New Delhi; (2010) *Let there be Light,* Wisdom Tree, New Delhi.

18. A Pathway Towards the One True Religion and Spirituality

JAMES D'ANGELO

James D'Angelo is an educator, composer, pianist, writer, course leader and formerly lecturer/tutor in music at New York University, The City University of New York and Goldsmiths College (London). A published composer, his works have been performed in the USA and Europe and were featured in two London music festivals. His 'Portraits of Krishna' have been recorded on Virgin classics. Since 1994 he has developed vocal sound therapy courses for self-development and has been an invited speaker at major sound healing and holistic science conferences. A regular contributor to the Caduceus Journal (UK), he is the author of Healing With The Voice *and* The Healing Power of the Human Voice.

Since the end of the Second World War the general standard of living in Europe and the United States has gradually risen. Food has become more plentiful as it is transported by aircraft from all over the world, consumer goods of all kinds are more affordable, standards of health have improved through medical breakthroughs, national healthcare schemes and the growth of alternative health practices and governments have provided all sorts of safety nets to keep people afloat who are unemployed and disabled. A significant ingredient in the acquisition of goods and services has been the credit card, allowing far more people, who formerly could not afford it, to have easily what they both need and desire. In short, the material world has turned into a kind of consumers' paradise fuelled by the competition of the mammoth corporate businesses.

The younger generation is particularly caught up in all that the material world has to offer — mobile phones, computers, DVDs, cinemas, discos, fast food establishments, a multiplicity of eateries, easy access to inexpensive alcohol and drugs, no taboos regarding sex, fast, low-priced holidays to almost anywhere in the world and, more than likely, their own easily obtained credit cards. All these things are subtly telling us that we can create a world where all our needs and desires are met and that this is the very core of life. To seek out these pleasures and thus avoid any feeling of lack within ourselves. But what deep down are they actually seeking? That is the great question.

At the same time many people are living out a life of insecurity, fear and depression which is inculcated in them by governments, media and businesses. In effect, people have abdicated their own power to them as though they were the gods. Added to this is cynicism when, for example, the greed of politicians and bankers is exposed. People envy those in the spotlight of the media and hence have developed what is called 'celebrity culture'. The acquisition of money becomes paramount as the media is obsessed with how much people earn and possess and how much things cost.

Fear, which has at its root peoples' sense of separateness and losing touch with themselves, has been the catalyst for eliminating all risk in our lives. Nothing untoward need happen. The word 'security' is writ large everywhere and yet, materially, it is such a hollow word. Everything that could disturb us is preventable and if it is not, then someone is to blame. Where does true security actually lie? More and more laws are enacted to stem the tide of what seems to be a breakdown in society: they hold us in check like fingers in a dyke that is forever leaking. Increasing numbers are imprisoned. In the workplace demands are put on employees to be more efficient and to work longer hours. In some cases, it could be described as a form of slavery. On the other side the unemployed lose their self-esteem or turn into layabouts on benefits. All of this can create a climate of ever greater separateness among people which places a strain on their mental health and their moral and ethical behaviour. If they are parents these vibrations infiltrate their children.

All these symptoms and more are indicative of a society which has been diverted powerfully from its natural spiritual state, a state that is most clearly seen in a young child. Children have a pure love, a simplicity of openness and an innate spirituality. Christ explicitly said to his disciples, 'Unless you become as little children, you cannot enter the kingdom of Heaven' Yet even childhood today is being eroded as children are robbed of their very innocence and sense of play and joy through being pressed into becoming little adults. Many parents, because of the pressures of our competitive world, send their offspring to nursery schools early on. Then there is the pressure to develop mental skills before children are emotionally ready. Two recent studies recommended that formal education in England should not begin until the age of six. Yet the government insists that children have to get on with it at four. Also the government attempts to be a surrogate parent as in the case of introducing compulsory sex education at an age when children should not be ready. Add to this their exposure to television, computers, DVDs and computer games against which their minds have no defence and you wonder what adult society will be like in twenty years' time.

All these aspects, to whatever degree they now exist in societies (and with globalization it is not just the West that is affected), leave a vacuum into which the values of religion and spirituality should enter. It should be said here that the words 'religion' and 'spirituality' as concepts are treated as synonyms in this essay. The derivation of the word 'religion' from the Latin means both 'to bond' and 'respect for what is sacred'. In this sense , to be religious is to bond with what is sacred, namely one's eternal soul/spirit. This is also the meaning of what it is to be spiritual. Unfortunately, many people create a religion out of their own self-interests and acquisitions which is a kind of drug to numb the feeling of separateness they experience in their daily lives. The fact is that, in varying degrees, we are all enmeshed in the material world and will find ways to have its pleasures and avoid its pains before death overtakes us. Almost none of us is exempt from this even if we have aligned ourselves with a religion or a spiritual path. Nonetheless the key to extricating ourselves and putting the care of our soul first lies in the very essence of religion and spirituality.

The traditional view of the Christian religion, for example, has been that you are a being of imperfection and thus a 'sinner'. However, as long as you aim at believing in the precepts of the church and what Christ preached, you could be offered a place in the heavenly paradise at death. You could continue to fail in this as long as you sincerely repented through confession and received sacraments. This held true for both the wealthy and the poor. This was what was meant by the salvation of your soul. As the pleasures and accessibility of the world greatly expanded in the last forty years, such ideas as receiving sacraments, saying prayers, the salvation of the soul and life after death lost their meaning. Why bother about an illusory, paradisiacal afterlife when you have a material heaven on Earth all around you?

Since the 1960s, as the Earth began to move across the point in the galaxy shifting us from the Age of Pisces to Aquarius, a new concept of spirituality, separate from traditional religion, has developed. That spirituality can be instilled and cultivated in someone without being connected to an established religious faith with all its trappings. It includes those who have adopted the practices and beliefs of certain Eastern religions. It is quite likely that the vibrations entering at this crossing point are the cause for this awakening, a discontent with the limits of a predominantly material existence and a corresponding hunger for transcendence. Of course, these souls have to have a strong magnetic centre and thus be highly pre-disposed to respond to the vibrations. As can be witnessed by the precarious state of the world, the majority have not. In fact, those who wield the power in this world, particularly in politics, business and the media, and influence society are actually quite resistant to the new vibrations. Filled with fear, they want to perpetuate the old ways and enmesh people in even greater materialism as though this path is endlessly sustainable. At best, they attempt to make the populace better off at the physical level but essentially continue the 'pleasure palace' mentality where consumption and the amassing of things, be it money or otherwise, reigns. Even the leaders of religions can get caught up in this mentality whereby their priority is humanitarianism and maintaining the church's status quo. However worthy this might be, their primary work should be the care of souls.

It is the care of our souls, assuming people feel this incorporeal aspect does exist within them, that is the essential activity of our lives. In Christ's words, 'Seek ye first the Kingdom of Heaven and all else will be added unto you.' To follow this way is the test for a spiritual being. If the rituals, precepts and the clergy of a religion can be of assistance in the care of the soul, then there is no reason to abandon it entirely as more and more have done. So, on the one hand, individuals who desire to care for their souls and consequently discover their true spiritual nature, do not have to distance themselves from the religion in which they were placed by their parents. In their wakefulness and mindfulness they could benefit from the established rituals and collective goodwill of the church and the congregation and yet not have to subscribe to its codified doctrines. For example, in Christianity, the receiving of the bread and wine in Holy Communion can become a powerful remembrance of union with the Divine, but not necessarily equating it with the body and blood of Christ. On the other hand, they can form groups of kindred spirits, practise meditation and prayer and follow the pure teachings of various Scriptures or a living fully Self-realized teacher. This is expressed in Jesus' words 'where two or three are gathered in My name I shall be present'. These two ways are not mutually exclusive. The crux of the matter is that the original great teachers of spiritual Truth did not set out to create a highly organized religion or institution. If these beings had come together to formulate the one true religion/spirituality, what would be their precepts? Here is one consensus:

1. All human beings have a non-material divine spirit and soul living within them that directly links to the Absolute (the Creator of Creators) and its creation. This is an absolute unity which individuals could come to realize.

2. Individuals, having accepted this first precept, see the same in others and this engenders in them love and compassion for one another's soul/spirit, thus moving far beyond their personalities and egos (simply defined as the impurities embedded in a soul).

3. This spirit/soul is eternal and goes on in space/time when the physical body ceases to be. Thus there is, at this level, no death.

4. The spirit/soul has come into the material world of Earth to experience and appreciate the beauty of the physical

world but not to become enmeshed in it. If the attachment to materiality grows and individuals feel separate from the source of Creation as a consequence, they will have to live many lives of physicality to come full circle and be restored to their original unity. This is known as re-incarnation.

5. The first objective of our lives is to be in touch with this inner reality at all times with its pure emotions (the real meaning of non-attachment) and to know an unbounded bliss in existence whatever the circumstances. This is what Christ called 'The Kingdom of Heaven.'

6. The second objective is for the spirit/soul, as expressed in Hinduism, to escape the wheel of birth and death. This means that the purification process is complete and there is no further need to inhabit a physical body. The individual then lives in another dimension of existence which cannot be described. Here we have inherited eternal life.

How does the care of the soul relate to these precepts? The soul or 'inner organ' as described in the Eastern tradition of Advaita (non-duality) has various functions. First, it a storehouse of our consciousness and has imprinted in it all our experiences throughout our lifetimes and also contains the memory of our true nature, thus reflecting the level of our consciousness. Another aspect is to make value judgments as to what will be of use and what will not in proceeding down the spiritual path. The third aspect is our sense of individuality, our particular way of approaching how we lead our lives. A fourth aspect is to receive impressions which are passed on to the other three compartments. All these aspects are subject to impurities and impediments built up not only from previous lifetimes but also in the current life. These dysfunctions are the result of the material world and our senses taking control and causing a loss of unity with the Absolute. In the simplest of terms the impeded ego becomes the master rather than the servant. This is what the Indian gurus call Avidya (ignorance of the Truth). In Christian terms this is the true meaning of 'sin' or 'missing the mark.'

How do we establish a universal spirituality in the world based on the care of the soul that serves as the great counterbalance to the materialistic 'pleasure dome' mentality that so dominates the globe? It cannot be met head on with cries of, 'Repent, the Kingdom of Heaven is at hand!' It has the possibility of coming into being as a 'grassroots' movement with individuals working on purifying their souls on a day-to-day basis. It could be helpful for such kindred spirits to bond together as groups but such organizations will only be as effective as its members grow in being through their own efforts. Doing 'good works' certainly has a role to play in preparing the ground for a true spirituality to flourish but ultimately, being just a 'do-gooder' is not enough. In other words, eventually we have to put our own house in order before we can do the same for others

Even those 'do-gooders' who have been affected by the Aquarian vibrations and profess to be spiritual can become identified with their own development and become stuck in the trappings of the so-called New Age. To put it one way: 'Rather than transforming into butterflies, they are only becoming bigger and better caterpillars.' They become vegetarians, eat only organic food, attend Yoga classes, use only alternative health practitioners, study astrology, use crystals for healing, go to lots of workshops and support a number of good causes. While any of these things can be of some value, it is not enough to root out the chief features in themselves which prevent the liberation that is the final goal of spirituality.

If future generations are to put their spiritual life as a priority, good works have to begin within education. The soul already knows its spiritual heritage and when it arrives fresh into this world it expresses this bliss. Whoever has seen a baby recognizes this and feels such great delight. In that moment our soul is cleared of its impediments and resonates with the purity of the child. However, as the child grows, how is its soul protected from all the influences of the external world? Gradually whatever impurities were brought into the world are activated as the material world imposes powerful impressions and re-enforces whatever pre-existed within the person. The antidote has to be a special kind of education, remembering that education means 'to lead out' or more to the point 'lead out of darkness'. The soul knows its ultimate source. It has to be given ways of remembering. To some extent this is what the visionary Rudolf Steiner did in establishing a programme of development for young people that became known as 'Waldorf education'. In educating the soul, the subtle world of our psychology is fertilized until such time that spiritual concepts and practices can be introduced that could take root. It is difficult to say at what age these can be introduced as individuals' readiness is so variable.

If education from an early age were designed for the care of the soul, then society would reach a natural spiritual unity that would not require the separation of religion from daily life. Metaphorically, we would be attending church every day but not in a building with its rituals. Rather it is the church of the gradually purifying soul that would correspondingly open up a loving heart. This spiritual education would consist of any or all of the following:

1. Meditation which could be linked to a preliminary stage of toning, chanting and the use of harmonious movement or postures, like Yoga or Tai Chi.

2. Prayer defined as holding oneself, someone else or something in the mental plane for healing, that is that their mind, body and spirit would be cleared of its infirmities.

3. Contemplation of spiritual knowledge either alone or in small groups. The sources for this can be drawn from all the great teachers who are representatives of the world's religions and philosophies. In groups this could be facilitated by someone who is acknowledged as having an expanded state of being, not someone who is just intellectually clever and has much knowledge stored in the brain.

4. Participation in artistic activity is a useful adjunct to the three main lines above.

5. Being of service to others.

The objective in all of these is to remove the impurities of the soul so that the ego assumes its rightful place only as a servant. This allows for more and more light to be reflected in the consciousness which in turn sees the unity of the one true spirituality. The consequence of such a state is a feeling of unbounded joy and bliss. If this were to be a permanent condition, it is but a short step to escape the wheel of birth and death as you witness the spiritual thread running through all Creation without being consumed by it.

As we move in space/time towards the midpoint of this transitional period, the year 2012, we witness a powerful polarity between the materialists and the spiritualists. One group resisting the new vibrations, the other responding to them. How do the latter — clearly in the minority — influence society as a whole so as to care for souls on their journey back to the Source or Absolute, the ultimate escape from the wheel of birth and death? That is part of anyone's role who takes to the one true religion/spirituality. The Christian churches have to reform themselves and concentrate on the realization of the teachings of Christ and put their trappings in perspective. This seems unlikely to happen. What could take place is that individual priests remove themselves from the church and establish their own 'little churches' with a special liturgy that directs people to the care of their souls. The forming of spiritual organizations could be of some value too, as a way of infiltrating society with positive vibrations.

As always it comes back to the individual. If we sincerely practise what we espouse in our daily lives we will influence others and let them know the secret of our inner life which could be reflected back to them. This is the best way to renew and promulgate the one true religion/spirituality. Those on the path should not be out to save the world as such and become identified with causes. Planet Earth is a way station, a school and a living being and it will well survive whatever humanity does. We care for the Earth simply because we love and respect all Creation. But, on another level, it is so powerful and could dismiss humanity at any time.

So, spiritually, we are faced with ourselves. Who are we? We are soul/spirits created by the Absolute for the purpose of knowing the bliss of Creation without ever being caught up in it. This is only possible through a spiritual education that reveals the illusion of the material world and the reality of our eternal nature.

References

Armstrong, Karen (1999) *A History of God. From Abraham to the Present: the 4000-year Quest for God*, Vintage Books, London, UK.

Chopra, Deepak (2008) *The Third Jesus: How to Find Truth and Love In Today's World*, Rider Books, UK.

Douglas-Klotz, Neil (1999) *The Hidden Gospel: Decoding the Spiritual Message of the Aramaic Jesus*, Quest Books, Wheaton, IL.

Epstein, Mark (2001) *Going On Being: Life at the Crossroads of Buddhism and Psychotherapy*, Wisdom Publications, Boston.

Freeman, Laurence (2009) *The Selfless Self: Meditation and the Opening of the Heart*, Canterbury Press, Norwich, UK.

Laszlo, Ervin & Currivan, Jude (2008) *Cosmos: A Co-creator's Guide to the Whole-World*, Hay House, Inc.

Moore, Thomas (2009) *Writing In The Sand: Jesus, Spirituality and the Soul of the Gospels*, Hay House, Inc.

Saraswati, Shantanand (2009) *Good Company II: An Anthology of Sayings, Stories and Answers to Questions*, The Study Society, London.

Tolle, Eckhart (2005) *A New Earth: Create a Better Life*, Penguin Books.

Waite, Dennis (2008) *Enlightenment: The Path Through the Jungle*, O Books, Winchester, UK.

19. Returning to Natural Mind

PETER RUSSELL

Philosopher and futurist Peter Russell originally studied mathematics and theoretical physics at Cambridge University, before studying meditation and eastern philosophy in India. He has a postgraduate degree in computer science, and conducted some of the early work on three-dimensional displays. His books include The Global Brain Awakens; Waking Up in Time, *and* From Science to God. *He is a fellow of the Institute of Noetic Sciences and an Honorary Member of The Club of Budapest.*

The following essay originally appeared in The View, *ed. Dave Patrick, published by Polair Publishing, and is reproduced with kind permission of the publisher.*

People are disturbed, not by things, but by the view they take of them. Epictetus

'In the final analysis,' said the Dalai Lama, 'the hope of every person is simply peace of mind.' As with many great truths, these words resonate with something we know deep down. Beneath all our endeavours, we all want to be at peace, to feel content, fulfilled, at ease. None of us wants to be in pain or suffer unnecessarily.

We may decide to change jobs, start a new relationship or take up a new hobby because we believe we will be happier. I may choose to go hiking because I expect to get some pleasure from it, a tangible endorphin rush from the exercise, or a feeling of warmth and closeness from spending time with a friend. I may spend time writing a book, forgoing other pleasures, because I gain satisfaction from my creative expression.

The gratification that we seek may not always be immediate. Most of us do not enjoy visiting the dentist, but we go in the hope that we will suffer less later. Or we may forgo some personal gain and devote our time to helping elderly relatives or others in need; yet we do so because it brings some inner fulfilment. Even the masochist, who sets out to cause himself pain, does so because he takes some comfort from it.

Seeking a better state of mind is the fundamental criterion by which, consciously or unconsciously, we make all our decisions. This is our ultimate bottom line. It is not a bottom line that can be measured in numbers, but it is nevertheless the true arbiter of all our decisions. We may think we are seeking an external goal, but we are seeking that goal in the hope that, in one way or another, we will feel better for it.

Why then do we seldom find peace of mind? After all, we are intelligent beings, we can look ahead and plan for the future. Moreover, we have many tools and technologies with which to create a better world for ourselves. One would think that we, of all creatures, would be content and at ease. Yet the very opposite seems to be the case. As far as I can tell, a dog spends more time at ease than its owner who is busy seeking the various things he or she thinks will bring satisfaction and fulfilment. Leave a dog with nothing to do, and it will probably lie down, put its chin on the ground, and watch the world go by. Leave us human beings with nothing to do, and it is not long before we complain of being bored, get restless, and start looking for things to fill the time. We worry what we might be missing and how we might improve things, or we go check off one more thing on that never-ending 'to do' list.

Paradoxically, it is our remarkable ability to change our world that has led us into this sorry state. We have fallen into the belief that if we are not at peace, then we must do something about it. We think we need to obtain something we don't yet have, get others to respond as we would like, enjoy a new experience, or, conversely, avoid some circumstance or person that is causing us distress. We assume that, if we could just get our world to be a particular way, we will finally be happy.

From the moment we are born our culture reinforces this assumption, encouraging us to believe that outer wellbeing is the source of inner fulfilment. As young children we learn from the example of our elders that it is important to be in control of things, that material possessions offer security. As we grow up, much of our education focusses on knowing the ways of the world in order that we might better manage our affairs and so find greater contentment and fulfilment. As adults, the daily deluge of television, radio, newspapers, magazines, and advertisements reinforces the belief that happiness comes from what happens to us. The net result is that we become addicted to things and circumstances.

Our material acquisitiveness may not look like a drug addiction, but the underlying pattern is the same. With drugs — whether they be alcohol, tobacco, coffee, tranquilizers, cocaine or heroin — people take them for one simple reason. They want to feel better. They want to feel happy, high, relaxed, in control, less anxious, temporarily free from some suffering. In this respect drug-takers are seeking nothing different from anyone else; it is just the way in which they are doing it that most societies find unacceptable.

Similarly with our addiction to having and doing, we are seeking a better state of mind. And, in the short term, it may appear to work. But any pleasure, happiness, or satisfaction we do find is only temporary. As soon as one 'high' wears off we go in search of another 'fix'. We become psychologically dependent on our favorite sources of pleasure — food, music, driving, debating, football, television, shopping, whatever.

When this fails to bring any lasting satisfaction we do not question whether our approach may be mistaken. Instead we try even harder to get the world to give us what we want. We buy more clothes, go to more parties, eat more food, try to make more money. Or we give up on these and try different things. We take up squash, or look for new friends. Yet true peace of mind remains as elusive as ever. We live in what Indian philosophies call the world of *samsara*, meaning 'to wander on'. We wander on, looking for fulfilment in a world which provides but temporary respites from discontent, a momentary pleasure followed by more wandering on in search of that ever-elusive goal.

Throughout human history, there have been those who have woken up from the dream that our state of mind depends on what we have or do. They are the rishis, roshis, mystics, saints, lamas and other 'wise ones' who have seen through the illusion that, if only we could get the world to be the way want, we would finally be happy. They have each, in their own way, rediscovered the same timeless truth about human consciousness: The mind in its natural state is already at ease.

By 'natural' they do not mean the state of mind in which we spend most of our time — which clearly is not usually one of ease and contentment — they are speaking of the mind before it becomes tarnished with worry, wanting, analyzing and planning. Time and again they have reminded us that we do not need to do anything, or go anywhere to be at ease. On the contrary, all our doing, all our seeking to change things, takes us in the opposite direction. We imagine something is missing, and with this self-created sense of lack comes discontent. Feelings of discontent cloud our consciousness, overshadowing the intrinsic ease of the mind in its natural, unsullied, state.

This was one of the Buddha's key realizations. He saw that we all experience what he called *dukka*. The word is often translated as 'suffering,' leading to the common misconception that Buddha taught that life is suffering. The word *dukka* is actually a negation of the word *sukha*, which has the meaning of ease (originally, a wheel that runs smoothly). So *dukka* means not-at-ease, and is probably best translated as discontent or unsatisfactoriness. Suffering, as we think of it, is an extreme form of discontent. Much more common — indeed, so common that it usually passes unnoticed — is the discontent that comes from wishing that things were different, worrying about what happened earlier, or hoping for a better future. Buddha realized that the root cause of this discontent was our clinging to our ideas of how things should or should not be. As soon as clinging enters the mind, we lose the natural state of ease.

Thus, to return to a state of ease, we have only to stop creating unnecessary discontent. That means letting go of our attachments as to how things should or should not be. Letting go never seems easy. This is because we treat 'letting go' as another task to do. We've become so enmeshed in the habit of doing that we mistakenly approach letting go in the same way. But you can't 'do' letting go — however hard you try. It is our doing that is the problem. To let go we have to cease the 'doing' of holding on. Letting go is allowing the mind to relax, accepting the present moment as it is, without resistance or judgment.

This is sometimes misinterpreted as accepting the world as it is, which can lead to a Pollyanna attitude of 'everything is OK': the world is perfect as it is. But there is a subtle, and crucial, distinction between accepting our experience of a situation and accepting the situation itself. Sadly, the world around us is rife with injustice, self-centredness and unnecessary suffering. No one, I hope, is proposing the kind of acceptance that says we can simply let such ills be. Accepting our experience of the situation, on the other hand, means not resisting what we are actually perceiving and feeling in the moment. There is nothing we can do to change our present experience. Wishing it otherwise is a pointless waste of time and energy. All it does is create additional discontent.

The most commonly recommended way to become more present is to bring our attention back to our physical experience, noticing how it feels to be a living being — the feelings in our bodies, the sensations of breathing, the air against the skin, the sounds around us. Our immediate sensory experience is always in the present moment. It is when we start thinking about our experience, what it means, and where it might lead, that our attention is drawn into the past or the future — and back into the world of *samsara*. The more often we can come back to the present moment, the more the mind is able to relax. When it is fully relaxed, totally at ease, we rediscover the mind in its natural, undisturbed state.

In Indian philosophy the profound and delightful ease of natural mind is called *Nirvana*. To many, the word conjures images of some blissed out, euphoric state of consciousness. But its original meaning is very different — and much more instructive. The word 'nirvana' literally means 'to blow out', as in extinguishing a flame. When we accept our experience of the moment, as it is, without lament or resistance, the flames of greed, hatred, jealousy and the many other unwelcome ramifications of our discontent die down; extinguished by a lack of fuel.

No longer blinded by self-concern, we are better able to see a situation for what it is. We are free from imagined lacks and needs and able to act in accord with what the situation requires. Whether it be helping others, righting injustices, working for some social cause, taking care of our health, raising children, whatever we choose to focus out energies upon, we can do so with greater commitment and deeper compassion.

We spend so much energy trying to find contentment in the world around us. If we spent a fraction of this energy allowing the mind to relax, letting go of some of our attachments, we would find more of the peace of mind that, in the final analysis, we all are all seeking. And the world around us would surely become a much better place.

PART 4

Global and Local Transformation: Governance, Economics and Education

20. Towards a Politics for the Twenty-first Century: Psyche; Polis; Cosmos

JEAN HARDY

Dr Jean Hardy has been a university teacher for most of her working life, in sociology, political philosophy and, later on, in transpersonal psychology. During the last twelve years she has lived in Devon, and is an active member of the Totnes community at Dartington Hall, Schumacher College, and latterly Transition Town Totnes, studying ecology and some holistic science. She is interested in the relationship of psychology and spirituality to politics, ecology and economics, in the search for a more whole world. She is the author of A Psychology with a Soul *which is now in five languages and has been selling well for the last 22 years. She has recently finished writing a book on the subject of this paper.*

> *And new philosophy calls all in doubt,*
> *The element of fire is quite put out;*
> *The sun is lost, and th'earth, and no man's wit*
> *Can well direct him where to look for it.*
> *And freely men express that this world's spent,*
> *When in the planet and the firmament*
> *They seek so many new; they see that this*
> *Is crumbled out again to his anatomies.*
> *'Tis all in pieces, all coherence gone;*
> *All just supply and all relation:*

Prince, father, son, are things forgot,
For every man alone thinks he hath got
To be a phoenix, and that then can be
None of that kind, of which he is, but he.

John Donne: An anatomy of the world (1621)

It seems perverse in an article about twenty-first century politics to start with a poem from the early seventeenth century — and even more so to add a sentence or two subsequently about the Middle Ages. But that's where I believe we can discern the root of our present political — and many other — problems. For John Donne was grieving about the lack of coherence felt in European society in his time, as people began to live in a different universe from the one generally assumed to exist in the medieval period.

> In 1500 educated people in Western Europe believed themselves to be living at the centre of a finite cosmos, at the mercy of supernatural forces beyond their control and certainly constantly menaced by Satan and all his allies. By 1700 educated people in Western Europe for the most part believed themselves living in an infinite universe on a tiny planet in (elliptical) orbit round the sun, no longer menaced by Satan, and confident that power over the natural world lay within their grasp. (Easlea 1980, p. 1)

But what people had *lost* by the seventeenth century was a coherent world, where the person, the society and the sense of the universe — the psyche, polis and cosmos of the subtitle — were given, and were experienced as one synthesized whole. As M.-D. Chenu writes in his scholarly study of the twelfth century, in past centuries it was possible to look to the Whole of your reality for guidance:

> To conceive the world as one whole is already to perceive its profound structure — a world of forms transcending the medley of visible and sense-perceptible phenomena. The whole penetrates each of its parts; it is one universe; God conceived it as a unique living being ... (Chenu 1997, pp. 6–8)

Chenu gives a passage from Honorius of Autun (AD 1130):

> the supreme artisan made the universe like a great zither
> upon which he placed strings to yield a variety of sounds ... a
> harmonious chord is sounded by spirit and body, angel and
> devil, heaven and hell, fire and water, air and earth, sweet and
> bitter, soft and hard, and so are all other things harmonized.

There was a conviction in the medieval period that the world made sense, and had been created by a 'supreme' hand, securely cradling the opposites.

But what Donne is saying is that by the seventeenth century you have to be able to make sense of the world as a unique individual on your own: you have to tolerate being unique — a 'phoenix' unto yourself, separate and lonely, unsupported by a comprehended and shared traditional society and a planet which provides spiritual certainties to the believer. Another voice that expresses the fear of that time most vividly is that of Blaise Pascal: 'the silence of the infinite spaces terrifies me', he famously wrote (Berman 1984, p. 40).

Though individual people amongst us in the twenty-first century may eventually achieve that sense of wholeness, the world we experience round us does not have a unified coherence. There is no over-arching belief that incorporates all reality — "Tis all in pieces', as Donne said, as true in the twenty-first century as it was in the seventeenth. The political philosophy and practice that we now have — the *polis* in Greek terms — rests uneasily and without true clear connections between its own separate political rationale and the 'psyche' — the person and all his or her complexities as an individual; and with the constantly astounding nature of the universe — the 'cosmos' — investigated by modern science.

Most organic societies, like the medieval period in Europe or most indigenous societies, do not have a political philosophy. Their power structure is already given, within a strong spiritual sense of reality, and a myth that makes sense. It may be a benign or a malign world, but the whole carries conviction. As Morris Berman beautifully puts it: 'throughout the Middle Ages men and women continued to see the world as a garment that they wore rather than a collection of discrete objects they confronted' (Berman 1984, p. 61). The story people were living out might be terrifying, like the Black Death or the Inquisition, but there was an inner connectedness of belief between the ordinary events of your life, the social structure and the nature of your understanding of spirit, or God.

Beginnings of modern political philosophy

When that coherence disintegrated, thinkers, philosophers had to construct and define the new realities, a new paradigm. Western political philosophy began in the fifteenth, sixteenth and seventeenth centuries with the great surge of original thinking and art in the Renaissance. There developed a new sense of individualism, a growing science and deeper investigation of nature, disputes within the Christian religion between the old Catholic Church and the new Protestants, a change in social power structures and an uncertainty about how life on Earth should be governed.

So it is no surprise that the best known early political philosophers, who have created our own world, were Niccolo Machiavelli in the disturbed and warring Italian states, and, a hundred years afterwards, Thomas Hobbes in the English Civil War 1642–49. What both men saw around them was war, and deduced from this that men are essentially war-like creatures. This Hobbes specifically saw as 'the state of nature': what, he deduced from his life experience, people are essentially like before societies existed. Western political philosophy is unashamedly myth-like in its presentation. Indeed nearly all the classic philosophers — Machiavelli, an Italian; Hobbes, John Locke, Edmund Burke, John Stuart Mill, all British; Karl Marx, a German; and Jean-Jacques Rousseau, a Frenchman — first state their views about what they assume we, as human beings, are like, and then construct their pictures of the political society they think we would best live in.

Their assumptions, and the theories that spring from them, are immeasurably important, because they have spread around the whole Earth with the spread of Western values. Our economics and our politics are inextricably linked together, and these are pervasive in virtually all world societies in the twenty-first century. They dominate the way we live, because they have formed the basis of Constitutions — like Locke's justification of individualism, freedom and property in the American Constitution: or formed the basis of governments like Marx's theories in all their varied interpretations, in Russia, China and South America: they have dominated the countries of the British Empire, which covered a quarter of the land and populations of the planet in 1900, including India, great swathes of Africa, Canada and the Antipodes. And because we rarely consider the validity of political stories at their source, they are largely self-fulfilling prophecies.

So modern political theory is a product of Western society, initiated of course first by the classical Greeks. In a situation of great change, such as we have experienced for the last four hundred years in the West, we have needed theories of stability, order and controlled change. Political philosophy has supplied these, though of course the different authors have hardly been in agreement with each other. There is a vast dialogue, a disputation, over time. But reading these philosophers again, as I did when I was teaching a year's undergraduate course at Brunel University in the 1980s, I found they are surprisingly like stories, even though several of the writers see themselves as 'scientific'. Political philosophy is not like any other subject; each philosopher, in the light of his or her own experience, has to start from scratch to create another picture of the nature of people and the world they therefore believe it desirable to construct politically.

It is not possible to give much detail about the dialogue between Western political philosophers from the sixteenth to the twentieth century in an article. There has been an English Parliament throughout that time, incorporating Scotland in the early seventeenth century until recently. We have been working towards a wider and wider representative democracy, with a very limited number of members in the sixteenth century — all men, all rich, powerful and mostly titled — through different stages and constitutions, to universal franchise for all adults in 1928. The monarch at the beginning was seen as having a 'divine right' to rule, but that was shattered at the execution of King Charles I in 1649 at the end of the Civil War, and the powers of the monarch have been eroded ever since by constitutional means.

Propositions in the politics we live with today

There has been a dominant strand among the philosophers from the beginning which assumed that people are naturally warlike. Machiavelli (1469–1527) in *The Prince* reckoned that human nature is despicable in general and therefore strong order is of paramount importance as an external curb. Men are at all times ungrateful, changeable, simulators and dissimulators, runaways in danger, eager for gain and able to be fooled. Hobbes (1588–1679) believed that the natural condition of mankind (he did not consider women) is war. This is because men are moved by appetites and aversions, and by a constant hunger for power. In Chapter 11 of *Leviathan* he writes: 'in the first place, I put it for a general condition of all mankind, a perpetual and restless desire of power after power, that ceaseth only in Death.' He believed that the whole society was arranged around war, even when it was technically peaceful. Indeed that was true in his day, and maybe it has justification as a belief in our own, with, globally, fifty wars in the last fifty years.

This strand of belief about human nature continues is in conservative writers to the present. Chris Patten in *The Tory Case* writes:

> Man was created in the image of God but he is flawed; he
> inherits Adam's mistake. He is capable therefore of great evil
> as well as great good ... without authority, government and the
> law, the impulses of an imperfect man are as likely to do what is
> wrong as to do what is right. (Patten 1983, p. 25)

The doctrine of original sin is basic to political as well as religious stories in the modern West.

A further dominant strand in political thought is what the theorist C.B. Macpherson called possessive individualism (Macpherson 1962). Capitalism was developing in the seventeenth and eighteenth centuries. Hobbes wrote in Chapter 10 of *Leviathan*:

> the value of Worth of a man, is as of all other things, his Price;
> that is to say, so much as would be given for the use of his Power:

and therefore is not absolute ... For let a man (as most men do)
rate themselves as the highest Value they can; yet their true
value is no more than is esteemed by others.

John Locke (1632–1704) in his Second Treatise of *Two Treatises of
Government* published in 1690, wrote that every man 'has a property in
his own person'. His labour is his and no one else's.

> Whatsoever then he removes out of the state that nature has
> provided, and left it in, he has mixed his labour with, and
> joined to it something that is his own, and thereby makes it
> his property ... Thus the grass my horse has bit; the turfs my
> servant has cut; or the ore that I have digged in any place
> where I have a right to them in common with others, become
> my property, without the assignation or consent of anybody.
> (Locke 1984, p.130)

Locke assumed God to be the great Property Owner. He did see that
at the time he lived, with the practice of interest given on loans being
legalized (before that in the early sixteenth century, usury had been an
offence for which you could be executed), this was leading to growing
and growing inequality, but he believed that society had tacitly agreed
to this 'side-effect' with the advent of the monetary system.

John Locke also argued for individual freedom, as our body is our
property:

> The natural liberty of man is to be free from any superior power
> on earth, and not to be under the legislative authority of man, but
> to have only the law of nature for his rule. The liberty of man in
> society is to be under the legislative power but that established
> by consent in the Commonwealth, nor under the dominion of
> will, or restraint of any law, but what the legislative shall enact
> according to the trust put in it. (Chapter 4, Second Treatise.)

This of course has been a very powerful doctrine for the United
States of America, where the sanctity of the individual is pre-eminent.
These views have also largely continued to this day in societies with
Western style democracies.

The urge for more equality in society has been a strong force in political thinking from the thirteenth century onwards, in protest, action, and eventually in the values underlying Fabian socialism, Marxism and State socialism. However, inequalities in the world flourish today on a global scale, from the affluent life style found amongst the rich in all countries, to the two dollars-a-day, or less, experienced by the billions of poor which is also ubiquitous.

What would be the values of an alternative politics?

Looking back over the philosophies which dominate our lives at the present time, certain huge gaps appear in the classical pictures. For instance, most of the theories were created by men for men. On a crude level, women did not have the vote on an equal level with men until 1928 in England: women certainly did not exist as a political force — many people would argue that they still do not. But more than that, the human nature upon which the theories are founded is decidedly male. It is also decidedly white, heterosexual and rich. Politics as we know it has been for and by the white European or American affluent man: the freeholder. Most of it was developed whilst the West believed itself superior to all other races and cultures; and most of it was written at a time when adult suffrage was restricted to the affluent few. The politics of today exemplify those 'yang' qualities of competition and aggression.

The picture of human nature at the base of these theories also assumes that human beings — particularly Western men — are at the apex of creation. In political philosophy, people are not generally seen as a limited and newly arrived species among the billions of other species sharing this Earth: rather, it is assumed that the natural world is there for humans to use as they wish. Only the odd philosopher, like Winstanley (British seventeenth century), Kropotkin (Russian nineteenth century) or Gandhi (Indian twentieth century), none of whom are taught in mainstream political philosophy courses as a rule, have any sense of humans as part of a greater whole, the Earth and all her creatures. The myth of human progress in the west is too dominating for that. Along with this assuredness of human superiority — which is present even in Hobbes and Machiavelli living in a more religious age — is the assumption that we are material not spiritual creatures, and have a living to make and powerful forces to control on this Earth. The human ego and the importance of the individual are paramount in conservatism and liberalism: the collective political force is dominant in Marxism and fascism. Political philosophy is about humanity alone, about material secular social forces, not about the spirit which may contain them regardless of form.

Finally political philosophy as we have it today is very adult and not at all self-reflexive — except of course for Rousseau in his book *Confessions*. It is interesting that most of the classic social philosophers — like most children in the West over the last centuries — had harsh, over-disciplined (or neglected) childhoods. Most write their philosophies as though they were an adult product — as, in one sense they are of course, because they usually ignore the child. But one of the things we can learn today is that much of the way an individual tends to see things is unconsciously determined, and much is rooted in childhood. If we begin to examine the interaction between the philosophers and their philosophies, we may see more about how they were constructed and why. The harshness of the picture of the world they generally draw is arguably a product of the harshness of their own lives. Rousseau was more aware of this than any other: he published his *Confessions* alongside his philosophy, knowing there was a connection — just as Carl Jung's *Memories, Dreams, Reflections* is a fundamental comment on his work. How much would be changed if modern political philosophy were written with self-awareness, profoundly affecting our picture of how things are? If political theorists wrote with more self-knowledge, including feeling as well as rationality, awareness of our whole lives and what has shaped us as well as logic, could we approach the assumptions of political philosophy differently, more deeply, more flexibly?

So what would a twenty-first century political philosophy look like?

Most fundamentally, I believe, we need a world in which there is once again a coherence between modern cosmology, modern sociology and politics, and a view of the nature of the person.

Our understanding of the universe has developed beyond all recognition in scientific terms through modern technology which has taken us near to the beginning of time. A new comprehension of the history of the planet offers us a quite a different view of how things are and have been on Earth in the five billion years of its existence. In addition to this, the geological knowledge of the Earth's history proffers a truly amazing picture, full of drama on land and in the sea, with long ice-ages and wildly moving landscapes. This knowledge requires a revised view of the significance of the human being on Earth where there have been five massive extinctions of species before this time and where humans have existed for the equivalent of little more than a minute in a twenty-four hour day. The civilizations we value so highly would not even feature in the few thousands of years of their existence, in this time scale: they would be the thin line drawn at the end.

At the same time, in terms of psyche, the twentieth century has brought us far more knowledge about human nature, particularly through the development of depth psychology. The growing understanding of consciousness and its rootedness in personal and collective unconsciousness, takes us far from the relatively easy assumptions of early political philosophers about who we are. Much of this knowledge which has been gathered particularly by Carl Jung and Roberto Assagioli and other transpersonal psychologists as well as Sigmund Freud, gives us a much more subtle picture of our nature, and how we can change with self-awareness. We have been greatly helped by learning of and being influenced by Eastern philosophies of the nature of the person and can more truly acknowledge and work with the contradictions in the person. 'Know thyself' was a maxim of classical Greek philosophy. It is this that needs to be at the roots of a different political philosophy.

As for the political, the polis, new ideas need to relate to the whole spectrum of modern knowledge, working, as all must do, towards a more whole world. Thinking locally as well as globally: accepting we are part of nature not opposed to her and using her: contemplating the differences in human religions and spirituality, in gender, in racial background as part of the political mix: accepting that all is but 'a woven web of guesses' in this mysterious and unfinished universe.

It is interesting to see that the Hansard Society, based in the House of Commons, is itself presently searching for a more participatory, more open system to replace the current discredited machinery. But this is hardly enough. We basically need a more three dimensional politics, which takes into account the greater subtlety of our present view of the person and all the opposed characteristics in our nature, with an acknowledgment of the awesomeness of the Universe. That requires a much more mature understanding of the terms under which we seem to be on Earth — an Earth that has experienced many major extinctions of species already and is of an extraordinary complexity and beauty.

We need to stop living out worn-out simplistic assumptions about who we are, and what should be the tenets of political thinking and action. As Paul Hawken points out in his recent book *Blessed Unrest*, published in 2007, there may now be over one million organizations over the world working to produce a new vision of how the human race may live here

> Across the planet groups ranging from *ad hoc* neighbourhood
> associations to well-founded international organizations are
> confronting issues like the destruction of the environment,
> the abuses of free- market fundamentalism, social justice, and
> the loss of indigenous cultures. They share no orthodoxy or
> unifying ideology; they follow no single charismatic leader; they
> remain supple enough to coalesce easily into larger networks
> to achieve their goals. While they are largely unrecognized by
> politicians and the media, they are bringing about what may one
> day be judged to be the single most profound transformation of
> human society. (Hawken 2007. Inside front cover.)

The politics we require, intrinsic to this change, should represent a holistic worldview which acknowledges the splendour of this universe and planet and the multiple forces within it, and the complex nature of the human person, part of the spirit of the whole, with all his or her contradictions. This politics needs to be reflective, coming from wisdom and not only from ego. As Plato said many centuries ago, the only person who is fit to lead a society is one that does not *want* power. Organizations should be mutual, hard though that is to manage, at all levels from local to international. And the world must be ever seen as emerging and changing. As William Kittredge writes in *The Nature of*

Generosity: 'a society capable of naming itself lives within its stories, inhabiting and furnishing them. We ride stories like rafts, or lay them on the table like maps. They always, eventually, fail and have to be reinvented. The world is too complex for our forms ever to encompass for long'.

We need to be creating new stories.

The gods did not reveal, from the beginning,
All things to us; but in the course of time,
Through seeking we may learn, and know things better.

But as for certain truth, no man has known it,
Nor will he know it; neither of the gods,
Nor yet of all the things of which I speak.
And even if by any chance he were to utter
The final truth, he would himself not know it;
For all is but a woven web of guesses.

Xenophanes (430–350 BC)

References

Berman, Morris (1984) *The Re-enchantment of the World*, Bantam Books, New York.

Chenu M.-D. (1997) *Nature, Man and Society in the Twelfth Century*, University of Toronto Press.

Easlea, Brian (1980) *Witch-hunting, Magic and the New Philosophy: An Introduction to the Debates of the Scientific Revolution 1450–1750*, Harvester, New York.

Hawken, Paul (2007) *Blessed Unrest*, Viking, London.

Locke, John (1984) *Two Treatises of Government*, Dent, London.

Macpherson, C.B. (1962) *The Political theory of Possessive Individualism. Hobbes to Locke*, Oxford University Press.

Patten, Chris (1983) *The Tory Case*, Longman, London.

21. Towards a New Renaissance in Good Governance

CHRIS WRIGHT

Chris Wright has had three non-fiction works published — Your Wake Up Call *(2006, The Community Press),* A Community Manifesto *(Earthscan, 2000) and* The Sufficient Community *(Green Books, 1997). He has also had three novels published* — Mayfield Park *(2007, Vanguard Press),* Completing the Charm *(2004) and* Sod 'Em at Gomorrah *(2002), both by New European Publications. He is a founder member of Action for Sustainable Living (www.afsl.org.uk* — *winner of the Guardian Charity Award 2008), which aims to support individuals and their local communities to take simple steps towards living more sustainably.*

Setting the scene

When asked how he came to understand that the Earth orbited the sun rather than vice versa, Galileo responded with a story. As a child, he had been taken out to sea in a boat and had been certain that the land was physically moving away from them; later, as an adult, he understood that it was the boat that was moving while the land remained stationary. At least that is what Brecht has him say in his play *Life of Galileo* (Brecht, Hare translation 2006), with the implication that a lot of what we see and understand in the world depends on the perspective from which we view it; the anecdote also suggests that humankind could benefit from growing up and discovering a more mature outlook on the nature of being.

A 'New Renaissance' requires just such a leap of imagination. We must look at both ourselves and the world we inhabit through new eyes and seek new answers to questions that have been long since been considered resolved. No aspect of human experience is sacrosanct and those elements we cherish most are likely to be least satisfactory from the new vantage point.

Any 'Manifesto for Change' must be clear about the issues it is trying to address and what makes their resolution so urgent. It must explore what is important and enduring in the human condition and explain why current ways of meeting these needs are failing and/or never likely to succeed. Finally, a revised set of priorities must be communicated in a way that provides an unambiguous sense of direction for those who wish to build a new future.

Decisions, decisions

There are many ways of trying to stand outside the status quo and begin to understand what it is that is no longer working. One of the most straightforward is through the notion of 'governance'. Put simply the term implies the way a group of individuals, an organization or a nation takes its decisions. As such it supports, and is supported by, the dominant mindset determining how people look at the world and the relationships that exist between them.

The most immediate and obvious example of the governance problems facing us is the economic crisis that we are living through. Flawed assessments of risk, built on financial products that few people in the industry fully understood, fuelled reckless decision-making in the mistaken belief that the good times could go on forever. The idea of the market place being fundamentally about exchange and the meeting of human need had long since disappeared. Even before the credit crunch people had become little more than information bytes in a vast global system that requires continuous growth to service the mounting debt on which it is based. It doesn't matter what is produced, or how, as long as it delivers a profit. Nothing is allowed to stand in the way of this growth imperative; rainforests are felled, sweatshops mushroom and regimes are toppled in the headlong rush to keep the juggernaut on the road. Climate change, environmental degradation, resource depletion, species extinction and an upsurge in war and terrorism are all direct and indirect consequences of this way of making decisions.

Similarly, the political decision-making process has ceased to be about the wishes and needs of real people — the basic assumption of the democratic process. Based on short-termism and expedience, prey to interest groups and lacking any moral compass, the message is endlessly massaged by the sound bite and the need for politicians to be seen to be responding to the latest, media-generated moral panic (even if what they do today reverses or contradicts what they did yesterday). Elections hang on swings in a handful of marginal seats and the 'value' of an individual vote is further eroded by the sheer numbers involved (the electorate has increased elevenfold in just over a century, while the number of elected representatives has actually gone down). The business of government becomes ever more complicated with a continuously expanding range of laws that reach into every aspect of daily life. Huge bureaucracies have evolved to implement and police them; top down, inflexible institutions fighting one another for funds and all operating to different, quasi-legalistic agendas which the individual supplicant must fit in with if they are to qualify for what is a public service.

These governance systems are simply incapable of responding to the challenges the world faces. They are no longer fit for purpose. However, the good news is that both the economy and political system are human constructs, rather than laws of nature, and can be changed if only we can find a fresh set of priorities on which to base them.

The organizational imperative

What becomes clear from even this very superficial analysis is that the needs of the individual and their communities, and their ability to make decisions about matters of significance to them, have all but disappeared from view. We live in a world dominated by organization and systems, in which people are the raw material to be shaped to the purposes of the institution. It has become a kind of virtual world that runs according to its own internal logic and has, in many cases, lost complete touch with reality.

Our ability as a society to make sensible decisions has been diminished accordingly. The individual has become largely defenceless in the face of these impersonal forces. People can no longer sort out the simplest of life's problems without recourse to experts and/or the law because any sense of community (the traditional resort of the aggrieved and disadvantaged) has been leached out by the centralizing forces that have encouraged this trend towards 'organization'.

To get a sense of what that means it is useful to juxtapose the qualities of organization and community:

ORGANIZATION	COMMUNITY
Emphasizes roles	Emphasizes relationships
Relationships based on contract	Relationships based on covenant[*]
Primacy of rules/procedures	Primacy of negotiation
Assumes conflict	Assumes cooperation
Emphasizes rights	Emphasizes responsibilities
Emphasizes uniformity	Emphasizes difference
Based on suspicion	Based on trust
Based on power	Based on mutuality
Based on position	Based on personal talents
Emphasizes authority	Emphasizes consensus

(Wright 2006, p.102)

Of course, there can be no community without organization of some kind and even within the most regulated organizations community will sprout within the gaps in the rules. In fact, it is a

---

[*] A covenant is an agreement based on trust and goodwill and a willingness to work towards a shared goal or vision. It is a joint commitment to set out on a journey the exact nature of which may be unclear at the outset.

sign of how impoverished our social opportunities have become that most people seek the comfort of solidarity in the unpromising soil of the workplace (which, in the extreme case, leads to the subverting of the organization and the growth of alternative loci of power). We are talking here about finding an appropriate balance between the two rather than the domination of the one by the other — an example of fruitful synthesis (the sum being greater than the parts) rather than the either/or thinking that is so prevalent today

Nevertheless, what this schema does suggest is that organization has relegated community to the margins, emphasizing hierarchy, rules and, most revealingly, the primacy of object relations at the expense of subject relations. For example, most of the interactions we have today are of the kind found at the supermarket check-out or on a telephone helpline. We do not expect to engage with or be engaged by the other person. Who they are and what challenges they face are irrelevant to what we want from them and we are wrong-footed or incensed if that boundary is crossed. Yet to be human is to engage. Perhaps all the unhappiness that characterizes life today, the increase in depression and anxiety, the rise in addictive behaviour and the general decline in physical and mental wellbeing can be explained in this one development. How has this state of affairs come about?

The answer is inevitably complex. There are immediate causes — increasing centralization, the collapse of Communism giving even freer rein to global capitalism, the social acceptance of individualism and indebtedness, increased mobility, and the sheer number of people to be 'managed', and so on — but there are also more fundamental drivers deeply embedded in the history of Western civilization.

A lasting legacy?

The classical world distinguished between *mythos* (understanding that is of the moment and gained through the coming together of different elements into a new whole that is difficult to describe in words; it is subjective and about feeling) and *logos* (understanding that results from careful definition and measurement and that can be explained and/or replicated; it is objective and about reason). Greek philosophers didn't see *logos* as a superior way of reaching the truth, but rather a more reliable way of approaching the unknowable and ineffable that *mythos* represented. They were two sides of the same coin.

In today's world these two ways of being have been reduced to the seemingly unbridgeable antagonism between religion/arts and science. The seeds of their separation can be found in the explosion of energy and creativity that was the 'Old Renaissance'. A new emphasis on what was actually out there in the world led to the study of the individual and a consequent high water mark in art and sculpture; developments in technology resulted in a wave of exploration which in turn promoted the militant Christianity that had first seen light in the Crusades; and, most fatefully, the schisms that resulted from the Reformation led to an emphasis on the certainty of and literal belief in the word (*logos*) of the Bible, as well as the need for *individual* salvation and a growing intolerance of heretical thinking. This insistence on individual belief contrasted with an earlier emphasis on communal faith — meaning a commitment to right living and ritual observance — as a way of approaching ultimate and unknowable reality *(mythos)*. This trend was not uniform and to this day there continue to be upsurges in the desire to submerge the self in the transpersonal ocean of *mythos,* but the Church has contributed immeasurably towards the West's acceptance that social reality is based on *logos* and its acolyte, 'organization'.

Meanwhile, Science was developing its own version of adherence to the Word. On the face of it science is quintessentially *logos.* Careful experimentation, data collection, hypothesis and replication are all reason-based activities and, as such, might be considered to be a refinement of what philosophers have always striven to achieve. As already noted, however, the Greeks in particular considered reality to be unknown and unknowable. Science as it developed through the nineteenth and twentieth century, while accepting that not everything is known, operates from the belief that everything is ultimately knowable because reality is material and science will therefore provide the means to know it.

That may not be the personal position of many scientists, but the institution of science operates on that assumption and it has taken root in the public and private imagination. Because of the prestige of science and the many tangible benefits it has brought, this certainty about the pre-eminence of *logos* has come to pervade all aspects of life, making it more likely that 'organization' and objective decision-making will be seen as the natural default mode. The observation that, in practice, the advance of science depends on many non-rational factors such as chance and intuition, or that career success means holding to the current orthodoxy despite the evidence (paradigm changes are usually bloody, internecine battles to the death) doesn't diminish the hold that the materialist worldview has on wider culture, nor that public and private bodies must act and to be seen to act from a purely objective point of view.

Breaking the mould

For five hundred years both religion and science, in their different ways, have been shaping society's perception of reality towards a way of looking that is based on *logos*. It has been a tremendously powerful perspective that has literally conquered the world. As individuals we are born and grow up with that assumption all around us, and it is hardly surprising that we both accept it unquestioningly and find it difficult to think of an alternative. But now we are seeing ever more clearly that the promise of certainty that scientific materialism holds before us is turning to dust in our hands.

We have much to learn, unlearn and re-learn. As literalists we have lost the ability to experience *mythos* in any meaningful way and our ever weakening communities have cut us off from the life-affirming sense of transpersonal identification with something outside ourselves. That does not mean that we should abandon *logos*; rather, we need to find new ways of seeking that age-old synthesis with *mythos*. The task is nothing less than to find a mindset that can encompass and value scientific orthodoxy (the material world) while at the same time giving true weight to subjective experience (the awareness of the non-material); that balances the exploration of 'self' with the need to identify with the 'other' and that shifts the emphasis away from 'organization' and back to 'community'.

How is such a seismic shift to be achieved? For a start major changes in perception don't happen very often and they don't happen overnight. The Industrial Revolution was perhaps the last such event (and even that was more a continuation of the Old Renaissance project than a truly new beginning). It is often portrayed as a nineteenth century phenomenon but, in reality, its immediate roots lie in the previous century with the upsurge of interest in and exploration of the natural world. Owing nothing to existing power and decision-making structures (it embraced all classes and conditions of people) this enthusiasm effectively laid the foundations for a way of looking at the world that would grow within the old order and eventually supersede it. By shaping a new language that increasing numbers of people came to share and understand, an ever growing impetus was given to the pursuit of a new set of priorities.

Language shapes perception. Introduce new words, change the meaning of existing words or bring redundant words back into play and reality changes. If enough people embrace the new terminology then you have the beginnings of a movement. It is like charging a social magnet. A piece of inert metal (the charges on the individual electrons are randomly distributed, cancelling each other out) can be transformed into a source of useful power (the electrons become aligned, the greater the degree of alignment, the greater the magnetic charge). In the same way, through the alignment of language, individuals acting independently on the same assumptions and seeking the same goals release tremendous energy that can both transform society and lead to great mental and physical achievement. In short, language provides a common sense of purpose (see covenant above).

So where is the new vision to be found and how does our fragmented and wounded world learn to pull together? It is important to understand that, on the cusp of change, the future really is an unknown country. What we can say is that social reality in ten, twenty or a hundred year's time will not be like anything we can imagine today. Who could have predicted how the Industrial Revolution would turn out? Plenty of writers and artists tried, but their analyses were more akin to science fiction and we should be wary of false prophets who point to the Promised Land and demand that we follow them there.

Change happens because people live it in their daily lives. Their immediate priorities have altered and so they do things differently. They take a step at a time and have to learn as they go along. It is that sense of direction, rather than a detailed route map of how to reach some objective on the horizon, that we need to capture and that can be best summed up by having a set of values to guide us: a set of values as clear as those that drove scientific exploration but leading us in a different direction entirely.

A new direction

Just as Old Renaissance thinkers and artists reacted to the obscurantism of the Middle Ages by shining the light of a re-discovered classical naturalism on their own times, so the New Renaissance is responding to the limitations of the scientific world view by re-engaging with the broader concerns of both classical antiquity and the Old Renaissance itself; namely what it means to be human. To do that we must put people and their communities back at the centre of everything we do by consciously adopting a human scale agenda in looking at how best to make decisions. Such a perspective can be approached by focussing on the following six aspirations:

RELATIONSHIPS
~ based on mutuality ~
COMMUNITIES
~ based on love and personal responsibility ~
LOCAL DECISION-MAKING
~ based on consensus ~
LOCAL FOOD/LOCAL WORK/LOCAL EXCHANGE/
LOCAL ENERGY
~ based on creativity and sustainability ~
IDENTIFICATION WITH PLACE
~ based on oneness with nature ~
LIVING WITH UNCERTAINTY
~ based on spirituality -

(Wright 2006, pp. 97–130)

Each dimension raises its own set of questions, but they are all inter-related and cannot ultimately be addressed in isolation. Thus, it will be difficult to achieve a high degree of, say, mutuality in relationships while at the same time ignoring the surroundings in which those relationships are taking place; awareness of and caring for a shared environment goes hand in hand with awareness of and caring for one another. As our understanding of one deepens so we are inevitably drawn to exploring the implications for the others. Inevitably, all six themes will feed into any discussion about governance but, in the light of the analysis so far, it is helpful to look briefly at four in a little more detail:-

Relationships — based on mutuality

If I am in a position of authority over you I can, in the final analysis, ignore you. In human terms that would be a lost opportunity because we only learn new skills and develop self-awareness through interacting with others. That is more likely to happen when we are genuinely engaged with them rather than as a consequence of occupying a role or being told what to do. Authority in this context comes from personal qualities rather than position in a hierarchy and it can therefore move from one person to another depending on circumstance. Mutuality does not necessarily imply equality in any given relationship, but it does require a whole-hearted acceptance of the other person.

Communities — based on love and personal responsibility

Any community depends on the skills, commitment and energy of its members being harnessed in a way that benefits everyone. And, if everyone is to grow and develop as individuals to the benefit of the community, there has to be a trade off between freedom and equality. If I am to be free to realize my potential I must extend that right to other members in equal measure. Freedom and equality are often seen as opposites but, by recognizing that we can only truly become ourselves when others are engaged in the same journey, they can be reconciled and reinforce one another. Love is the glue that makes such a virtuous circle possible and the acceptance of personal responsibility is the means by which it is achieved. The quality of relationships is what defines a community rather than the quantity of people who can be coerced in a certain direction.

Local decision-making — based on consensus

As well as providing a context within which individuals can thrive, a community must address issues that arise both in the short and longer terms. Although much of what happens on a day to day basis may be handled by giving individuals or groups authority to act on behalf of the community, such authority can only work if it has the continuing acceptance of all the members. A covenant has to be agreed and has to be reaffirmed on a regular basis to ensure that the thinking that is active in people's lives is still shared and vibrant. That can only be achieved through consensus, a careful exploration of what is important through a respectful engagement with others so that language becomes re-aligned and the social charge reinforced. Decision-making becomes dispersed and focussed rather than centralized and haphazard.

Living with uncertainty — based on spirituality

The emphasis on relationships, community and consensus implies accepting uncertainty. We, as individuals, do not know what other people are thinking and feeling, or what is best for our community at any one time. We have to engage and we have to accept that it is us who may have to change (and hopefully grow in the process). Often discussion will centre on how people are feeling and why, rather than the immediate issue that has brought them together. Both reason and emotional literacy are required. It is a short step to recognize that Life is inherently uncertain and ultimately unknowable but that, in community, the individual can experience something of its harmony and grace. It is possible to conceive of scientific communities sharing that kind of transpersonal experience while individually and collectively continuing to explore the physical laws threaded through that reality. In the process, logos and mythos will have been finally reconciled rather than being forever in conflict.

Final thoughts

What is being described is a small-scale, bottom-up approach to governance. Of course, such communities will also need to co-exist with their neighbours and there will be many initiatives that can only be sustained by several communities working together. Local, bio-regional, continental and global systems of governance will evolve based on the human scale principles. At each level participants drawn from the constituent communities will work together 'in community' but will only tackle those issues that cannot be satisfactorily resolved at a more local level. Such an approach has the potential to become a self-regulating, holistic organism that reflects what is best in the human spirit.

There are many groups and individuals today who are trying to shift the balance back towards the whole individual and their place in the community. From community allotments to clothes swap shops, from neighbourhood recycling schemes to energy cooperatives, people are trying to do things differently. Many of those schemes will fail but, in the process they are not only grappling with what works, but how to make it work (that is the most appropriate decision-making processes) and that in the end is what will drive change forward. It is not so much the 'what' as the 'how' that is important, based on the relationships between people and the way they take decisions together.

As Margaret Mead said: 'Never doubt that a small group of thoughtful, committed citizens can change the world: indeed, it is the only thing that ever has.'

Maybe we are about to realize once again that it is the ship that moves and not the land. And, just maybe, Humanity is about to take one more step towards maturity.

References

Brecht, Bertolt (2006) *The Life of Galileo*, trans. David Hare, Samuel French.

Mead, Margaret (n.d.) Quotation on p. 246. Although firmly attributed to Margaret Mead, there is no record of when or where this often quoted observation first appeared. It is likely that it came into public circulation through a newspaper report of something said informally and spontaneously.

Wright, Chris (2006) *Your Wake Up Call — Signposts to Sustainability*, The Community Press.

22. Transforming the Economy

PETER BOWMAN

After graduating from Oriel College, Oxford, the author spent a number of years teaching science at St James Independent School at Twickenham. He is now science coordinator of the University Preparatory Certificate at the Language Centre of University College, London. He has a wide range of interests from atomic physics to the nature of consciousness and has been a member of the Scientific and Medical Network for a number of years. He studies economics at the School of Economic Science, is a director of the Henry George Foundation of Great Britain and vice-chairman of the Coalition for Economic Justice.

Introduction

Although the calamitous events of Autumn 2008 did not in the end result in total collapse of the financial system, fifteen months later the sense still remains of an economy in crisis. Those events were symptomatic of a deeper malaise. It was certainly not the case that before that time all had been well. The appearance of growing prosperity over the previous decade proved to be largely a sham. When the bubble broke, the underlying instability of the present system was revealed. Even if the goal of a return to growth of gross domestic product (GDP) is achieved, two deeper issues that rankle beneath the surface will not be driven away by simply reinstating 'business as usual but with more regulation.' The first is the growing gap between the rich and the poor that is present both between different countries and also within each country itself. It is this inequality rather than poverty that is now recognized to be the source of a whole range of gradually worsening social ills, particularly in the developed world (Wilkinson & Pickett 2009). The second is the effect of growth-impelled economic activity on the environment. This is resulting in both the rapid depletion of natural resources and the excretion of growing quantities of pollutants that the world's eco-system cannot cope with.

The crisis has produced for some a waking up to the reality of our present situation. In so doing it provides the opportunity to examine critically our whole economic system and review the depth of reform needed to deal effectively with these underlying issues as well as the inherent instability. Is it the case, as some have suggested, that the free market hypothesis is inherently flawed and that our system is rotten to the core? Behind the drive for growing material prosperity at any cost that our present market economy facilitates is an overtly materialist worldview. Could it be that this is a cultural crisis and that nothing short of a change of this fundamental stance can provide the change of direction that is needed? After acknowledging the possibility, this essay will leave that question to others and focus just on the economic realm. It will attempt to look holistically at the present situation to uncover its underlying shortcomings and what could be done to remedy them.

The most helpful tool in such an examination would be a model or framework that is capable of fulfilling three functions simultaneously:

1. To provide a basis for analyzing the underlying faults in the present system that have led to the destructive crisis;
2. To provide a basis for a better system, one that is fairer, more stable and sustainable; and
3. To provide a 'road map' to take us from the former to the latter.

Karl Polanyi and the Great Transformation

The thesis is that such an analysis of our present free market system was provided by the political economist Karl Polanyi, in his classic work, *The Great Transformation,* written some sixty years ago (Polanyi 1944). Through his comprehensive analysis that combined social, economic and historic perspectives, he identified the critical weakness that would inevitably lead to the self-destruction of the free market system. When, contrary to his prediction, the world's economy got back to its feet after the Second World War, there seemed to be a good reason to ignore his analysis but sixty years on its prescience is again being recognized (Spratt *et al.* 2009).

In its essence Polanyi's argument is very simple. It cuts right to the heart of the present crisis. Polanyi did not criticize the market system in itself. He recognized that markets have been a social phenomenon throughout human history. What he gave original thought to was the natural limit of the market system, what should be included in it and what excluded.

The traditional function of a market is the exchange of commodities, a term which implies man-made goods. These range from extracted raw materials and agricultural produce through intermediate goods to complex finished products. According to Polanyi what happened to sow the seeds of self-destruction in our present free market system was a *deception*. It was the pretence that the primary elements of the economy, namely land, labour and credit, are commodities that can be traded in the market in the same way that actual commodities can. He pointed out that these primary elements of the economy are patently not commodities in that they are not man-made goods. Markets in labour, land (the distinguishing aspect of 'property' and 'real estate') and credit are artificial and will behave totally differently to markets in commodities. These basic elements are of an entirely different category to man-made goods and the economic laws they follow are entirely different. For Polanyi, the admission of this pretence that these factors would follow market theory was not only unreasonable but ultimately destructive.

Here is the heart of the problem with the current free market system. This underlying pretence is the cause of its inherent instability and has given rise to the (often unrecognized) characteristic feature of its history which is a series of cycles of 'boom and bust'. It is in the markets in these primary elements that the difficulties of our present economic system lie. Note the main features of the last crisis: the self-destruction of the credit market, the stagnation of the closely connected property (that is, land) market, shortly to be followed by a significant increase in unemployment. With the primary factors so destabilized, the real market economy then suffers consequently as an innocent victim.

Since economists themselves have taken up the pretence, the subject of economics as it is presently taught has rendered itself incapable of describing the real working of the economy and hence of explaining and predicting the recurring cycles of boom and bust that frustrate it (Bezemer 2009).

Why is it fundamentally wrong to have markets in these basic elements?

Consider land. In economics this term is used to include all natural resources. In other words, it denotes the part of the economy that is not man-made. It is, in the words of Alfred Marshal, the 'free-gift of nature.' It follows that because it is not man-made one of its fundamental economic characteristics is that its supply is inelastic ('They're not making it anymore,' to quote Mark Twain). Therefore land does not respond to the law of supply and demand in the way that manufactured goods do. Unlike motor cars or toothbrushes, when the demand for land increases the supply cannot be increased to match, it is perfectly inelastic and all that happens is the price goes up.

To be traded land must first be claimed. To many cultures of the world, such as the North American Indians, the notion that land can be owned and hence bought and sold was incomprehensible but it has become ingrained in Western thinking despite the reasoning of philosophers such as Locke. In his view (see Mazor 2009), the basis of a claim to a property in anything lies in the work done (directly or indirectly, for example, through trade) to produce it. There can be no such claim for land, since by definition; man does not make it. However the tendency to ignore this and claim land as private property is difficult to resist. Because it is such an essential pre-requisite to all human activity and has an inelastic supply it is one of the most valuable of assets. In addition there is the fact that at this time on this planet, with its current human population, land of quality good enough to sustain a high level of human wellbeing is scarce. As such it enters the market place to become an irresistible object of speculation and because it is so fundamental, since everyone needs somewhere at least to live, the asset bubble has to follow and take precedence over the real needs of the economy. The market in land can never come to equilibrium in the way that markets in manufactured goods do.

Credit is almost as fundamental to economic production as land. Its essential function is to provide a bridge to cross the time gap between the start of any economic activity and its point of completion when it can provide a return for the producer in the marketplace. The farmer has to sustain himself between the time he plants his crop and when he harvests it, the craftsman and builder must purchase their materials before they can even start their work. Even the shopkeeper must purchase his goods before he can sell them on to his customers. For all these and other productive activities credit is absolutely essential.

In the hands of the banking system this primary function has become privatized and effectively monopolized. It has been distorted from an essential economic service into a method of making returns for its owners and a few select employees at the expense of the rest of society. One effect of this distortion is that credit is directed not where it is actually needed but where it can gain the largest returns for its issuers. Even where it is for productive purposes these are usually of a large scale and of questionable overall social and environmental benefit: mechanized energy intensive large-scale agriculture, large-scale production of short-lived consumer goods driven by advertising rather than real need, and large centralized energy schemes. A high proportion of credit issued is not for production at all but for speculation on assets or even just to finance consumption. The removal of the separation between the credit-creation of conventional banking and the operation of investment banking has led to the use of bank credit in leveraged operations to greatly expand the power of financial institutions to engage in highly profitable transactions, in what was recently described 'socially useless activity' (Hosking 2009).

In the hands of the private banking cartel, credit has been transformed from an essential economic service into the pretence of a commodity whose price is the rate of interest. The pretence overlooks the underlying economic truth that, like land, credit does not obey the law of supply and demand in the way that manufactured goods do. The 'cost of production' of credit is negligible and its supply is without any natural limit. Once the agreement with the customer has been made, a bank 'loan' can be produced simply at the stroke of a pen or the pressing of numbers on a computer keyboard. The market in credit can never come to equilibrium, it can never clear in that way that markets in goods do, and hence it always remains under the control of its producers, the banks (Werner 2005), until they overreach themselves.

The existence of a 'labour market' where human beings are themselves treated as little different from a commodity contributing one of the costs of the productive process is largely a result of the monopolies of privatized land and credit. Under conditions where the land and the other natural provisions of nature are no longer freely available but only accessible at the monopolist's price and the basis of the extension of credit is to maximize the return to the issuer, the relative bargaining power of employers and employees is so uneven that the latter have little choice but to accept what is offered. In most modern economies it has become acceptable to maintain a significant proportion of the workforce unemployed. Having excess 'supply' helps to keep the cost of labour low. In developed countries the worst effects of this commoditization of labour have been ameliorated through social provision by the state but taking humanity as a whole the effect of this has simply been to export the worst effects to less developed countries. In the process known as globalization, multi-national companies continually move their production to where lower wages can be paid and poor working conditions remain acceptable. This has generally depressed earnings of labour everywhere. In the developed countries, to maintain what they regard as an adequate standard of living, workers have been pressed to supplement their inadequate earnings with debt using their homes as collateral.

The effects are worsened by the way most governments have chosen to use wages as the basis for taxation, diminishing yet further the proportion of the wealth that workers produce that they are able to retain for themselves.

These are the economic effects of the commoditization of labour. The human consequences go much deeper. The nature of work has fundamentally changed. For many it is no longer something that is fulfilling and satisfying in its own right; it becomes just a means to an end. People now work not for what they can contribute but for what they can get out of the system and attempt to seek their satisfaction in other avenues.

What is the solution?

If Polanyi's analysis is correct, then, in addition to indicating the underlying causes of the present crisis it can also point to a remedy. This would be a move to an economy in which the market is limited only to commodities and the primary elements: land, labour and credit are excluded. For this to take place governments would need to enact their fundamental duty to protect these components from exploitation and thus enable them to fulfil their respective primary economic functions. This does not require centralized state control. On the contrary, it offers the possibility of a truly free market with economically free people having unexploited access to the land and credit that is needed for genuine prosperity. The route to achieve this would be to take the primary factors out of the market system. They need to be 'de-commoditized'.

First consider credit. To begin to stop thinking of credit as a commodity and start thinking of it as an essential economic provision requires a fundamental change in attitude. In the developing world this step was taken with the introduction of the micro-financing schemes starting with the Grameen Bank (Yunus 1999). The transformative effect on many thousands of poor people able to take advantage of the scheme has been to begin to lift them out of abject poverty.

In the developed world there is much public confusion and misunderstanding over the way the money and banking system work. As the proportion of money that exists in bank accounts rather than as cash has grown so also has the proportion of the money supply that is produced by the private banks rather than by the government. On the basis that 'every advance creates a deposit' the proportion of the UK money supply that has been privately produced as bank credit has now risen to 97%. The nation's money supply has become interest-bearing bank credit. An essential government function and all the economic privileges that go with it has been gradually and unwittingly handed over to a privately owned cartel. However, as was demonstrated recently by state intervention to rescue crippled banks in Europe and the US, the ultimate responsibility for the money supply remains with government, so it is left to pick up the pieces and the taxpayers the bill when these private institutions, through their greed, and incompetence fail.

Credit is essential for economic activity. Where it is directed will prosper and where it is restricted cannot flourish. With the present private banking system and 'commodity' model of credit the basis of where it is directed is not how socially or even economically useful the recipient's purpose is but rather what achieves maximum return at minimum risk for the issuer. When credit is used for investment in 'real' economic activity such as manufacturing then the effect can be real economic growth. When it is used for the purchase of assets such as real estate in the hope that they will increase in value then the long-term result must be inflation. Similarly, if credit is issued for consumption, although this may have a short-term stimulating effect, in the long term it is not likely to produce a sustainable increase in economic activity. The differing effects on the economy of these different uses of credit are highly significant but it is not in the interests of private banks to recognize them.

Even in this age of electronic money there is good reason to return the function of issuing money to the government and restrict the banks to what most people think they do now — not creating credit but putting their customer's deposits to good use by investing it in productive enterprise. With the adoption of the policy of quantitative easing the central banking has recently been openly creating new money, but it could be put to much more productive use. Financing much needed infrastructure projects — particularly low carbon energy production — would have a much greater impact on the real economy than its present use of buying back debt. Under the present conditions with the private banks showing great reluctance to extend credit for productive purpose whilst they rebuild their balance sheets there is a real need for an institution to take on the traditional function of banks and supply credit to the real economy, for the sake of the economy rather than its own gain.

Such is the fundamental importance and therefore high price of land that in our present commoditized arrangements, well over two thirds of the credit issued by banks is for mortgages on domestic or commercial property. Redirection of credit away from speculative purchase of assets either directly or through leverage takeovers would be a first step of removing land from the market mechanism. A further significant step could be achieved in a less direct way as a consequence of reform of the way Government collects its revenue. To appreciate how this could be achieved requires taking a fresh look at what the basis of the value of a plot of land is, particularly in an urban environment where the more valuable land is now found. One sees that it is not the land itself as a piece of earth which is where the value lies but rather with the access to public goods and services, markets, and an environment propitious for business or domestic occupation, that owning that site provides. In the present system of privatized property all these benefits come free of charge to the owner once he has acquired the plot. The public aspects of these services do have to be paid for by someone. At present it happens indirectly through the system of taxation, mostly levied on labour as income tax but on various other taxes as well. Perversely, as a community grows and the location is enhanced so the owner receives greater benefits but this enhancement is also reflected in the growing (land component of) property value and increased equity accrues to the private owners as well as the benefits of the location. This was illustrated quite vividly with the extension of the Jubilee Line in South London in 2000 where an infrastructure development costing £3.5 billion and financed by taxation raised property prices in the locality by an estimated £13.5 billion (Riley 2001). It can also be seen in the way property prices around a good school command a premium.

On this analysis the value of all services and other benefits a particular site receives by virtue of its location can be equated with the rental value of the site (stressing strongly that for any building this is only the site component, not the full market rent for the premises). If the landowners had to actually pay the community back for these services the site-related component of their unearned rental income would be now matched by this expense (Burgess 1993).

The ramification would be that no unearned income would any longer accrue from merely having property in land. It would become particularly disadvantageous to hold land out of use in the hope of making speculative gain since the service expenses would still have to be met but without any corresponding income. The only reason for having property in land would be to actively make the best use of any advantages a given location offered. The best sites, would be available at a premium, but with the payments now going to the suppliers of the services, that is, the community as represented by either local or central government. For the enterprising, marginal sites would be available at very low cost.

Here is the second step of reform, the charging for public services by location using land rentals as a means of evaluating the overall value. The overall effect of this would be to de-commoditize land. It would no longer be worthwhile to treat it as a good that can be bought and sold. It would remain a valuable primary factor of production, which would have to be put to good use for it to be retained.

A similar system could be applied to natural resources. The extractor would be paid the costs of extraction including normal profits. (The value of this could be decided by auction as recently happened in Iraq). The resource rental, the difference between the extraction costs and the market value of the resource would then fall to the local community. This could provide a much-needed source of public revenue for many developing countries.

An additional advantage of using land and resource rents as a major source of Government revenue is that the burden of taxation could be taken away from labour and enterprise.

Setting the economy free

The combined effect of de-commoditized credit directed towards productive economic activity, de-commoditized land freed from speculative valuation and the burden of taxation removed from production, would have a huge impact on the conditions for engaging in economic activity and hence on the 'labour market'. With the possibility of self-employment and associated meaningful work so much more accessible there would be a shift in bargaining power from the employer to the employee. A viable alternative to 'wage slavery' would be much more realistic. The possibility could also arise of full employment. More and more of the workforce could begin using their working life as a means of utilizing their innate talents rather than just earning enough to keep body and soul together. From this follows the possibility of a general uplift in society. There would be the opportunity for a move away from cheap, low quality manufactured goods that the circumstances of the debt-based economy forced upon us, back towards the production of quality goods that actually provide the purchaser with some lasting satisfaction. This shift would also have positive effects for the environment. In the long term longer-lasting quality goods require fewer raw materials taken from nature and less pollution. The freeing up of the labour market would encourage a general increase in the quality of service offered including the rejuvenation of a maintenance industry. The incentive could be for quality rather than quantity. For example the new labour and land tenure arrangements would make quality domestic food production much more viable. With credit sensibly directed there would be the possibility of bringing low carbon energy production into play.

In addition, and of the greatest importance, is the effect these changes have on our social welfare. The removal of the special privileges accruing to the effective monopolies on land and credit in combination with greater opportunities for productive employment would directly address the underlying causes of the inequalities in wealth and income we see in both developing and developed economies. This in turn would bring about a considerable reduction in the gap between the richest and poorest with the consequent wide-ranging social benefits that are now recognized to accrue to more equal societies.

Polanyi's insight offers an analysis that is both simple and deep. The aim here has been to no more than sketch out how it could provide a basis for the transformation of the economy towards something that is more stable, more just and less damaging for the environment; one that continues to embrace the extraordinary technical achievements of the age whilst at the same time offering the opportunity for a much greater proportion of humanity to find fulfilment and satisfaction through their everyday work; one in which the rewards obtained for honest endeavour are preferred to those achieved through exploitation.

References

Bezemer, Dirk (2009) *No-one Saw This Coming: Understanding Financial Crisis Through Accounting Models,* Munich Personal PePEc Archive.

Burgess, Ronald (1993) *Public Revenue without Taxation,* Shepheard-Walwyn, London.

Hosking, Patrick (2009), quoting Lord Turner of Ecchinswell: 'FSA chairman says City is too big', *The Times,* August 27.

Mazor, Joseph (2009) *A Liberal Theory of Natural Resource Property Rights,* PhD thesis for Harvard University.

Polanyi, Karl (1944) *The Great Transformation: The Political and Economic Origins of Our Times,* Beacon Press, Boston, MA.

Riley, Don (2001) *Taken for a Ride: Trains, Taxpayers and the Treasury,* Centre for Political Studies, London.

Spratt, S., Simms, A., Neitzart, E. & Ryan-Collins, J. (2009) *The Great Transition,* New Economics Foundation, London.

Werner, Richard (2005) *A New Paradigm in Economics,* Palgrave.

Wilkinson, Richard & Pickett, Kate (2009) *The Spirit Level: Why More Equal Societies Almost Always Do Better,* Allen Lane.

Yunus, Muhammad with Jolis, Alan (1999) *Banker to the Poor. The Autobiography of Muhammad Yunus, Founder of the Grameen Bank,* Aurum Press LW.

23. Music and the Arts in a Possible Future

CLEMENT JEWITT

Clement Jewitt was born into the London blitz of 1940, giving him childhood experiences which he says have informed his life. Coming from an artistic family, he was destined for a career in architecture but the course was not completed. He went on later to work in libraries, and this led to specializing in library automation in the early 1970s, eventually designing and project managing the first automation of HMSO catalogues and the EU Technical Directorate equivalent. He was elected subsequently to the Institute of Information Scientists. Following redundancy, he looked for a more formal expression to his deep interests in, particularly, Jungian psychology, and in the arts of music. Music won (on the surface), and he trained in composition, taking his PhD in 2004 on the creational uses of a post-Jungian model of flows in the psyche. His website is: www.clement-jewitt.co.uk

The subject before us is the concept of a New Renaissance. That thought immediately prompts remembrance of the great artists, inventors and thinkers of the historic Renaissance such as Alberti, Brunelleschi, Leonardo, or Michelangelo. The concept of 'renaissance man' has long been familiar in our language: one who transcends, bridges, the compartmentalizations of our fractured world. So are we implying a new world where the all-too-often misunderstandings and rival status claims, even active warfare, between boundaried domains envisioning and exploring the world have eroded these now traditional attitudes in favour of co-operative cross-fertilization and mutual respect and support? I take it that we are so implying, and take as focus of exposition in this endeavour music and the arts.

My vision of the New Renaissance world has the practices of music and other arts integrated into the cultural fabric. Integrated, and, importantly, centrally meaningful as valued and valuable to all aspects of life including the practical, as non-verbal, or — in order to include literature, particularly poetry — as non-linear, expressions tending to the holistic, inclusive as opposed to the narrowly focussed, affirmative of values other than the economic and material. This is in contradistinction to the marginalization and commodification of music and arts apparent in our present profoundly unbalanced *soi disant* civilization. Marginalization (in the UK despite, or arguably because of, Arts Council grant policies) is now so pervasive that in equations of what is officially held to matter in our mainstream culture arts tend simply to be overlooked, despite their (commodified) economic value — seen as meaningless and disposable add-on entertainments: bread and circuses. Art therapies, for example, are often held to be expensive luxuries which NHS Trusts cannot afford, yet they may be less costly in some cases than the lifetime of medication which their success can banish (Casson 2004, Appendix 4). Nevertheless the conventional attitude prevails, while Big Pharm protects its investments.

A more extreme version of this outlook was articulated by Steven Pinker:

> Cheesecake packs a sensual wallop unlike anything in the
> natural world because it is a brew of megadoses of agreeable
> stimuli which we concocted for the express purpose of
> pressing our pleasure buttons. Pornography is another pleasure
> technology. In this chapter I will suggest that the arts are a third
> ... I suspect that music is auditory cheesecake. (Pinker 1997, pp.
> 525–32, quoted in McGilchrist 2009, p. 483, note 43)

Such cultural norms percolate down (or through), however much at an individual level one's musical preferences or art classes are treasured. Less tangible values therefore become hard to assert against such prevailing unanchored misperceptions, to say nothing of the here evidenced shadow side of liberalism, where there are no values in the vertical dimension, everything accepted as equal: flatland.

With that in mind we note a pervasive theme in Iain McGilchrist's new book, *The Master and His Emissary*, the somewhat schizophrenic attributes of the left hemisphere outlook:

> Alienation, fragmentation, decontextualization: the defining features of the modern world were as problematic for art as they were for society ... The predicament of art in the modern period could be said to be how to respond to this challenge And its problem is made more intractable by a different sort of deracination — more than just the severance from place ... but the inevitable consequent severance from the roots of all meaning in shared values and experiences, the vast implicit realm from which imagination draws its power. (McGilchrist 2009, p. 409)

Anne Wilson Schaef provided a telling parallel, calling our mainstream worldview addictive:

> ... like any addiction, *this world view absorbs positive attributes like love and then presents them as if they were its own, feeding off nonaddictive energy and, at the same time, seeking to overpower and destroy it.* (Wilson Schaef 1992, pp. 96–7, emphases in the original)

And there is a further slant to this, seen through the lens of art:

> ... one can surely agree with Virilio that the unanchored re-presentation of reality as art, however dislocated or disturbing — an extension of the aesthetic creed, art for art's sake — which is endemic in modernism is part of a much more profound failure of compassion and an erosion of pity. (McGilchrist 2009, p. 411, discussing Virilio 2003)

The failure of compassion and associated loss of pity can surely be discerned in almost any news report, and in ordinary encounters in public simply lacking what used to be called common politeness.

But of course the art and music worlds are not entirely sterile, devoid of empathy and feeling. Heiddegger commented on great art that 'the artist remains inconsequential as compared with the work, almost like a passageway that destroys itself in the creative process for the work to emerge'. And Merleau-Ponty similarly considered that an authentic work of art (and this also applies to music) was not about the work as invention, nor about the artist, but enabled the world to be envisioned (reheard) anew. There are always some for whom their creative work has nothing to do with ego flattery and everything to do with passionate endeavour to convey deeply held and felt convictions about the world, probably better not verbally articulated, whose works are compellingly 'seen through' to the lived world itself. Anyone who has visited Sandham Memorial Chapel in Hampshire without being profoundly moved by Stanley Spencer's visionary murals of his First World War experiences was surely sleepwalking. In a different though related vein the contemporary English composer Jonathan Harvey has transcended the modernist style he works in, and is regarded by some as producing deeply spiritual music. In both cases the experience is drawn through perception of the message, not the messenger. Such life-enhancing values are precisely what my vision of our coming world finds to be *its* mainstream: a world where distancing by conceptualization, mostly verbal, is paralleled and complemented by holistic direct sensual interaction with what is encountered — Maslow's 'peak experiences' as not exceptional, but commonplace.

As exceptional experiences we feel impelled to make special note of them. David Abram, now carrying forward the phenomenalist enterprise, writes extensively on this topic, and has several tales to tell. Here he is in the Himalayas:

> Across the dry valley, two lammergeier condors floated between
> gleaming, snow-covered peaks ... I took a silver coin out of my
> pocket and aimlessly began a simple sleight-of-hand exercise,
> rolling the coin over the knuckles of my right hand ... [in] the
> dazzling sunlight I noticed that one of the two condors in the
> distance had ... swung out from its path and began soaring back
> [towards me] in a wide arc ... As the great size of the bird grew
> apparent, I felt my skin begin to crawl and come alive, ... and
> a humming grew loud in my ears. The coin continued rolling

along my fingers. The creature loomed larger, and larger still, until, suddenly, it was there — an immense silhouette hovering just above my head, huge wing feathers rustling ever so slightly ... the coin dropped out of my hand. And then I felt myself stripped naked by an alien gaze infinitely more lucid and precise than my own. I do not know for how long I was transfixed, only that I felt the air streaming past naked knees and heard the wind whispering in my feathers long after the Visitor had departed. (Abram 1996, pp. 23–4)

This description of oneness precisely illuminates the connections with art and music I am trying to put across. Despite its prose form, there is I think a poetic sensibility at work in the quoted passage which gives me and hopefully you that 'seeing through' to the lived world mentioned above. Much despised tree huggers can know this feeling, as can musical improvizing groups focussed wider than the notes and away from egoic virtuosity. Practitioners of Goethean science should also recognize it.

There are, as may be expected, many art and music creators with similar intentions, unconscious or not, as Spencer and Harvey, but with less skill, talent, or luck of circumstance, who do not gain attention from mainstream culture arbiters, but nonetheless attract devoted intelligent local appreciators of their work. This contrasts with the legion of lesser talents currently enjoying high profile media favour because they are assiduously following the cultural fashions, often entirely consciously, and even cynically. I am here taking it as a given that art and music production focussed entirely consciously — too easily becoming self-consciously egoic — almost necessarily excludes that 'vast implicit realm from which imagination draws its power' to re-use McGilchrist's telling phrases. The works of these latter are life denying, because self-regarding, and produce only the shiny surface to focus on, no depth to 'see through' to the lived world: mirrors which reflect nothing except the smirk of the inventor. Too many in our sick culture have lost the perception to spot the inauthenticity of such work, or the courage to challenge the 'experts'. My wished-for future redeems that loss, via the regaining of mutuality, mutual trusting, through the lenses of authentic music and art, authentically perceived, seen through. And this is spiral, for a revelatory experience opens us up to expectation, which affects what we can (and will) create, and via inter- and transpersonal connections, what others will create, and so round, all of which widens our perceptions of 'the other' as a feeling being like us, open to trust. True art *is* life, non-verbal metaphor as it were, and co-creates with us the better, more authentically felt parts of our life; it is life enhancing.

The vision of verbal, linear thinking demoted to be equal to a promoted non-linear is not at all new, appearing here and there in many forms, places and times, which there is not space here to explore. However, a recent series of published documents on the state of the world can be seen to exhibit a tenuous trajectory through time in the admission into their reports of considerations other than the material. Indeed their changing definitions of possible content show, I submit, and this is why I choose them for illustration, something of the recent history of new thinking and concern for the state of our culture leading to this present publication.

The MIT 1972 report for the Club of Rome's Project on the Predicament of Mankind firmly adheres to discussion of material resources and socio-political trends, though the absence of consideration of value systems was noted by commentators on the draft, answered by: 'The present model considers man only in his material system because valid social elements simply could not be devised ...' (Meadows 1974, p. 188) The word 'devised' here suggests eloquently a focus on measurement as sole validity. Similarly in a UK government discussion paper on Future World Trends the potential, even practical values of non-material factors are simply not considered. (Cabinet Office 1976).

Two years later UNESCO published a report of a Round Table on 'What kind of world are we leaving our children?' This topic left room in its formulation for consideration of music and arts values, which were taken up by a couple of contributors. Philip Noel-Baker, recalling perhaps Rousseau's *Emile or On Education*, called for 'investment to combat the darkness of the mind ... I would found our education on music', citing Kodaly, Suzuki, and a now largely forgotten English educator, Charles Fry, who founded his academy for merchant navy officers on music and gymnastics, among whose old boys during WWII were no less than seven Royal Navy admirals. (Noel-Baker 1978, p. 81) Elsewhere in the report Aurelio Peccei asserted that 'the concept of responsibility *and beauty* must take precedence over the concepts of needs and rights ... responsibility regarding what we are doing and planning'. (Peccei 1978, p. 121: my emphasis) The importance of beauty cited here arrests because of the rarity of such assertion in our materially oriented world. The personal disciplines required for meaningful musical and artistic expression cannot help but inculcate responsibility for self, which then infuses all other actions, an inculcation tragically subverted by the frustrations of living in a depersonalized and over-materially oriented world.

I am talking about authentic music and art here, not the self-serving cynical constructs, surfaces without depth, metaphorical or literal, which gain plaudits in our sick culture for providing The Shock of the New, a concept displacing beauty, falsely equated with creativity. However the unexpected award of the Turner Prize in 2009 to Richard Wright's understated filigree works rooted in fine art beauty traditions might indicate a welcome change of direction on the part of art grandees and hopefully also other arbiters of culture.

And then the Club of Budapest report in 1997, written by that fine inclusive mind Ervin Laszlo, in a chapter on resources for revisioning devotes an entire section to art and religion. The coupling is noteworthy, recalling Joseph Campbell's insight that purposes and actions in the domain of religion were taken over by the arts during the modern period. Laszlo writes:

> In great art and literature, and in the foundations of the spiritual experience, we can experience a deep source of inspiration for living and loving, and harmony with nature. ... Despite [art's] different modes of expression and its own criteria of excellence, it is nourished by the same fundamental source as science: insight into the nature of human experience. ... Great works of art and literature ... attain universality. They socialize us ... giving us insight into the relations that bind us to each other, and to nature. Achieving the true potential of art ... *may be crucial for our future.* (Laszlo 1997, p. 87, my emphasis)

If the pessimistic conclusion of McGilchrist is right, that the atomizing narrowly focussed left hemisphere is succeeding in blocking off the more life affirming and holistic attitude of the right hemisphere, as the oscillations through the history of the Western world of left and right brain hemisphere views-of-the-world proceed, then Laszlo's insight in the last phrase quoted above is correct, and highly important, for the right hemisphere has important roles to play in the mediation of art and music, which can therefore be an aid in warding off that fate of impoverishment and culture wide schizophrenia which in the end cannot but lead to full cultural collapse. (McGilchrist 2009, pp. 103ff and elsewhere)

More recently, though, there are further signs that our culture is changing towards a broader understanding. Archaeologists have in recent times begun to consider the acoustics of ancient sites, which might give clues about their original builders usage intentions, thus attending to a non-visual sense. Paul Devereux produced the first survey of this work (Devereux 2001). He is also on the editorial team of a new journal accepting papers exploring ancient consciousness through archaeology (Devereux *et al.* 2008). Issue 1 included an interview with landscape archaeologist Peter Fowler, who has taken to imaginatively painting landscapes as a complementary way of approaching his work. A movement away from interpretation of the past purely via material remains is clearly underway, and it would be reasonable to expect it to develop that growing inclusiveness in further ways as yet unspecified: a step, I submit, towards integration of the arts and work worlds.

The trajectory I have tried to indicate as inhering in those reports could be perceived as intrusions in the mainstream world of 'authority' (reported though it often is by the powerful media as unassailably homogenous) by smaller cultural streams on the other side of the watershed, emerging from underground. Under various names ('New Age', Alternative lifestyles, Cultural progressives) these streams are cutting channels in our culture which taken collectively begin to add up to at least the possibility of a better future, a future which seeks to empower local communities as opposed to centralizing tendencies by government, privileges interpersonal relations as antidote to sweeping generalizations of 'citizens' as 'workforce' and 'consumers', and pays attention to psychic development (self improvement stream) and therefore, as corollary, arts and music are perceived as more than mere entertainment, but integrated into the fabric of life. Laszlo has this to say:

> While there is undoubtedly a lunatic edge to this vast
> movement that is escapist, introverted and narcissistic, there is
> also a core that is intensely significant and hopeful ... It indicates
> the emergence of a different mindset: the evolution of a new
> vision. (Laszlo 1997, p. 89)

And in more recent times the signs are that, in parallel with widening perception of the crises facing us, largely now focussed through the lens of climate change, these conservatively dismissed movements are moving closer to mainstream approval: 'downsizing' one's mode of living, for example. What is also illustrated though is how slowly new ideas, mindsets, propagate into the world of power-over, consequence of the inevitable clinging to stasis in fear of loss of that power.

Returning to art and music, examples abound of events and organizations aimed at empowering young persons (our future) by nurturing their creativity. The founder of one, The Power of Hope, which runs vacation workshop camps for teenagers, with drums figuring prominently in activities, commented: 'We can become creators of the culture we want and not just consumers of the culture we have'. To give another example, the Khayaal Theatre Company tours England with plays and music striving to represent Islam positively, consulting young Muslims in order to popularly present complex issues, with the mission to draw out faith to enrich art and draw out art to enrich faith. In other words, precisely the kind of integration discussed in this essay; nothing new really, but arguably in danger of oblivion at mainstream level, though burgeoning in the so called 'alternative' world.

Both these examples of purposive uses of arts (not mere entertainment) are taken from the current issue of the occasional newspaper *Positive News,* and these pointers to the world we have discussed sit with empowering endeavours aimed at adults, such as at the Findhorn Foundation, and many other establishments hosting 'alternative' courses and workshops throughout the land. Similarly we find community building activities such as the work inspired by Participative Spiritual Inquiry, and communal musical improvizations as approached by, for example, Rod Paton's Life Music and the Music & Psyche Network. Such work can have practical applications as well as creating and maintaining strong interpersonal links. The Music & Psyche Network finds that an initiatory improvization before business meetings creates harmony and respect in the ensuing verbal discussions, not unlike the moments of gathered silence before Quaker business meetings. The Participative Spiritual Inquiry work specifically aims at building communal working structures without hierarchy, though it is not as yet, so far as I know, using any art or music modalities to facilitate its work.

Such creative endeavours are too easily perceived as educationally supplemental, separate from the 'important' acquisition of pre-digested information designed to make its receivers useful to the economic body politic: schooling instead of education. Compartmentalization is powerfully endemic. The findings, confirmed in later work, that listening to music positively enhances learning, has made no noticeable dent in mainstream education provision: sales of Mozart recordings sky-rocketed though, since his music was used in the experiments — to the unnecessary detriment of vast quantities of other music (Rauscher 1993).

Much of what is written above points to a possible (re-)integration of music and the arts into the fullness of life. There is a profound rift currently between the official, mechano-economic body politic and what each individual counts as necessary for a satisfactory life. We all (barring various modes of pathology) spend some time creatively, from a level as simple as keeping pot plants to as complex as may be found among dedicated artists, musicians, architects, engineers, to name but some. We need to discard our narrowly divided culture and its excessive bureaucracy: being a musician as I am does not mean I am incapable of (say) servicing a car, looking after a baby, painting a portrait, or understanding scientific method. The common prejudice that I am 'only' a musician denies that capability.

I am suggesting here that there are grounds for admitting music and the arts into a more integrated way of living, a way which does not make arbitrary distinctions between with what tools and beliefs our society governs itself or is governed and with what tools and beliefs we live our private lives. Not an intrusion into privacy by unwelcome officialdom, but an expansion of individual ways of living into co-operative governance, replacing an unfeeling and overweight bureaucracy which acts as if 'citizens' are untrustworthy. Show a person trust and they will be trustworthy; deny that and they will strive for personal autonomy in whatever ways are still open, anarchic, psychopathological, or not.

And I am suggesting that this wider, more rounded individual and communal living can be helped into being, and maintained, by practical applications of authentic music and the arts, working naturally with their sheer life-giving enjoyment, so that they become manifest in the meaningfulness of life at the same level that we currently pay attention to our employment and household, for the good of our psychic balance, for the good of our souls.

References

Abram, David (1996) *The Spell of the Sensuous: perception and language in a more-than-human world*, Random House.

Cabinet Office (1976) *Future World Trends*, HMSO.

Casson, John (2004) *Drama, Psychotherapy and Psychosis: drama therapy and psychodrama with people who hear voices*, Brunner-Routledge.

Devereux, Paul (2001) *Stone Age Soundtracks: the acoustic archaeology of ancient sites*, Vega.

Devereux, Paul et.al., (eds) (2008) *Time & Mind: the journal of archaeology, consciousness and culture*, Berg.

Findhorn Foundation: www.findhorn.org

Khayaal Theatre Company: www.khayaal.co.uk

Laszlo, Ervin (1997) *3rd Millennium: the challenge and the vision: The Club of Budapest report on creative paths of human evolution*, Gaia Books.

McGilchrist, Iain (2009) *The Master and his Emissary: The Divided Brain and the Making of the Western World*, Yale.

Meadows, Dennis L. (1974) *The Limits to Growth: a report for The Club of Rome's Project on the Predicament of Mankind*, Potomac 8 Pan Books. First pub 1972.

Music & Psyche Network: www.musicpsyche.org

Noel-Baker, Philip (1978) *The worst kind of poverty: poverty of mind. In* UNESCO 1978.

Participative Spiritual Inquiry:

www.oasishumanrelations.org.uk/pdfsnew/CG1%20Report.pdf

www.wrekinforum.org/wrekin_forum/rtrlo.html

Paton, Rod: www.lifemusic.org.

Peccei, Aurelio (1978) *Man, An Abandoned World. In* UNESCO 1978.

Pinker, Steven (1997) *How the Mind Works*, Norton.

Positive News: www.positivenews.org.uk

Power of Hope: www.powerofhope.org

Rauscher, Frances *et al.* (1993) *Music and Spatial Task Performance*, Nature Vol. 365, 14 October.

UNESCO (1978) *What kind of world are we leaving our children?* Amadou-Mahtar M'Bow & others.

Virilio, Paul (2003) *Art and Fear*, Athlone Press.

Wilson Schaef, Anne (1992) *Beyond Therapy, Beyond Science: a new model for healing the whole person,* Harper Collins.

24. The Virtues of Uncertainty: A Character Curriculum for the Learning Age

GUY CLAXTON

Guy Claxton is an internationally acclaimed authority on the development of young people's learning and creative capacities. He is currently Professor of the Learning Sciences and Co-Director of the Centre for Real-World Learning at the University of Winchester. He is the author of a dozen well-respected books on the mind. A new book, New Kinds of Smart: How the Science of Learnable Intelligence is Changing Education, *written jointly with Bill Lucas, was published in April 2010. His Building Learning Power approach to creating learning cultures in schools and colleges has influenced youngsters' lives throughout the UK as well as in Singapore, Sweden, Dubai, Brazil, Australia and New Zealand.*

We seem to live in a morally bashful age. Perish the thought that anyone might try to 'impose their values' on anyone else. Education colludes with this squeamishness by pretending that the only serious questions it faces are technical ones. How are we going to raise standards? What are the most appropriate methods for testing students, and when, and how much? Should we have 14–19 diplomas, or a six-term year?

But words like 'standards' and 'appropriate' merely finesse the underlying moral questions. They have only the appearance of neutrality, for we have only to ask 'Standards of what?' and 'Appropriate to what end?' and their value-laden nature is hauled to the surface. Only if we assume that 'standards' refer, self-evidently, to performance on national tests — with a sprinkling of statistics about 'attendance', and 'exclusions' — do the moral questions subside. But that assumption is looking increasingly flimsy. If, after one hundred years of tinkering and innovation, half of all young people still don't get a clutch of good GCSEs; if millions of school-leavers still can't read well; if thousands of students vote with their feet every day — not because they are inherently lazy or stupid, but because they can see no value in what school is offering — you might have thought that a slightly deeper look at aims and values was timely.

The idea of 'personalizing learning' is the latest from the stable of Morally Weaselly Ideas. Who could be against 'choice'? Surely you do not prefer bondage? But choice of what? Choice for what end? Is it obviously a 'good thing' that students and their teachers be able to customize their curriculum, like they can their lattes? 'Double shot with skinny milk and a cinnamon shake, please'. 'World Wars I and II minus the Balkans, and extra Palestine, please'. Shall we quietly drop the Holocaust lest it arouse any genuine dissent, or provoke the expression of repugnant views? Is that the extent of our moral vision?

Education for character

Education has always been about much more than the mastery of self-evidently valuable bodies of knowledge, skill and understanding — though you have to search quite hard, in ministerial pronouncements, these days, to find the 'more'. We can argue at the edges about what is 'self-evident' (another weasel word) and what isn't, and create wonderfully engaging distractions by arguing about the relative merits of Shakespeare and Dickens and J.K. Rowling. But the real moral heart of education is about character. What kinds of adults does a nation want its children to become: not just with what skills, but with what dispositions and interests and concerns, do we want them to grow up? And that means valuing some traits over others, and being clear and up-front about which ones we don't think matter so much. Dropping

Dickens is not the point; it is, do we drop 'neatness' in favour of 'discerning consumption of internet-based information', and are we going to favour 'resilience' over 'honour'?

In the nineteenth and early twentieth centuries, they didn't pussyfoot around. The public schools talked happily of developing qualities for the leaders of the future such as team spirit, fair play, judgment and rationality. It was assumed that we only needed so many Leaders and a great many more Followers, so mass education (for the Followers) sought to develop obedience, punctuality, precision, honesty, neatness and hygiene, as well as a degree of basic literacy and numeracy.

Nowadays, quite rightly, we no longer want to be associated with a school system that sorted children so divisively into potential 'winners' and 'losers', and trained their characters differentially, and so we have become nervous about talking about character-formation at all. But the problem was not in talking about character *per se*. It was only the *particular* sets of valued characteristics that needed challenging and updating, and we should not have thrown out the baby of value-judgments about desirable characteristics, along with the bathwater of colonial patriarchy and inherited privilege.

Actually, there *are* signs of a resurgence of interest in character. Countries round the world have recently been busy drawing up wish-lists of the kinds of qualities they would like education to develop in young people. From Australia's 'new basics' (Queensland) and 'essential learnings' (Victoria, Tasmania) to the UK Qualifications and Curriculum Authority's 'personal learning and thinking skills' and the Royal Society of Arts' 'key competencies', the world is now buzzing with fine-sounding phrases like 'respects the environment' and 'plays an active role in the community'. These may be a start towards something more robust, but they can often seem more like paving slabs for the road to hell than well worked out guidelines for a revitalized education.

First, they are often phrased so vaguely that no-one could possibly disagree — but at the unacceptable cost of no-one knowing what they really mean either. Does 'respecting the environment' mean lobbying the G8? Demanding James Lovelock come and talk to the school? Insisting that school meals are organic? Or merely watching *An Inconvenient Truth*, not dropping litter and trips to the bottle bank? And second, the gulf between these fine sentiments and the daily reality of life in lessons remains, for the vast majority of students, huge. Schools may pay lip-service to such ideas on the opening pages of their prospectuses and strategic plans, and then tacitly ignore them. Students, of course, are wise to these disparities and hypocrisies, and their main effect, when they are honoured in the breach rather than the observance, is to fuel cynicism.

Maybe education could learn from another area where values have made a comeback — the 'positive psychology' movement inspired in 1998 by American Professor Martin Seligman. Fed up with the fact that psychology had a vast vocabulary for describing pathology, but very little to say about wellbeing and happiness, he and Chris Peterson trawled the world's literature for a preliminary list of 'character strengths and virtues'. Some apparently timeless ones kept recurring, like integrity, generosity and forgiveness. Others, however, seemed to be particularly suitable to certain kinds or conditions of society, like physical valour or aesthetic sensibility. Given that we too would like our kids to grow up kind and honest, what then are the special virtues that twenty-first century living seem to require?

It is a cliché that we live in times of escalating uncertainty, complexity, ambiguity, choice and individual responsibility. Through the electronic media children are bombarded daily with conflicting models of what to value and how to live, and their communities often offer little strong, unanimous guidance about how to choose wisely — or little they are willing to heed. It is also increasingly obvious that young people (especially in the UK, according to a recent UNESCO report) are not coping well with this freedom and diversity. Classic symptoms of stress are high — escapism, recklessness, drug abuse, anxiety, depression, self-doubt. If stress reflects a widening gap between the demands of one's life and the resources one has to cope, clearly many young people are feeling badly under-resourced. Those resources are psychological, as much as they are material or social.

As the core function of education is precisely to develop in young people the mental and emotional resources they will need, to cope well with the real demands of their real lives, it is clearly not doing its job. And one of the reasons it is floundering is because it has no clear understanding of what the virtues are; no agreed vocabulary for talking about the tolerances, interests and habits of mind that are the bare necessities, if they are to flourish in the midst of uncertainty.

It is impossible to 'improve' the running of schools unless we have a clear idea of what those virtues are. 'Where' and 'why' have to come before 'how' and 'what'. Without that clarity, all innovation falls back obsessively on 'raising standards' as traditionally, and inadequately, defined. The requisite discussion about values and character is what has been grievously lacking so far.

Character strengths and virtues for the learning age

So in the spirit of positive psychology, let me offer for debate a set of Character Strengths and Virtues for the Learning Age. Some of these are drawn from Peterson and Seligman's list; some are derived from asking teachers and young people themselves; some are suggested by the burgeoning literature of the learning sciences. They are, as I say, merely a provocation, an invitation to argue. I propose eight, that I call the Magnificent 8 (or magn8, in text-speak). They are: curiosity, courage, exploration, experimentation, imagination, discipline, sociability and mindfulness. Each of these, in turn, comprises a number of sub-dispositions that I shall illustrate briefly.

Curiosity

Curiosity is the starting point for learning. If you are not interested in things that are difficult or puzzling, you won't engage. Curious people have a sense of wonder. They wonder about things: how they come to be, and how they work. They live in a wonder-ful world, not a world of dead certainties and cut-and-dried rules. They know how to ask good, pertinent, penetrating questions. They can be challenging. They may not take Yes for an answer. They have a healthy scepticism about what they are told.

Courage

Young people surely need *courage*; not necessarily physical valour but the courage to engage with uncertain things, 'to boldly go' (the world's favourite split infinitive) where they are not yet sure how to respond.

They need to be up for a challenge, willing to take a risk and see what happens, not always playing it safe and sticking to things they know they can do. Courageous learners have the determination to stick with things that are hard, even if they turn out to be harder than they thought. (Though it is also a virtue to know when to quit, not because you are feeling stupid but because it really isn't worth it.) They can be patient and persistent. They bounce back from frustration; they don't stay floored for long.

Exploration

Exploration is the active, inquisitive counterpart of curiosity. Inquisitive people are good at seeking and gathering information. They can attend carefully to situations, taking their time if needs be, and not jumping to conclusions or producing slick answers just to 'look good'. They enjoy the process of finding things out, of researching (whether it be footballers' lives or particle physics). They like reading, but they also enjoy just looking at things, letting details and patterns emerge. They can let themselves get immersed in a book or a game; absorption in learning is often a pleasure. They can concentrate. They like sifting and evaluating 'evidence', not just reading or surfing the net uncritically, and their exploration usually breeds more questions. Explorers are also good at finding, making or capitalizing on resources (tools, sources of information, people) that will support their explorations.

Experimentation

This is the virtue of the practical inventor, actively trying things out to see if they work. Experimenters like tinkering, tuning and looking for small improvements. They don't have to have a grand, ostensibly foolproof, scheme before they try something out; they are at home with trial and error. They even spend a good deal of time just 'playing' with materials — paint, cogs, computer graphics — to see what they will do, uncovering new 'affordances'. They are happy practising, taking time to 'get it right', even putting in the effort (maybe the long boring hours) to pick out the hard parts and master them. They enjoy drafting and re-drafting, looking at what they've done — a garden bed, an essay — and thinking about how they could build on and improve their own products and performances. They don't mind making mistakes (learning matters more than being 'right'), and, as Billie Jean King said, they 'look on losing not as failure but as research'.

Imagination

Imagining is the virtue of fantasy, of using the inner world as a test-bed for ideas and the theatre of possibilities. They are at home in the world of 'What If' and make-believe, of playing with possibilities. Good imaginers have the virtue of dreaminess: they know when and how to make use of reverie, how to let ideas 'come to them'. They have mixture of healthy respect and scepticism toward their own hunches, intuitions and 'feelings of rightness' (even if they can't justify them yet). They use mental rehearsal to develop their skills and readiness for tricky situations. They like finding links and making connections inside their own minds. They use imagery and metaphor in their thinking. (All this is true of many Nobel science laureates, creative artists and international sportsmen and women, for example.)

Discipline

The creativity of imagination needs to be yoked to the virtue of *discipline*; of being able to think carefully, rigorously and methodically, as well as to take the imaginative leap. 'Reason' isn't the be-all and end-all of learning by any means, but the ability to follow a rigorous train of thought, and to spot the holes in someone else's argument, as well as your own, is invaluable. Disciplined learners can create plans and forms of structure and organization that support their learning — like the Scouts, they can 'Be Prepared' — but can also stay open to serendipity, and throw away the plan if needs be. Discipline enables knowledge and skill to be used to guide learning, to allow the painstaking 'crafting' of things that usually needs to follow the 'brainwave'.

Sociability

The virtue of *sociability*, and of judiciously balancing sociability with solitariness, also seems essential. Effective learners seem to know who to talk to (and who not), and when to talk (and when to keep silent) about their own learning. And they are good members of groups of explorers. They know how to listen, how to take turns, what kinds of contribution are helpful. They have the knack of being able to give their views and hold their own in debate, and at the same time stay open-minded to and respectful of others' views. Collective learning is more important to them than point-scoring. They can give feedback and suggestions skilfully and receive them graciously. They are generous in sharing information, ideas and useful ways of thinking and exploring; and they are keen to pick up useful perspectives and strategies from others.

Mindfulness

Finally there is the virtue of *mindfulness*, in the sense of being disposed to reflection and contemplation, taking time to mull things over, take stock and consider alternative strategies and possibilities. Not paralysed by self-consciousness (which is a pitfall) but capable of self-awareness, reflective learner can take a step back every so often and question their own priorities and assumptions. They somehow know the strategic moments when this useful (and are not seduced by the current fad for 'metacognition' which seems to make the mistake of supposing that 'thinking about your own thinking' is always a good thing, which it isn't.) Mindfulness means giving yourself the time to go deeper, to see to what conclusions you may have leapt, to let a bigger picture emerge.

A new framework for learning

One of the benefits of this list, as I have tried to construct it, is that the virtues seem broad enough to apply to a good deal of out-of-school learning. Dealing with the real-time uncertainties of modern life, and developing one's own passionate interests and vocations, is usually not at all like school. The carefully planned, pre-digested, sequenced and graded kinds of bite-size learning in which conventional schooling trades are not the kinds of learning for which young people need to be prepared, and an apprenticeship in exam-passing leaves even the most successful with a skill for which there is little call, once they have left university. So we need to focus on developing qualities of mind that do have real-life currency, and the first step is to talk about what they are.

The second step, of course, is to design schools that offer an effective, systematic apprenticeship in those qualities and virtues. How do you teach courage, or inquisitiveness, or sociability? The first stage of Step 2 is to realize what doesn't work, and not do it. What doesn't work is stand-alone lessons on those virtues. Being able to talk *about* thinking is not the same thing as being a better thinker, and it may not even be necessary. (I have watched lessons in which youngsters have been parroting back Howard Gardner's Multiple Intelligences, without any evidence of them becoming more multiply intelligent.) And even being coached in the skills of 'questioning' or 'self-evaluation', for example, and being able to demonstrate the benefits when asked, is very far from having those abilities become part of one's learning *modus operandi* in everyday life.

What is needed are schools that have three things. First, they use the language of the learning virtues all the time. They find multiple ways to notice and acknowledge students' 'virtuous' development. Second, they create frequent, genuine, attractive opportunities for students to discover for themselves not just the power of these virtues but their pleasures. That means creating sizeable chunks of time where they can, both alone and in collaboration, get their teeth into real hard learning challenges that engage and intrigue them. So it means trusting them more. And finally, the school and all the adults in it need to model the virtues in their own professional lives. Headteachers need to let the students know that they do not have all the answers, and that the school as a whole is being curious, inquisitive and exploratory about its own operation, tinkering its way imaginatively, thoughtfully and courageously towards improvement. And every teacher, governor and midday helper should be actively looking for and welcoming opportunities to display their own learning virtues.

None of these three requirements is impossible. None of them need to jeopardize hard won levels of control or of examination results. None of them means — God forbid — that we have to chuck out Shakespeare and start doing a new subject called 'the learning virtues'. What it does mean, as a first step, is that we all start experimenting with thinking and talking about young people and their development in a different way. I've offered a first shot at a 'primer' for that conversation. Now, please, help me get it better.

References

Claxton, Guy (1997) *Hare Brain, Tortoise Mind: Why Intelligence Increases When You Think Less*, Fourth Estate, London; (1999) *Wise Up: The Challenge of Lifelong Learning*, Bloomsbury, London; (2005) *The Wayward Mind*, Little Brown, London; (2009) *What's the Point of School?* Oneworld, Oxford.

25. Why Schooling is a Major Contributor to the Crisis — And What Can Be Done About It

IAN CUNNINGHAM

Ian Cunningham BSc, MA, PhD, FIoD, FRSA, Chartered FCIPD, FCMI, is Visiting Professor in Organizational Capability at Middlesex University; Chair of Strategic Developments International Ltd, and Chair of the Centre for Self Managed Learning. Previous positions have included Chief Executive of Roffey Park Institute; Senior Research Fellow in International Leadership at Ashridge Management College; Visiting Professor in Education Management in the Graduate School of Education, University of Utah; Visiting Fellow in Innovation in Education at the University of Sussex. He has published seven books and over one hundred articles and papers in areas such as education, learning, leadership, strategic management, organizational change and social change.

Introduction

In this essay I will use as my starting point the Scientific and Medical Network's 'Manifesto for Change' elaborated by Robinson, Clarke and Lorimer, 2009. Each of the nine points in this manifesto summarize exceedingly well the basis of the global crisis explored in their paper.

Others have commented on a range of aspects of the socio-economic-ecological crisis affecting the planet — and all species on it. Here I will explore schooling and possible antidotes to the effects of current practices. Note that I am concerned about an alternative to current institutional schooling. Education is a broader concept, as is learning. Indeed one mistake official bodies make is to conflate learning and schooling as though they are synonyms for education.

All available research on learning shows that most of what we learn that is of value in our work, and lives in general, is outside school. The best summary of all the evidence suggests that, for instance, schooling in all its modes (and I will include here college, university and formal training courses) contributes at most 10–20% of what makes a good professional person effective. (See Burgoyne and Reynolds 1997; Cunningham *et al.* 2004; Eraut 1998; Eraut *et al.* 1998; McCall *et al.* 1988; Wenger 1998.) Most of the useful learning that we gain comes from what tends to be dismissed (by officialdom) as informal learning, such as from peers, family, travel, reading, etc, etc. In our own research we have identified over eighty useful learning modes outside schooling. Some of these are summarized in Cunningham *et al.* 2004.

In what follows I will take just two examples of the nine 'questionable assumptions' challenged in the SMN's Manifesto for Change and make comments about their validity as applied to schooling. I will add some notes about alternatives that do work. The first questionable assumption is:

> Separation of the individual from the social nexus and from
> nature, and the corresponding affirmation of individualism,
> individual success and self-interest (by contrast with ideals of
> community, co-operation and social responsibility). (Robinson
> *et al.*, p. 3. See Appendix here.)

We become our selves through our relationship with others. We need to be in productive relationships with other human beings. Hence the notion of co-operation and community is central to how we develop. We know from the extensive researches of Wilkinson and Pickett (2009), Marmot (2004), and others that the greater the social distance within a society the greater are the problems of health, crime and psycho-social distress. An individualistic society where there are large differences in income and social status is bound to contribute to the social crises we face.

My argument is that schooling plays a major role in this and if we do not change the nature of current schooling practices there is no chance of addressing these social ills. As an example — in England seven year olds in school are assessed by what many educationalists recognize as a crude methodology. Parents eagerly discuss these ratings (SATs) and children quickly learn where they stand in the class. From then on children absorb the notion that some people are valued more than others and that if you have low SATs scores you are less likely to do well in school — and life.

A learning centre

We run a learning centre in Brighton for 11–16 year olds who have chosen not to be in school. The reasons for this choice vary — some have been home educated prior to joining us; some have been bullied in school; some have found the classroom an impossible environment; some have been rejected by school. In the latter category is Tina. She came to us at fourteen having had a range of difficult experiences in local schools. One of the things we do is to ask new students about themselves. In Tina's case one thing we asked was about what she was good at. She replied 'Nothing' — and she meant it. It was not false humility; she really believed that she was useless at everything. The messages that she had gained throughout her schooling were that she had no abilities of any value.

In working with her she has come to recognize that she will never succeed with high-level academic qualifications. However she makes a real contribution to our learning community. She is prepared to ask the difficult questions; she has a strong moral sense; she has learned to challenge others appropriately (she didn't when she first came to us); she has developed her dancing and dramatic skills and become a good singer. And so on. She has developed the capability to work with others and to work independently — and these are qualities that employers say many young people coming out of school lack.

The role of the learning community has been crucial in supporting

Tina's development. Within the community each person is allowed to develop their own voice and to pursue their own learning. However they have to work with others to achieve their own learning. For instance resources in the learning centre have to be shared and students and staff together work out how the resources are used. There is no formal imposed content curriculum — the students negotiate with adults and their peers what they want to do during a typical week. As an example students meet in small groups (a maximum of six students with one staff member) on a Monday morning to consider what they want to do in the coming week. Students are assisted to write their own timetables and to negotiate with adults and with peers on what they want to do.

Three of the girls play wind instruments and they have worked with Alison (a staff member) to form, with her, a wind quartet. Alison has arranged music for the quartet. All four need to agree when they will play together — and therefore agree with others in the community as to when they will have the music room. They also need to work together so that the quartet can create the lovely music that it produces.

This latter is a simple example of the need for students to be able to learn on their own (to be good on their own instruments) and to work together. Learning needs to balance the *independent* element and the *interdependent* element. The problem in schooling is that it encourages a different balance — that between *dependence* on others and *counter-dependence* (for example, when a son says: 'I am not influenced by my father — I just do the opposite of what he says').

Schools tend to value the dependent learner: the one who is quiet in class, does what teacher tells them, doesn't question the work that they are set, does all their homework on time, and so on. Some young people rebel (exhibit counter-dependent behaviour) — they mistake this for independence, when usually they are not actually doing things of value for themselves but merely getting into trouble.

Working with schools

We get asked to assist schools where they have students that they label as problems. The process we use both in schools and with young people out of school is Self Managed Learning. In this process the aim is to develop independence and interdependence — and in doing so help young people to be able to lead good lives. At the start we get the students to join a learning group of six students and one adult (as learning assistant). Once the group has agreed its rules for working and how it will operate we ask the students to answer five questions, namely:

— Where have I been? What has been my experience of life up to now?

— Where am I now? What kind of person am I, what do I care about, what interests me, what am I good at, and so on?

— Where do I want to get to? What kind of life might I want to lead, what kind of work might I want to do, what goals for learning should I set myself now?

— How will I get to where I want to be? How will I learn what I want to learn?

— How will I know if I have arrived? How will I measure my progress and my development?

In answering that first question we often unearth major reasons why particular individuals are having difficulty in school. For instance in a group of fourteen year olds in a local school, Rochelle talked of her family experiences to date. Her parents split up when she was very young. Her mother had gained custody but her father had kidnapped the children at one point. The family feuding had culminated in the father smashing up the family home in the preceding week and beating up her sister. The school was getting annoyed with her because she was not doing her homework — but had no idea why there was a problem. For Rochelle doing her school work was not high on her agenda, given her home circumstances. And this story could be repeated a hundredfold in local schools — none of whom seem organized to understand the real problems that many of their students face.

One reason that Rochelle was in the Self Managed Learning programme was that her year head had identified that Rochelle was mixing with what the year head labelled 'a bad crowd'. Rochelle had been reasonably successful (by the school's standards) in her first two years in the school but had been perceived to go downhill as a result of the changes in her friendship group. Interestingly the year head was aware enough of the influence of a peer group but seemed unable to act on the issue.

We know from our research that the peer group is usually the greatest influence on young people, especially teenagers. Adults such as teachers and parents are generally less of an influence, even though they may not recognize this. Schools promote an individualistic culture where, for instance, learners helping each other with their assessed work is punished (as cheating). However this can be undermined as students create their own subcultures inside school — and these generally dominate in terms of the behaviour of students.

In Rochelle's case the learning group (of six students) was able to discuss the ways in which each person might want to develop (using the five questions indicated above). This led on to considering what might be difficulties for each person in achieving their life goals. In Rochelle's case she realized that she wanted to work towards a professional career (her interests led towards the law). One piece of work the students did was for each to write out what the school would say about them now and what they would like the school to say about them when they left at age sixteen.

Rochelle summed up her current situation very well — citing, for example, her difficult behaviour and the bad influence of her new friends. In writing what she hoped the school would say about her in two years' time she suggested that she would still occasionally be difficult but that her behaviour had improved and that she had changed her friendship group. The others in her learning group agreed that what she was looking to change was the right thing to do and they pledged to assist her.

This is an example of how we look to balance *independent* and *interdependent* learning. Each young person needs to be assisted to develop ideas about what life they want to lead and how they will achieve this. However the role of the group is crucial in being initially a test bed for these ideas and later both a support and a challenge for the person.

An example of this latter dimension is of the role of the group for thirteen year-old John, who was in a learning group in another school. He had been having a difficult time and was in and out of exclusion from school. He committed to some significant life changes. One of these was to give up smoking. At the penultimate meeting of the group, Mike (another group member) started to sniff at John and alleged that he had been smoking. John denied this saying that he had just been with others who had been smoking. The group members decided to search John's bag and his pockets to see if they could find any cigarettes. John agreed to this. Having failed to find any incriminating evidence they decided to accept John's assertions.

This provides an example of how individuals may need support — and sometimes challenges to their behaviour. The rule we have is that you *support the person* while sometimes challenging *what they do*. The separation of who the person *is* from what they *do* is crucial. Because the group cared about John as a person they challenged suspected behavioural transgressions. In the process of challenging they demonstrated a significant level of support for him. And the overall role of the group demonstrated how it was important to develop a peer group that could act for good rather than ill.

Schooling

Schooling emphasizes a range of structures such as classrooms, an imposed content curriculum, an imposed timetable and imposed rules. While some schools attempt to leaven the influence of such structures, the general process is one which creates a context for promoting individualism and self-interested behaviour. A counter to this has been the growth of democratic schools in many countries. There is increased interest from parents in the UK in such approaches, though officialdom tends to frown on democratic schools, as evidenced by the Government's attempt to close Summerhill School in Suffolk.

The argument made by many supporters of democratic schools is that they better prepare young people for playing an active role in democratic society, since young people have to learn to make a democratic community work effectively. Another reason for support for democratic schools is exemplified by the need to counteract the second of the questionable assumptions from the SMN's 'Manifesto for Change', namely:

> The separation of knowledge specialism in science, philosophy and humanities, leading to the fragmentation of knowledge (as opposed to a more interdisciplinary, co-operative and integrated approach). (Robinson *et al.*, p. 3. See Appendix here.)

I remember in my first degree in chemistry asking my professor of physical chemistry — 'What actually is an electron?' (My question was prompted by the complex maths that we were asked to grapple with while never actually dealing with the oddities thrown up by quantum theory.) The professor pretty much told me to shut up as he indicated that my question was about philosophy (and therefore not legitimate in a chemistry lecture).

Later doing a Masters' degree in occupational psychology we had a lecture within which was given a purely psychological explanation of some recent research. I suggested an alternative explanation for the same data and was pretty much told to shut up as my explanation was sociological and therefore not legitimate. And I could go on with other examples of the separation problems in education. What is clear is that this fragmentation has serious consequences.

In schooling (including higher education) the separation of subjects means that learners are encouraged to think in fragmentary ways. This means that we may never solve ecological problems as young people are discouraged from thinking systemically and holistically. Schooling's hidden curriculum is that learning has to be compartmentalized if you are to succeed academically. This learning has more impact than the actual subject learning as it is hidden from the learner. For the learner it is part of the way things are and is not therefore available for challenge. Even where teachers recognize the problem they seem to feel powerless to act to change things. One headteacher said to me that he would ideally love to get rid of all his science teachers because of the way science was being taught in his school. Yet he could not realistically do it — even though he was the head.

Modes of learning

Ideally learning needs to start with what I have called the 'P MODE'. P stands for:

— PERSONS: we need to understand the person if we are to assist their learning. Each person is different and they have different needs.

— PATTERNS: each person will have patterns of behaviour and of thinking.

— PROCESSES: each person has their own processes of working and living.

— PROBLEMS: one way of thinking of learning is as a solution to a problem. For example if you can't speak French and you need to, then you have a problem and the solution is to learn French. Or if you need to write well to progress in life and work, then the solution is to learn to write well. And so on.

Note that in the latter example, problems come before solutions. In our approach, the P MODE comes before the S MODE.
The S MODE stands for:

— SOLUTIONS: to respond to the person and their problems there may be a need to look for solutions;

— SUBJECTS: subject knowledge may help to meet the 'P' needs;

— SKILLS: may be needed to progress;

— SPECIALIZATIONS: may contribute; as may

— SYSTEMS: such as IT systems.

Schooling too often starts with 'S' — young people have imposed on them Subject knowledge and Solutions to Problems that they have not yet formulated. Or the Solution distorts the way the Problem is addressed.

As a chemist, presented with the problem of mental health, my training (schooling) would have oriented me to create a pill. Later, from working in the field of psychotherapy, my solution to the same problem would be to talk to the person. As far as I can gather chemists and psychotherapists don't talk to each other yet they are dealing with the same problems. Schooling is predominantly in the 'S Mode' and distorts how we deal with the 'P Mode'.

In our learning centre we try to avoid these issues. Tim came to us at age twelve with a passion for the TV series *Dr Who*. Through this interest he started to write his own scripts for a *Dr Who* series. This also prompted an interest in visual representation and he worked on a Mac to develop videos and comics. He decided that he needed to know more of the science underpinning *Dr Who* and this led into serious explorations in a range of sciences. For instance he wanted to explore the reason for the Doctor's altruism and that led to the two of us discussing philosophical issues around altruism as well as ideas from Darwinism, genetics and evolutionary psychology.

Tim started in the P Mode with his Personal interest and this linked to his own Patterns of thinking. One of his Problems was to write better scripts hence needing better scientific knowledge. He also developed his ability in English through his writing. Given the time-travel dimension of Dr Who he developed his historical knowledge (again so that he could write better scripts). The learning mode here is 'P' before 'S'.

Two errors can occur in learning. Firstly starting with 'S' before 'P' leads to motivational problems, as many young people find it difficult to see the relevance of learning subject knowledge abstracted from their needs to live and work in society. Also 'S' mode thinking creates anti-ecological and anti-systemic thinking. The other error is for learners to start in 'P' and stay there. They do need assistance to see how to use what is available in the 'S' mode, hence a role for adults. However our role is first to understand the person before assisting them to make the link to the 'S' mode, such as via subject knowledge and skills.

The curriculum

The standard educational (schooling) model for thinking about the curriculum has become a list of subjects and skills to learn ('S' Mode). However the choice of content is a purely subjective one. There is no objective basis for the school curriculum — the content is created by adults who live in a different world from young people.

When adults say that they were young once and can therefore understand the needs of young people, Margaret Mead (see Howard 1984) famously responded something along the following lines: 'Yes, you were young once but you have not been young in the world that young people are young in. You were young in another world totally different from that of today.' To add to that it is clear that adults are not in a strong position to predict the world that young people will inhabit when they are adults.

The alternative to a content/subject curriculum is a process curriculum. Here the emphasis is on a systemic, holistic model where, through the process of learning, young people are prepared to deal with whatever the future may hold. Sometimes this emphasis is labelled 'learning to learn' though I would argue that it is bigger than this. We talk of Self Managed Learning (see Cunningham *et al.* 2000, and www.selfmanagedlearning.org) as we emphasize the need for people to be self managing — though our model of self managing is one of balancing independent and interdependent thought and action.

An example of a real situation

The global financial crisis of 2008/9 is an interesting example of how the two questionable assumptions (individualism and knowledge fragmentation) have played out in a real situation. The best analysis of the roots of the crisis is in Gillian Tett 2009. As a social anthropologist working as a journalist for the *Financial Times* she had access to the facts and an anthropological approach which exposed the lack of systemic thinking amongst the bankers and others who precipitated the crisis. She commented:

> ... regulators, bankers, politicians, investors and journalists have all failed to employ truly holistic thought ... a 'silo' mentality has come to rule inside banks ... with shockingly little wider vision or oversight. (p. 298–99).

The dimension of self-interest amongst the culprits (for example, excessive bonuses based on dubious criteria) has also been extensively explored. What is often missing from these analyses is the role of schooling in creating this mindset. If schooling rewards self-interested behaviour, and gives no credence to behaviour that has a social dimension, it is clear that this links to the way in which these and other organizational actors play out their roles.

The teams that created the toxic financial instruments not only did not connect to wider societal issues; they did not connect to other operations within the banks. They betrayed the kind of arrogance exposed some time ago by Chris Argyris (see, for example, Argyris 1990). What he showed is that people who have been successful academically, such as via élite business schools, can develop a mindset where their mistakes are reframed as the mistakes of others. An example was his research on young management consultants who made inappropriate recommendations to clients and then blamed the clients when things went wrong.

Argyris' demonstration of the need for double loop learning has largely fallen on deaf ears, as did Bateson's earlier (1972) exposition of the value of second order learning. Schooling is committed to single loop/first order learning where the ability to step back and analyze one's own learning, and the values and beliefs that underpin it, is discounted — and even discouraged.

People *learn* to think and work in silos. It is not an inborn feature of humans. Clark's (2002) in-depth study provides ample evidence on this. Furthermore anthropologists studying hunter-gatherer bands comment on how such bands behave in a more ecological way (see, for example, Brody 2001; Clastres 1989; Gall 2002; Gowdy 1998; Lee & Daly 2004). Hunter-gatherer people do not fragment the world as supposedly developed people do.

All humans lived in hunter-gatherer bands for over 90% of human history. It is therefore only relatively recently that we have moved away from this more holistic life-style. As evolutionary psychologists (for example, Nicholson 2002) argue, our brains and general make up are still what they describe as 'Stone Age'. And in this mode we were able to keep our thinking connected to action. The abstract-thinking analysts in the banks disconnected their models from the reality of Mr and Mrs Smith and their sub-prime mortgage.

Indigenous peoples on islands in the way of the tsunami that hit South East Asia were able to survive because they could read the many signs from animal and bird behaviour that there was an oncoming disaster. They survived when others, such as tourists not used to holistic awareness, did not.

Conclusion

In this essay I have only taken the first two of the 'questionable assumptions' identified by Robinson *et al.* 2009 (see Appendix). However other items on their list could also relate to issues in schooling. What I have wanted to demonstrate is that we have to address what goes on in formal institutional educational settings. If we fail to make changes in such settings then other worthy efforts may fail. Schooling has a significant impact on how people approach global crises and how they address them.

References

Argyris, Chris (1990) *Overcoming Organizational Defences: Facilitating Organizational Learning*, Allyn and Bacon, Boston.
Bateson, Gregory (1972) *Steps to an Ecology of Mind*, University of Chicago Press, Chicago.
Brody, Hugh (2001) *The Other Side of Eden*, Faber and Faber, London.
Burgoyne, John and Reynolds, Michael (eds) (1997) *Management Learning*, Sage, London.

Clark, Mary E. (2002) *In Search of Human Nature,* Routledge, London.

Clastres, Pierre (1989) *Society Against the State,* Zone Books, New York.

Cunningham, I., Bennett, B. and Dawes, G. (eds) (2000) *Self Managed Learning in Action,* Gower, Aldershot, Hants.

Cunningham, I., Dawes, G. and Bennett, B. (2004) *Handbook of Work Based Learning,* Gower, Aldershot, Hants.

Eraut, M. (1998) *'Learning in the workplace,'* Training Officer, Vol. 34, No. 6, July/August, pp. 172–4.

Eraut, M., Alderton, J., Cole, G. and Senker, P. (1998) *Development of knowledge and skills in employment, Research Report No. 5,* University of Sussex Institute of Education, Brighton.

Gall, Sandy (2002) *The Bushmen of Southern Africa,* Random House, London.

Gowdy, John (ed) (1998) *Limited wants, unlimited means,* Island, Washington DC.

Howard, Jane (1984) *Margaret Mead: A Life,* Simon and Schuster, New York.

Lee, R.B. and Daly, R. (eds) (2004) *The Cambridge Encyclopedia of Hunters and Gatherers,* Cambridge University Press, Cambridge.

Marmot, Michael (2004) *Status Syndrome,* Bloomsbury, London.

McCall, M.W., Lombardo, M.M., and Morrison, A.M. (1988) *The Lessons of Experience,* Lexington Books, Lexington.

Nicholson, Nigel (2000) *Managing the Human Animal,* Texere, London.

Robinson, O., Clarke, J., and Lorimer, D. (2009) 'Crisis as Opportunity: Seizing the Moment for a New Renaissance', SMN Network Review, No. 100, pp. 3–5.

Tett, Gillian (2009) *Fool's Gold,* Little, Brown, London.

Wenger, Etienne (1998) *Communities of Practice.* Cambridge University Press, Cambridge.

Wilkinson, Richard and Pickett, Kate (2009) *The Spirit Level,* Allen Lane, London.

Appendix

Crisis as Opportunity: Seizing the Moment for a New Renaissance
A Manifesto for Change

OLIVER ROBINSON, JOHN CLARKE, DAVID LORIMER

Originally published in the Scientific and Medical Network Review, volume 100, 2009.

The Scientific and Medical Network (SMN) was founded in 1973 by a group of scientists, doctors and professionals as a response to an almost exclusively materialistic outlook in science and medicine and a marginalization of a spiritual perspective. Over the course of thirty-five years we have organized conferences, courses and lectures, published written and online materials, and formed discussion groups to explore alternatives to a purely materialist worldview, while maintaining the highest scientific and ethical standards (see www.scimednet.org).

However, the context in which we have been active as an organization over the three and a half decades has radically changed, creating an even greater imperative to pursue our aims. Many other organizations across the world are now also exploring new roles for spirituality, values, contemplative insight and consciousness in relation to science, medicine and philosophy, thus creating a wider movement exploring the frontiers of conventional orthodoxies.

There is also now a growing and wide-reaching socioeconomic-ecological crisis which is widely seen to have its roots in a predominantly materialistic outlook as a philosophy and as a value system. This assessment is not confined to 'alternative' commentators, but has in recent years been expressed by many who would be considered as part of the socio-economic establishment. Given the pressing urgency of the crisis and the need for a progressive voice, we feel compelled to take up the challenge and make creative use of the opportunities with which the current crisis presents us. Our intention, outlined in this manifesto, is to expand the SMN's traditional remit of open-ended discussion into an active consideration of appropriate responses to the crisis and the promotion of a worldview that enhances much needed wisdom and balance.

The presence of an all-embracing and growing crisis

The current global financial crisis and its associated frantic media coverage represent the visible tip of a deeply rooted socio-cultural crisis, the many filaments of which reach out into all corners of our society and knowledge systems. The ecological destruction caused by industrialized economies is now evident for all to see, with the imminent possibility of major climate change, continued deforestation and extinction of many species. There is a crisis in the social fabric, shown by the gradually decreasing level of trust and cohesion in the UK over the past fifty years. The uneven distribution of income across society is worse than at any time in history, with Britain being one of the most extreme cases in the developed world. There is also a psychological crisis, as rates of depression and anxiety continue to rise, while reported levels of wellbeing are in decline. Despite advances in recuperative medicine, physical health is declining as levels of obesity, diabetes, liver disease, alcohol abuse, heart disease, stroke, cancer and other lifestyle-related disorders increase, leading to intolerable demands on the National Health Service and other health systems.

The roots of the crisis

A crisis that manifests itself in so many domains simultaneously emerges from deep-seated beliefs and values in the affected cultures. There is strong evidence that a fundamental paradigm has been a major contributor to the current impasse. Questionable assumptions underlying this paradigm are:

1. The separation of the individual from the social nexus and from nature, and the imbalanced emphasis on individualism, individual success and self-interest (contrasted with the ideals of community, co-operation and social responsibility).

2. The separation of knowledge specialism in the sciences, philosophy and humanities, leading to the fragmentation of knowledge (as opposed to a more interdisciplinary, co-operative and integrated approach).

3. The adversarial separation of reason from feeling and practical living, leading to the belief that science is a process devoid of feeling and intuition (which cries out for a new approach to knowledge which takes account of the full range of human experience).

4. The prioritizing of economic growth, material gain and quantitative profit as ultimate ends in themselves, linked to a narrow model of laissez-faire capitalism (by contrast with an economics enlightened by a moral commitment to compassion and social justice).

5. The deterministic and reductionist view of living beings as machines leading to the view that consciousness is an illusion (in contrast with the recognition of the distinctive nature of life and mind and their central place in our world).

6. Nature and living beings as resources to be treated as objects for exploitation and consumption (rather than as a spiritual community of all beings).

7. Science as the only path to reality, and empirical evidence as the sole criterion of truth (by contrast with a more embracing epistemology which recognizes that there are many paths to truth).

8. Matters of value, goodness, love, quality and beauty as merely personal and subjective, and therefore subordinate to the physical sciences (rather than as embedded in the fabric of life and the cosmos).

9. Science and scientific evidence as requiring or implying a world devoid of spiritual depth and spiritual knowledge (by contrast with a science which is seen as a part of the perennial search for wisdom).

Promoting new opportunities: towards a 'New Renaissance'

According to the historian Arnold Toynbee, new cultures and worldviews emerge as a response to the challenge of wide-reaching crises that require unprecedented solutions. The new direction that we are promoting is one which has the potential to transcend many of the divisions and false assumptions outlined above. In pursuit of this we believe that a reconceptualized, more realistic view of science is essential, one which sees science as a lived human activity in which the first person 'I' and second person 'you' positions are as important as the third person 'it'. The practising scientist knows that inspiration, intuition, imaginative insight, dialogue, politics and conflict are as much part of science as experimentation and data-collection. All these aspects of being can be seen as operating in the scientist without loss of rigour or validity of findings.

Alongside a broader view of science, we need an emerging spiritual ethos, which is free from the straightjacket of outdated religious dogma, one in which we do not hark back to a lost age of truth and perfection, a proverbial Garden of Eden, but accept the optimistic and humbling Enlightenment axiom that human progress is possible but not certain, and that the ever greater realization of human potentiality lies open for us.

We believe that it is of utmost importance to move towards a greater sense of equilibrium and harmony in our approach to nature outside of us, to the spiritual world within us, and to the relation between these two. Our world is saturated with antagonistic polarities and either-or disputes, which need to be embraced in a new synthesis that honours both sides and seeks a higher level of understanding and toleration. A new worldview will therefore grasp the need for a balance between dialectical opposites such as matter and spirit, head and heart, reason and feeling, individual and collective, and local and global. In this pursuit of balance and healing, both allopathic and complementary forms of medicine have a role to play.

This approach has implications for social and political practice. The modern emphasis on nationalism and on partisan and parochial human identities, along with the pervasive development and employment of military force, has proved increasingly unsustainable and a threat to our very existence. Any worldview which is adequate for our survival and future flourishing must give a central place to the ideal of global community and co-operation, and must involve a commitment to the ideals of universal human respect and equality, to global justice, and to the attainment of a world without war.

The goal of human survival and flourishing also depends on wise and sustainable attitudes towards our relationship with the natural world. Thinking globally, we need a philosophy of life which integrates the human within the natural, seeing our individual spiritual aims as integrated into the spiritual qualities of the world and the cosmos at large. At the same time we must recognize the importance of the local where, for example, low-impact technologies and locally co-ordinated actions are appropriate responses.

A growing worldwide movement

The research of Paul Ray has found that up to a quarter of the population already holds elements of the emerging worldview outlined briefly above. He refers to this group as the 'Cultural Creatives'. The emergence of the Cultural Creatives can be seen as an important development in world historical terms because it is the first time in recorded history that a value shift has emerged at a global level simultaneously. It is a bottom-up rather than a top-down movement which has arisen spontaneously in many contexts of human experience and endeavour.

This emphasizes the fact that the Scientific and Medical Network is one manifestation of a much larger movement, and that a shift in worldview can only occur through the combined action of many groups and individuals. This is a challenge to our future, and it is also an opportunity for us to seize and embrace. It is our intention, therefore, to create close links with organizations that are similarly aligned towards a transformed worldview and towards bringing about positive change. We envisage building partnerships with associates in order to enhance co-operation in regard to practical action and education, in order more effectively to cross-fertilize ideas, and more explicitly to embed our activities in this wider movement of change. With our uniquely interdisciplinary emphasis, our wide-ranging and high-calibre membership, our history of frontier thinking our pedigree of cutting-edge conferences, the SMN has a unique contribution to make to this movement.

A programme of action

It is important that this vision of a New Renaissance should move boldly from theory to practice, and with this in mind the Network will develop a programme of action which will reach to our members, to other like-minded organizations and to the community at large. We envisage that the campaign will initially comprise four elements:

publications, online resources, outreach (in schools, universities and business) and conferences/events relevant to the contemporary situation. The fruitful development and detailed working-out of these and other activities will require the participation of our worldwide SMN membership. As we develop and concretize our programme of action, we will keep members informed by way of updates in the *Network Review* and on our website (www.scimednet.org) .

This campaign rests on the belief that the world needs a new integration of modern science, philosophy and ancient spiritual wisdom, a 'New Renaissance', inspired by the 'Old Renaissance', the latter with its sense of renewal and synthesis, but created anew to confront the needs of our own time. We believe that the Scientific and Medical Network has a unique role in formulating and realizing this vision of the future.

Index

Rome 65, 74
Rousseau, Jean-Jacques 226, 231, 265
Royal Society of Arts 96, 274
Russell, Peter 99, 215
Ryle, Gilbert 193

Sahtouris, Elisabet 34
SATs 284
Saul, John Ralston 169
Schaef, Anne Wilson 262
schooling 283, 288
Schumacher College 129
Schumacher, E.F. 12
Schweitzer, Dr Albert 11
Science over scientism 138
Scientific and Medical Network (SMN)
    8, 76, 129, 157, 282, 299, 304
scientism 138, 143
secular worldview 168
Seligman, Martin 275
Shackleton, Patrick 8
shamanic cultures 172
Sheldrake, Rupert 131, 142
Shelley 12
Shell Oil 40
Singleton 151
Skolimowski, Henryk 199
Slow Food 184
Smith, Adam 26
sociability 278
socialism 230
social philosophers 231
Society for Psychical Research 137
Spencer, Sir Kelvin 8
Spencer, Stanley 263
Sperry, Roger 107
Sri Aurobindo 32
Strickland, William 10
subjectivity 126
Summerhill School 288

Tarnas, Richard 48
Taylor, Charles 96
Teilhard de Chardin 197
Thatcher, Margaret 75
therapies, art 261
Thomas, Lewis 110
Toynbee, Arnold 41, 302
trickster 161–164

tsunami 46, 89, 294
Turner, Edith 151
Twain, Mark 251
Twist, Lynn 40

UK Qualifications and Curriculum
    Authority 274
UN 100
UN Environment Programme 20
UNESCO 265, 275
universe, expanding 76

Velmans, Max 132
Von Neumann, John 123
voodoo death 108

water 22
Watson, Thomas J. 29
weapons, nuclear 183
Wei-Ji 27
Weltanschauung 148
Wheeler, John 77
Wigner, Eugene 107
Wilber, Ken 99, 120
Wilson, E.O. 70, 80
wisdom, perennial 186
World Bank 18
World Trade Centre 183
worldview, modern 48
worldview, transmodern 92, 97
World Wide Web 147
Wright, Chris 235
Wright, Richard 266
Wundt, Wilhelm 137

Xenophanes of Colophon 234

Zeh, Hans-Dieter 123